THE TWO JULYS:

The Fourth and The Fourteenth

Peter de Bolla
and
Christopher Prendergast

Cam Rivers Publishing

First English Edition Published in Great Britain

By CAM RIVERS PUBLISHING LTD 2024

THE TWO JULYS
THE FOURTH AND THE FOURTEENTH

Authors: Peter de Bolla and Christopher Prendergast

Honorary Editor: Professor Alan Macfarlane FBA
Editor-in-Chief: WANG Zilan
Editor: WANG Zilan, Levente Koroes, QIN Yuchen

Cover Design: GE Dalong (MUYE)
Design and Typeset: GE Dalong, QIN Yubin (MUYE)

The publishing of this book is supported by
the Vanishing Worlds Foundation, U.K.

A CIP Catalogue of this book is available from the British Library

ISBN: 978-1-916858-45-9
Contact: press@cambridgerivers.com
www.cambridgerivers.com

List Of Contents

Introduction

It surely cannot be that, relative to all the other months, July has some special status in the calendars of active history making. It is of course remembered as a creation of the early Roman calendar, when the Senate voted to honour the dead Caesar by renaming Quintilius (the fifth month in the calendar and the month of Caesar's birth) as Julius. Then there are the two Julys that furnish the title of this book, separated by thirteen years and a vast ocean, joined together by virtue of their signal participation in two of the most enduring and robust attempts at revolutionary nation or state building. Each plays the card of commemoration; both exploit the affordances of myth and collective fantasy. Both announce a desire for a better polity, more respectful of its citizens, even if in both cases the dream of a universal franchise would remain, perhaps for ever, just that: a politically opportune and intransigently unrealisable dream.

Why tell their stories together, back to back? Certainly not to imply that the one, in 1776, which announced the then colonists' intentions to sever ties with the 'mother country', was in a significant sense a precursor of the other, in 1789, when the creaking wheels of the *ancien régime* finally fell off, and a new, distinctively modern political entity began to form and express its views, anger and aspirations. Even if, as we note below (following in the footsteps of Patrice Higgonet's comparative history of the two revolutions, *Sister Republics*), a strong case can be made for echoes and borrowings from the American experiment in founding a republic on principles including the rights of man and popular sovereignty, being deployed as the newly liberated (if soon to be shackled once again) populace in France stumbled into revolutionary Republicanism. Echoes that powerfully determined some of the terms of debate, the discourses of Republicanism and Federalism, as well as the institutions which both countries slowly and in some cases painfully created for their new republics: the Convention or Congress, a written constitution, oaths of loyalty among them. Nevertheless, and notwithstanding the two-way echoes, and influences, it would surely be a mistake to claim that the one July *caused* the other.

Even if the outcomes of both Julys can be seen, not as mirror images, but (citing Higonnet) as 'mirror opposites: the centrality of individualism that triumphed in the one [America] was badly shaken in the other [France]', the effect of the radical contrast is to direct our attention to the larger political disturbances caused in each case. The two Julys we present are not intended to contribute to the history of ideas or to the copious literature on both revolutions as political events. Rather we wish to direct attention to the fabrications of a date, a time, both in July and only ten days apart, which intricately weave fact and fiction, myth and ideology in ways that in both cases have turned out to be extremely durable. And seeing the two dates in the light of each other helps us identify the mechanisms which enable the perpetuation of the fantasies and socio-political desires that each year, when July rolls around, are once again agitated like an itch that will not settle down. If both the Fourth of July and the Fourteenth are involved, even invested, in social and political acts of commemoration, of a past and origin that must be remembered and in at least one case unambiguously celebrated, they both also signal the fact that what is blithely commemorated has as yet to become fully manifest. Acts of commemoration, then, wrapped up in the folds of aspiration: rehearsals of a past, both good and bad, as a means of continuation, looking forward to an as yet to be achieved futurity.

Notwithstanding these orientations, the conjoining of our two stories does provide the occasion for noting similarities and differences. To begin with, the two moments and their associated immediate contexts share some actors, individuals who played roles, even if minor, in the outcomes of both revolutionary events—men such as Franklin or Lafayette, Tom Paine or Gouverneur Morris. And both moments share a common European heritage of ideas, broadly conceived as 'Enlightenment' principles of rationality, individualism and religious toleration. But the differences at the level of close detail are perhaps more striking. To begin with, the precise historical and political contexts of each moment were very singular. The Declaration of Independence expressed, or more exactly performed, the rejection by the American colonists of rule from afar, specifically the authority of the king, George III, though, as subjects under the Crown whose right to the colonies was secured by royal warrant, they were not explicitly anti-monarchical as such. Neither of these considerations applies to 14 July. The issues surrounding the Parisian uprising were entirely internal to the nation. And although there was much mistrust of Louis XVI's intentions, no one, at least at this stage, apart from a few firebrands, conceived the project of an end to monarchy. In so far as 14 July was animated by any clear political aspirations at all, the aim was to temper not liquidate royal authority, by replacing absolutism based on the doctrine of divine right with a constitutional arrangement under which the monarch ceded a large measure of sovereignty to a national assembly of representatives.

The second major difference concerns the terms on which the respective Days have been commemorated. There have been attempts to link them. Two of the besiegers of the Bastille were soldiers who had fought in the War of Independence, while the most illustrious French combatant in the American war, Lafayette, was later to present George Washington with the keys to the Bastille. Yet this produced no enduring commemorative kinship. In France 14 July became an occasion of state, and remains such. In the United States, although most presidents make a speech somewhere, 4 July is not an official state ceremony. There is good reason why it is not, connected as it is to the long history of federalism and anti-federalism that informed both the founding and the making of the United States. The terms 'federalism' and 'anti-federalism' were understood quite differently in France, and where points of contact between the two commemorations are concerned, this has often lead to curious, and confused, affiliations. For instance, in the United States it was the anti-federalists in Boston and Philadelphia who incorporated the fall of the Bastille and the tricolour flag into their own 4 July festivities. But this reflected a misunderstanding: in France it was the 'federalists' (keen on regional autonomy) who approximated most closely to what in the United States went under the banner of anti-federalism (states' rights), while the main thrust of the anti-federalist cause in France pulled in the opposite direction, towards an ever more centralised state. In short, across the divide of the Atlantic, we encounter, around a roughly common vocabulary, very different political conceptions reacting to and informing very different circumstances.

It is, however, the third difference that is the most striking of all, in the character of the events themselves that took place. In the case of 4 July, there is from the word go a disjunct between what actually occurred (or rather what did not occur) and the celebratory fiction. Every American schoolchild is taught that a significant act took place in Philadelphia that day which involved the appending of signatures to a document that is now preserved in an airless box in Washington. The document—velum and manifestly real—is an historical artefact, but the act that supposedly created it is part fiction and part fact. The precise sinews of the moment are murky, difficult to ascertain. By contrast, there is no doubt whatsoever that something both determinate and dramatic took place in Paris on 14 July. The latter had its own raggedness, but it was far more cohesive as a day on which something definitive and defining took place: the Bastille was taken, an event in itself, as Georges Lefebvre put it, 'of minor importance' but momentous in consequence.

The modality of the events of 14 July was the brandishing not of bits of paper but of guns and pikes. It was an armed insurrection, an action on the streets backed by force of arms and as such entirely illegal. While we must be alert to the traps of reading 'backwards' from the perspective of subsequent developments, especially given the huge differences of both scale and intensity, 14 July is often seen as a dress rehearsal for the great *sans-culotte* uprisings of the period 1792–5 (although the view that 'the Terror was merely 1789 with a higher body count' is closer to headline-seeking journalism than to responsible historical inquiry). America was of course to plunge into violence on an epic scale, above all with the Civil War. The Declaration of Independence, however, though of course illegal from the point of view of the king and his ministers, was intended as a legal document, outlining why George III had abdicated his rights over the colonists. The latter were well versed in the legal literature and were essentially saying that, as in 1688, the king had acted 'illegally' in respect of his subjects. July 14 was not like this at all. No lawyerly arguments were made by those who stormed the Bastille. It was a day of violence, of a type which was to yield a new meaning for the word 'day' itself: what the historical actors were shortly to call the revolutionary *journée*.

These differences in the textures and meanings of the two events as precisely world historical events, are the legitimate concerns of good history. If, however, we examine not the events as such, but their long tails and tales, as mythopoetic objects, the similarities begin to emerge in fascinating ways. This is why we see the merit of running the two stories together as drawing attention to them as precisely stories. The one July, supposedly locked in to a singular day, the Fourth of July, 1776, when something, it is commonly assumed, momentous happened. The other, 14 July 1789, when events in all their messy incoherence and inconsistencies certainly did happen, but what and where, and who and when is as much a feature of a fiction, or set of fictions, as it is of historical record. Stories, in both cases, that have had and continue to have political valence: stories we want to believe in and stories we suspect as potentially damaging, obfuscatory props in continuing projects of state building and ideologies of belonging and exclusion. Stories to this day we have to negotiate, process and work with.

Such a contemporary vitalism can immediately be perceived when we turn our attention to the uses to which the two Julys are currently put, the one in the United States and the other in Republican France. Not only each to its immediate national context, but also each in the world at large, in the international context of geopolitics. In the case of 4 July, the uses to which the myths of the founding moment are being put are deeply embedded in an ongoing and deeply divisive battle whose conclusions are, of this moment, difficult to predict. Far from using the myths of founding as a means to rectify the glaring omissions of the actual founding moments, the slower process of constructing the modern polity that is the United States of America, contemporary arguments about the nature and constituency of that polity play fast and loose with the trump card, pun certainly intended, of origin. The supposed ineluctable authority of the true past, the supreme fiction of inhabiting the moment of origin and continuing to live by and uphold its supposed commitments, beliefs, laws and modes of civility, polity, person. Such a ploy, rhetorical for sure, but also powerfully irresponsible, can be seen at work all over contemporary America, from legal arguments spuriously based on 'originalism' to social justice campaigns seeking to draw their moral and political authority from different myths of origin, as in the 1619 Project created by *The New York Times*, which, for reasons that some may find excusable, seeks to rewrite the myth of founding of the nation so as to claim a different moment than that commemorated in the received story, whereby a bunch of men, mostly well off and professional, who had their own interests firmly to the fore, debated and argued in a stuffy room with its doors closed so as to prevent others overhearing their deliberations, one hot day in July in Philadelphia. No, they claim, this was not the founding moment. It was in August 1619, when a ship whose cargo included twenty enslaved Africans, landed and these people were sold to the forebears of the colonists who just over a one hundred and fifty years later would go on to put in place the administrative and political structures that to this day continue to uphold and create discrimination among the peoples of the nation. The observation regarding discrimination is irrefutable, but the myth of origin is no less fantastical than the one it seeks to supplant. To reinforce our point above, we do not seek to offer a better narrative, or more correct history, rather we aim to make as transparent as possible the ways in which myths of founding are created, and, more importantly, how their uses have real, all too seductive, effects and consequences.

In the case of the Fourteenth, the state-sponsored celebrations that occur throughout France every year reimpose and reaffirm a set of expectations and obligations to a particular political entity called 'The Republic' which may, to some extent, honour the spirit of the moment of origin, but which also fails to advance the revolutionary ideals that gave rise to it. The stories of the Fourteenth are used, each year, as a means for perpetuating the myths of a revolution that dismantles and then reassembles the sinews of power that construct the polity on behalf of all its citizens, without prejudice. Memory and commemoration shape and repeat a tale saturated in controversy, politically and ideologically fraught, while increasingly becoming an exercise in showmanship, starting with the late nineteenth-century institution of Bastille Day, culminating in the extravagant spectacles of the Bicentennial.

But for now, let us return to beginnings and, from the narrative point of view, to a major point of comparison, namely, the role, at once pivotal and seminal, played by very special forms of the political Meeting, the first in Philadelphia, the second at Versailles. On 4 July 1776, the great and the good of the Second Continental Congress assembled in the Philadelphia State House to frame and debate the terms of a Declaration. On 20 June 1789, the representatives of the Third Estate, having provocatively announced their formation as a National Assembly on the 17th, gathered to swear an Oath in a tennis court. What followed from both is broadly the story of this book.

First we go to Philadelphia.

PART ONE

THE FOURTH

Peter de Bolla

1

The Philadelphia Gathering

If there is any one thing that has singularly determined the shape and focus for the story of the Fourth of July, it is this image. It depicts a moment which in many of the narratives recounting the creation of the United States of America is said to be the originary moment. There are other moments, for sure, which might make a similar claim: the resolution of Congress to adopt the Constitution, for example. But none have been represented in so varied media and contributed so significantly to the iconology of the United States. The painting itself has three versions and it has been reproduced at various times on postage stamps, currency and china, not to mention the hundreds of thousands of prints and photographs which have been taken from it. It is easy to understand why its dissemination has been so extensive since it documents the birthday of the nation. It is a snapshot of what transpired on 4 July 1776. Many, certainly millions of people, have seen this version of the painting which hangs in the Rotunda of the Capitol in Washington, DC. It was commissioned by Congress in a vote of 6 February 1817 authorising the fourth president, James Madison, to approach the artist John Trumbull with a request that he create four paintings commemorating the history of American independence. The title of the painting is *The Declaration of Independence.*

Many of the men depicted, life size, seated around the edges of the room, are no longer prominent characters in the common

1. Declaration of Independence (1819), by John Trumbull

knowledge of contemporary Americans, notwithstanding the voluminous literature, both scholarly and popular, on the founding of the nation. Some of them, even in their own lifetimes, were never particularly well known outside, perhaps, the colony or even town in which they lived. But collectively they are notorious. This is the body of men who comprised the Second Continental Congress: these are the Signers of the Declaration of Independence. Each of them (excepting the man with the hat—the only man wearing a hat—standing in front of the door on the left-hand side), painstakingly rendered in portrait likeness by the artist, assented to the irrevocable step of signalling to the world at large the separation of the colonies from the mother country, thereby instituting the process that was to lead to the creation of the first modern republic: The United States of America. In so far as any snapshot can encapsulate a process, this image conveys the signal moment in the story of the Fourth of July.

Although the events of that day in 1776 have been celebrated, for the most part continuously, since 1777, understanding has varied of what precisely did occur in the State House in Philadelphia when these men collectively agreed to the wording of a document that had been drafted primarily by one man, the tall figure in the central group of the painting standing closest to the left side of the desk with a document in his hands, the man who would become the third president of the republic, Thomas Jefferson. Over the course of the following chapters the extent of this variation will become clear. But let us begin with our own moment in time, with what one might reasonably expect most people today to know about 4 July 1776.

The land mass we now refer to as North America was, in 1776, home to thirteen colonies, all of them independently founded at different times over the previous 169 years and each administered by separate institutions within each colony. All were beholden to the British government under the provisions of their own distinct charters and legal instruments which collectively determined that relationship as colonial. By the middle of the eighteenth century those relations had become very strained, so that by the time of the Stamp Act in 1765, which levied a tax on documents, newspapers and nearly every form of paper used in the colonies, many citizens were beginning to advocate independence from the mother country.

Although each of the colonies administered its own affairs, it had become clear by 1765 that acting in concert over the Stamp Act would be advantageous. In October of that year thirty-seven delegates representing each of the colonies met in New York to draw up a plan of action. Ten years later, when the Second Continental Congress first met in May 1775, irritation and dissatisfaction with the King's behaviour towards the colonies was running at such a pace that the political will to launch a revolution was in the ascendant. His Majesty's attempts to steer a course away from confrontation were less than half-hearted: as far as many of his ministers were concerned, the hotheads in the colonies were 'rebels' and needed to be brought back into line by military force. When the shot heard around the world was fired in April 1775 both sides began to be locked into a confrontation which was unlikely to end amicably. And so by the summer of 1776, 'independency', as it was referred to at the time, was seen by many as the inevitable next step. This is where the story of 4 July makes its entrance.

Of all the things that might be within common knowledge about that day in 1776, the one that appears to be a constant is the fact that something momentous occurred in the State House in Philadelphia. Here, in words taken from a book entitled *The Declaration of Independence* by Hal Marcovitz, one of a series of books for young students called 'American Symbols and their Meanings', is how that story is told:

> On July 4 the Congress intended to vote specifically on the declaration drafted by Jefferson. ... The delegates entered the Philadelphia State House through the large doorway facing Chestnut Street. Above the door hung the royal coat of arms—the final reminder to them that they were still living under the oppressive will of the King of England. The delegates met in the white-paneled meeting room on the east side of the building. Above, an elaborate crystal chandelier provided candle light. There were two fireplaces in the room and tall windows lining the walls. Displayed in the room were a British drum, swords, and flag captured in 1775 by Continental Army soldiers under the command of Ethan Allan at the battle of Fort Ticonderoga.

The detail of the description gives it a sense of accuracy that helps transport the reader to the physical location, the very room in which the Declaration was made. For many readers it must have an air of familiarity about it since Marcovitz is essentially describing the image millions have seen in the Capitol, the image with which I began. A painting which itself is clothed in the rhetoric of authenticity and historical exactitude: Trumbull, as the evidence of his correspondence and sketches demonstrate, went to extreme pains to produce a documentary image. He travelled across the states tracking down those people who had been present on 4 July 1776 in this room in Philadelphia in order to accurately portray their faces in his painting. Of course, his subjects had advanced in years by the time Trumbull came with pencil, pen or brush in hand, since he only began studies for the painting in Paris in 1785. It was not completed until 1818. No wonder so many of them look so august. Similarly, the room he positioned them in, with its drum, swords, flags and doorways, is presented to us as an accurate depiction of the Assembly Room in the State House. But when he began his initial sketches of the composition for the painting in the company of Thomas Jefferson—in fact it was Jefferson who had suggested the subject for the painting—he had never visited Philadelphia. He was, therefore, completely reliant upon the sketch of the room that Jefferson made for him, and, as we now know, Jefferson had misremembered many of the details, including the positions of the doorways and the adornments to the walls. Trumbull, in a later version of the same painting, took great care to correct these errors.

Leaving aside the accuracy of the depiction of the room, Marcovitz's narrative then moves into what transpired that day:

> At the front of the room stood the president's dais—a raised table and chair usually occupied by the speaker of the Pennsylvania Assembly. On July 4, 1776, delegate John Hancock of Massachusetts sat at that table, having been named president of the Congress by the other delegates. Hancock dropped the gavel to open the

debate. One by one, delegates from the 13 colonies took turns making their arguments on independence.

Then, following a preamble about the discussions held on the days leading up to the 4th, he states that 'the declaration was read'. Finally, after further discussion and changes to the document that Jefferson and his committee had submitted, 'a roll call vote was taken' in which 'all delegates but those representing New York cast their ballots for independence'. Then, Marcovitz states, came the moment which, for a complex set of reasons discussed in the chapters following, essentially marks the beginning of the nation: the document was signed. 'At first', he writes, 'the declaration received just two signatures—those of Hancock, the president of the Congress, and Charles Thomson, the secretary.' Later—how much later he does not say—'the signatures of the other delegates were added'.

This can be said to be the kernel of the story of the Fourth of July. Although some people today, be they Americans or citizens of other countries, might struggle to capture much of its detail—indeed they may even have forgotten why celebrations take place that day—very few would contest the basic fact that the Declaration of Independence was made on 4 July 1776. There are countless representations of this fact and the painting with which I began provides evidence of a kind for it. Yet if we look at it with a little more historical information at our disposal and with a cool, keen eye, we can begin to see some of the multiple threads woven throughout the story which begin to unsettle what can be said to be common knowledge.

Is this image really presenting a moment to us and, if so, can we be certain which moment it might be? It may be the case, for example, that Trumbull did not have in mind the depiction of a single moment at all; he may have set out to collapse a number of significant moments into each other as he struggled to produce an iconic image to fit the brief Congress had given him. But let us leave this possibility aside in order to see how Trumbull's painting might be read as recording either of two quite different acts which are part of the history of the document we know as the Declaration of Independence. On the one hand it might be depicting the first time that Jefferson and his four accomplices presented to Congress the draft they had prepared of that document. This took place on 28 June. Since the five-person team that was the drafting committee occupies the centre of the image it might be understood in this way. But in the subsequent history of the Declaration no one has ever made a strong case for the significance of 28 June, so it would seem to be unlikely that Trumbull intended to depict that moment. It is much more likely that the artist, in discussion with Jefferson in Paris in 1785, began to formulate how he might depict the moment which, even by then, had come to be seen as a defining moment in the history of American independence, the moment at which the Declaration was signed. And this, as everyone knows, took place on 4 July.

This would seem to be a more plausible account of what we see. It explains why Jefferson is depicted gesturing with his left hand, pointing to the place at the bottom of the document where

2. John Hancock's Signature

the person seated on the other side of the table, John Hancock, was supposed to sign his name.

And here, in this illustration of the document we now know as The Declaration of Independence, is how Hancock left his signature to history and in the process bequeathed a figure of speech used to refer to the mark we call a signature: a 'Hancock'. But if Trumbull's painting depicts what happened on 4 July, Jefferson cannot be holding the document whose facsimile appears above since that was only made later, under instruction from Congress in a resolution of 19 July 1776. Furthermore, there is no record of the signatories to that sheet of parchment ever coming together as a body in the room depicted by Trumbull for the express purpose of signing the document now preserved in the State Archives in Washington, DC. Nevertheless, to millions of viewers, what is seen, frozen in time, is the moment at which the declaration was made, and what is understood by 'making' the declaration is naturally and effortlessly assumed to be the same thing as *signing* the document.

If many of the faces around the outer edges of the room are only now familiar to historians and amateurs of the revolutionary period, the group in the centre of the painting depicts at least three men who have subsequently become heroic actors in the story of the formation of the republic. Known to us as Founding Fathers, they were instrumental in the founding of America.

At the left of the group is John Adams, the second president of the United States and one of the most important figures in the colonial struggle for independence. He was forty-one in 1776 and had by that time made his reputation in Massachusetts as a lawyer and a man of considerable learning. He did not mince his words and argued his case with passion and energy. Within his own lifetime he was dubbed 'the Atlas of American Independence'.

At the far right is Benjamin Franklin, perhaps the most variously talented and gifted of all those who played a role in the founding of the nation. He was the oldest Signer of the Declaration, well into his seventieth year in July 1776. Printer, member of the Assembly in Pennsylvania, scientist and diplomat, Franklin's humour and intelligence were indelibly scored across the political debates which eventually brought independence to the colonies.

And heading the group, standing in closest proximity to the table and holding the document he was to come to think of as his own property, is Thomas Jefferson. The story of the founding of America that it tells would be almost unimaginable without him.

2

The Event and the Myth

Philadelphia, 4 July 1776

It wasn't, in the overall scheme of things, such a big deal. The weather all summer had been sticky but rarely swelteringly hot. Conditions had been a little different inside the chamber of the State House in which the Second Continental Congress held its meetings since sessions were held with windows closed and doors locked to prevent anyone overhearing the deliberations. On the morning of the 4th, at 6 a.m., Thomas Jefferson recorded that the temperature was 68 degrees Fahrenheit. There was a modest south-easterly breeze and it looked as if it would be another humid day, although the future third president noted in his diary that he distrusted his thermometer and needed to buy a new one.

About fifty delegates to the Congress were in Philadelphia that day—the exact number is not known—those from Pennsylvania, not surprisingly, outnumbering the representatives from the other twelve colonies. Some of the most important spokesmen for independence, such as Richard Henry Lee and George Wythe, had left the city nearly a month earlier on 13 June. The previous day, on the 12th, Congress had appointed yet another committee—this one to draft proposals for a putative confederal structure for the thirteen colonies.

Independence was in the air, though no one at that moment

could have predicted precisely when the majority of delegates from each colony would finally sign up for separation. Some of them, like John Adams, had been gasping for the ratification of what they believed to be inevitable for months. Others were only slowly coming around to accepting the final and decisive step into a new era. And then there were those delegates whose personal or professional lives were in the immediate term taking their full attention: Oliver Wolcott from Connecticut, for example, had left Philadelphia on account of illness. Some, like Lewis Morris, the tall, handsome Yale-educated aristocrat from New York, had to deal with local crises back in their home towns or colonies—Morris had been called away to take command of a local militia. There was, then, no sense that 4 July would become, in John Adams's words, the 'epochal' moment. Those who remained in Philadelphia rose early since the meeting was scheduled to begin at 9 a.m. and the agenda was lengthy. No one doubted that these were dangerous times.

Uppermost in everyone's mind was the intelligence that had arrived five days earlier: around one hundred and fifty of His Majesty's ships had been sighted off Sandy Hook. For some time now, it had been clear to the Committee of Safety that the strength of individual militias in each colony would not be sufficient to repel the forces of the British. They had, therefore, recommended to Congress that a 'flying camp' be formed. This was to comprise the various town militias from a number of colonies which could move swiftly to wherever a military crisis seemed imminent. It was fortunate that Congress had adopted this recommendation without too much debate since the current situation was becoming critical. For—on the morning of 3 July—news was abroad that the fleet had landed on Staten Island. Most of the delegates reasoned that an immediate attempt on New York was likely to be deemed too hazardous by His Majesty's forces, and, this being so, the most proximate colonies of Pennsylvania and New Jersey would become prime targets. As day broke on the 4th the four men who served on the Committee of Safety—Benjamin Franklin, Robert Livingston, Francis Hopkinson and John Dickinson—knew they would have to assess the risk of imminent hostilities within the colony and recommend a course of action to their colleagues. And each delegate knew that the committee's proposals would undoubtedly be the main business of the day.

And so it proved to be. The four men met with great urgency. One of their number, Robert Livingston, was instructed to draft a letter to the Lancaster Associators setting out the plan to form a flying camp. A second committee, the Committee of Inspection chaired by Thomas McKean, a young lawyer from Delaware, also met that day and conferred with the field officers who were in Philadelphia. During the afternoon of 4 July Congress ratified the letters that each of these committees proposed and instructed that they be printed as a single document and dispatched by rider to Lancaster. This was the only official written communication issued by Congress that day. It begins:

> Gentlemen,
> The congress this morning directed us to confer with the Committees of Safety and Inspection, and the Field Officers now in town, about the proper mode of collecting the militia of this province, in order to form a flying camp, to cover Pennsylvania and New-Jersey, from the Attacks of the Enemy, who have landed on Staten-Island, and will probably direct their March this Way, if they should imagine the Attempt on New-York too hazardous.

It is true that some business from two days earlier needed to be dealt with. At the conclusion of the discussion of the draft declaration which had begun on 1 July it had become clear that unanimity was now in sight and the resolution beginning 'these colonies are, and of right ought to be, free and independent

States' was likely to be passed. But by the end of the long second day, Tuesday 2 July, it was still unclear as to how this intention to signal the colonists' separation from the mother country ought to be broadcast and acted upon. This was to take up the first hour or so of the business on the 4th. By 11 a.m., the entire thing was done and dusted. A local printer by the name of John Dunlap was to be instructed to print up the text they had approved two days earlier and instructions for its public dissemination were to be sent to the various colonies and to the army that was under the direction of George Washington. Then discussion of a further fourteen items of business commenced. The noble words we now revere which begin 'When in the course of human events' were not proclaimed from the steps of the State House. No bells rang. No fireworks were sent into the blue sky. It was another Thursday in the long march towards independence. That was it.

It must be said that throughout the summer the idea of revolution had been gently simmering away. The delegates collected together in Philadelphia had been pushing around the arguments for and against 'independency' for months. Some, like John Dickinson, a brilliant lawyer from Pennsylvania, were yet to be convinced that complete separation at this moment was timely, and these men, though certainly not loyalists, kept open the possibility of voting against the declaration right up to the last. But by the turn of June into July there were too many now minded to embark upon the adventure of what would come to be seen as the first truly modern republic. And although no one was in any doubt about the danger of separation, or in any doubt about the illegality of it according to the laws in place in each of the colonies, most were also now firmly committed to the revolution in government that the firebrands had been promoting since the Stamp Act eleven years earlier. Trepidation and excitement in equal measure were certainly in the air in Philadelphia that summer in 1776, so when it was finally done, when all the colonies excepting New York, which had abstained in the crucial vote on 2 July, voted for independence there was some cause for celebration. At least to those who were now sold on the idea of creating a new nation. But of course throughout the colonies, for reasons of vested interest, sentimental attachment to the mother country, dyed-in-the-wool loyalty to authority and tradition or just plain fear of the consequences of embarking upon what could still be regarded as a treasonable act, many remained opposed to the hotheads in Philadelphia. Above all else we must remember that in 1776, on 4 July, the outcome of the declaration seeking to announce the intention to 'dissolve the political bands' which had, heretofore, connected one people with another was unknown.

For those like John Adams, who had been advocating separation for so long and whose views were a matter of public record, the vote on 2 July was the culmination of years of persuasion and debate. Even those delegates, like John Witherspoon, the president of the College of New Jersey at Princeton, who came late to the political struggle were now fully convinced that it was time to seize the day. Witherspoon, who was said to be one of the very few men of his era whose weight or force of presence rivalled that of Washington himself, had risen to his feet on 2 July to support the move for independence by claiming that the country was 'not only ripe for the measure but in danger of rotting for the want of it'. So yes, there was reason for celebration when the die was finally cast on 2 July.

But even then, on that rather hotter Tuesday when the Congress had once more rehearsed the arguments, now overly familiar to everyone, the decision felt anticlimactic. At least it did so to John Adams who wrote to his wife the next day: 'Had a Declaration of Independency been made seven Months ago, it would have been attended with many great and glorious effects ... We might before this Hour, have formed Alliances with foreign States.' For Adams the cost of delaying the decision had been significant. It had, for example, resulted in the loss of Canada for the Union. Notwithstanding these differences of opinion he nevertheless rather grudgingly granted that the slow process had also had its advantages: 'time has been given for the whole People', he wrote in the same letter, 'maturely to consider the great Question of Independence and to ripen their Judgments, dissipate their Fears and allure their Hopes, by discussing it, in Assemblies, Conventions, Committees of Safety and Inspection, in Town and County Meetings, as well as in private Conversations, so that the whole People in every Colony of the 13, have now adopted it, as their own Act.'

As far as Adams was concerned the progress leading towards independence had not been particularly smooth. There had been moments when the general drift in the direction of independence got stuck, and then others when it looked more likely. But although he had lived the political process which resulted in an act that was to be decisive, he would have been hard pressed to say when, exactly, that process had come to its resolution. On 1 July, when the debate at last came formally to the Congress? Or the following day at the conclusion of that debate? Adams had not doubted the outcome for weeks. As far as he was concerned the only remaining impediment was the slow progress towards unanimity of all thirteen colonies.

But history, in the sense of what happened, always comes to us in the form of punctual moments—this happened on that day, at such and such a time, in this place, and so on. When we attempt to reconstruct the sequence and consequence of past events it is inevitable that history seems to be full of such decisive moments. But there are many kinds of 'event' in history. Some, of a cataclysmic kind, like earthquakes or the beheading of a monarch, can be precisely dated, even timed. One might say that their temporality is that of the instrument we use for registering the spinning of the earth on its axis: the clock. But most of those things we like to think of as 'historical events' are not like this, and as we know from our own lived experience, these kinds of events have a different kind of temporality. When we look at them closely we see that they have no singular moment of 'happening'. In the sense that 4 July 1776 was an 'event', that something happened that day which by long tradition is celebrated each year, it can be said to have never happened. It is a peculiar, though not unique, kind of historical event.

While it is certainly true that something connected to the Declaration of Independence did happen on 4 July 1776 in Philadelphia, it is also true that from that day to this the celebration that is entered into on the Fourth is not of *that*. For what happened that day in Congress was the agreement to print and publish the Declaration whose form of words had first been presented two days earlier. But, as we shall see below, even if a case can be made for assigning the 'punctuality' of the event to 2 July, there are problems here too. In fact, once we begin to trace carefully the origin of any political act, the idea that there might be a *moment* at which such acts come into being begins to feel like sand in the outstretched palm of the hand. Such and such a decision may have been taken at such and such a time—even precisely date- and time-stamped—but then this decision turns out to have been built upon or implied by an earlier one, and so on.

Of course, it might be said in riposte to this kind of thinking that we are merely splitting hairs, or standing too much on an obstructive principle of accuracy. So what if the Declaration was actually made two days earlier? Surely the point of the celebrations on the 4th is to mark the moment at which a new nation came into being. Or to honour and reaffirm the principles upon which that new nation was founded. And this is undoubtedly so. But there is also a more interesting story to be told. For what the history of the tradition of the Fourth allows us to see is the past and present significance of the celebratory act. Furthermore, it brings into sharp focus the fact that honouring the Fourth *does* something; it is not, in itself, an inert political act. Thus, as will become evident, although the moment of the Declaration was to those who lived through the time of its enunciation a matter of no real importance—note, this is not to say that what the Declaration set out to achieve was insignificant; nothing could be less accurate than to propose that—the fact that subsequently it became possible to claim that it was a *punctual moment*, and moreover that its significance substantially lies in that punctuality, has become one of the most important features of its continuing political resonance. The claim, indeed the belief, that the Declaration happened at a stroke, as it were, when the words of the document were first enunciated provides the scaffolding for a new kind of political agency. A republic whose legitimating institution is the collective speaking as one: we the people.

John Adams, as we have seen, thought that the final debates were nothing more than pro forma. Writing to Samuel Chase on 1 July he reported that the first day of the momentous discussion was 'an idle mispence of time, for nothing was said but what had been repeated and hackneyed in that room before, a hundred times, for six months past'. But even he fell into the rhetoric of the punctual, recognising that even if the movement towards separation from Britain and the consequent foundation of a new political entity was now inevitable, this first step into an uncertain future nevertheless needed its moment of ratification. So, on the same day that he wrote to his wife in terms effectively saying 'no big deal—we should have done it months ago', he also says:

> Yesterday the greatest Question was decided, which was ever debated in America, and a greater perhaps, never was or will be decided among Men. A Resolution was passed without one dissenting Colony, 'that these united Colonies, are, and of Right ought to be free and independent States, and as such, they have, and of Right ought to have full Power to make War, conclude Peace, establish Commerce, and to do all the other Acts and Things, which other States may rightfully do'.

And then in a second letter the same day, obviously having had some time to mull things over, air his sense of frustration, commiserate perhaps with some of his colleagues from Massachusetts over the length of time it had taken, he eventually finds a residue of energy and excitement. 'But the Day is past,' he reflects on the struggle to achieve unanimity, 'The Second Day of July 1776, will be the most memorable Epocha, in the History of America.' Then, warming to his theme: 'I am apt to believe that it will be celebrated, by succeeding Generations, as the great anniversary Festival. It ought to be solemnized with Pomp and Parade, with Shews, Games, Sports, Guns, Bells, Bonfires and Illuminations from one End of this Continent to the other from this Time forward forever more.' Well, he may have got the day wrong, but he was pretty firmly on the button with everything else. Just how prescient will become clear as we follow the invention and adoption of the various rituals comprising the tradition of celebration that is the Fourth.

But if Adams thought that 2 July marked the moment at which the course of human history changed, others who had also lived through the weeks, months and years of political debate felt the pressure of different moments along the way. Congress had met on 28 June to read the draft of the Declaration that had been prepared by Thomas Jefferson, and the consideration of the text that day can, to some extent, be said to mark the moment when separation from the mother country moved from the hypothetical to the realisable. We do not know what was said once Congress formed itself as the 'Committee of the Whole' since no minutes of these meetings were taken. But we do know that the draft prepared by Jefferson was altered and that on 28 June Congress decided to postpone its ratification of the document for another three days. So expectations were already building about the potential significance for the *first* of July, the day when the matter, it was thought, would be resolved. John Penn, one of the many delegates who practised law when in his home colony, in his case North Carolina, wrote from Philadelphia on 28 June.

> The first day of July will be an era of great importance as that is the day for debating the great and important question of Independance and from what I have seen there is no doubt but a total separation between Britain and her Colonies, that were, will take place as all the Provinces but Maryland are for it, and the Inhabitants there are coming over fast. I fear most people are too sanguine relative to commerce, however it is a measure our enemies have forced upon us. I don't doubt but we shall have spirit enough to act like men, indeed it could no longer be delayed.

As things turned out it took another day to get to the actual resolution, but many of those present recognised that by the end of Monday 1 July it was a fait accompli. This was certainly the view of the man who is said to have cast the first vote for independence, Josiah Bartlett, the physician from New Hampshire. He had written from Philadelphia to John Langdon on 1 July: 'The affair of Independency has been this day determined in a Committee of the Whole; by next Post I expect you will receive a formal declaration with the reasons ...' So a case could be mounted for proposing 1 July as the significant punctual moment, especially given the fact that notwithstanding the secrecy which surrounded the deliberations of the Committee of the Whole—or at least its desire to prevent anything incriminating getting into the record—it would appear that the entire city was aware of what was happening. As the 32-year-old Elbridge Gerry, one of the Massachusetts delegation, wrote to James Warren on 2 July, 'I have only time to inform you that yesterday was agitated in Congress the great question of Independency'. But this, he makes clear, was hardly a secret: 'as the facts are well known at the Coffee-House of the city as in Congress, I may go on to inform you that, in a Committee of the whole House, it was carried by nine Colonies.' Surely it is reasonable to assume that if the talk of the coffee houses had been this explicit it would have been likely for such intelligence to spread far and wide, its progress determined merely by the speed at which a horse and rider might travel between towns across the colonies.

If a case for the decisive moment can be made for the Monday or Tuesday of the first week in July it begins to erode the sense one might hold onto that a political act of this kind has a precise origin. Just as the debate that took place on 1 July—not conclusive in a technical sense, but nevertheless definitive in outline and consequence—had been proleptically signalled at the meeting on 28 June, so that meeting had been foreseen by the earlier resolution made on 10 June which states 'that the consideration of the first resolution [regarding separation] be postponed to this day, three weeks [i.e. 1 July]'. Although at this time a number of colonies had yet to fully instruct their delegates to vote in favour of the resolution, it is clear from the Journal of the Congress that the drift was towards a declaration of independence, since on that day, 10 June, it is recorded that Congress also agreed that 'a committee be appointed to prepare a declaration to the effect of the said first resolution, which is in these words: "That these United Colonies are, and of right ought to be, free and independent states"'. And the next day it is recorded that Congress duly appointed a five-man committee with instructions to draft a document expressing the colonists' desire to separate from the mother country. It could be argued that in setting up such a committee to draft the document the move towards independence had in effect been decided.

But, again, the appointment on 11 June of Jefferson, Adams, Franklin, Sherman and Livingston to a drafting committee with instructions to draw up the document that was to become the first text of the new nation was itself the outcome of a discussion held three days before, on 7 June. It is, in fact, on this day that for the first time independence can be said to have been within the reach of the colonists as an achievable political act. Since we do not know what was said the day Richard Henry Lee got to his feet and proposed, under instruction from the Virginia convention, 'that these United Colonies, are, and of right ought to be, free and independent states: that they are absolved from all allegiance to the British Crown; and that all political connection between them and the state of Great Britain is, and ought to be, totally dissolved'—words that were inserted by Congress into Jefferson's final paragraph of the document that is now revered as his—we can nevertheless surmise that, since further discussion of his proposal was postponed so that delegates could return to their colonies in order to ascertain the measure of support for such a bold step, it must have been the case that a significant number of delegates present on 7 June were minded to vote for independence. It could be said, then, that the decisive moment was 7 June.

The first time the text of the Declaration was, in a simple sense, 'declared' in public occurred on 8 July when a member of the Committee of Safety—probably John Nixon—stood in the State House yard and read the document aloud to a large crowd of people. According to John Adams, cheers rose up; the battalions paraded on the common and fired into the air. He claimed that 'the bells rang all day and almost all night'. And so the tradition of celebration that was to become The Fourth of July began, on 8 July.

The Fourth of July 1776

History tells a different story. At least the history which has become woven into the fabric of the nation's founding promotes a rather more climactic version of what happened that day. Although the account of events that follows is certainly inaccurate as far as we are able to reconstruct them, it is also, simultaneously, an accurate rendition of the myth that, through repeated telling over the stretch of time between then and now, millions of Americans have learnt as the truth. It is a story that helps one come to an understanding of an extremely complex political and conceptual event: the birth of a nation. Even if, as shall become clear, the notion that nations have singular moments of birth is recognised as suspect, it nevertheless remains the case that without the transforming aid of narrative, history in the sense of what happened remains inert, beyond or beside the reach of understanding.

In point of fact, to this day most Americans believe that the celebrations on the 4th do not commemorate the moment when the Declaration was *made*, howsoever that might be understood, but the act of *signing* the document itself. That this is so tells us something about the power of the signature and its assumed guarantee of veracity. It is not enough, in a curious way, that the words of the Declaration might have been spoken at a particular moment—in the State House, outside in the yard, from the steps of meeting halls all over the colonies. For what seals the authenticity of the origin, what allows it to be elevated to the status of the moment of origin is the fact of the signature. And, given that this was a collective act—Congress issued the document we know as The Declaration of Independence—it requires more than one signature. At least its declaratory power would be diminished were it to have been signed by only one person, say John Hancock, the president of the Second Continental Congress, even if he was the delegated representative of that body. Consequently, as we know, the 4th was the day on which fifty-five members of the Congress that was to secure the fate of the colonies *signed* the declaration (the fifty-sixth, John Dickinson, having declined to add his signature).

It is true to say that the record of the Congress is itself contradictory on this point, but for reasons that will be explained below it is relatively easy to reconcile the discrepancies. In any case it is very unlikely that the various versions of these early congressional meetings, with minutes and resolutions taken in something approaching Masonic code, kick-started the story that has been learnt by millions. It is almost certain that the source of the claim that the Declaration was signed on 4 July is to be found in the writings of Jefferson, who stated in a letter written to S.A. Wells on 12 May 1819 that he had kept notes throughout the meetings in Philadelphia during the summer of '76. These were subsequently written up in his own Journals at a distance of time that is unknown. Jefferson's notes, as preserved, are in fact pretty sketchy but it is the following entry that gave birth to the story countless generations of Americans have passed down as lore. Jefferson states: 'The debates having taken up the greater parts of the 2d, 3d and 4th days of July, were, in the evening of the last, closed', and he continues, 'the declaration was reported by the commee[*sic*], agreed to by the house; and signed by every member except Mr Dickinson.'

Jefferson was writing to Wells seven years before he died, and at that time, late in life with his future reputation much in mind, he was vigorously constructing a platform to support the edifice that was to become his legacy and memorial: Thomas Jefferson, author of the Declaration of Independence. He was also remembering events that happened forty-three years earlier. There is a great deal of evidence, albeit some of it circumstantial, pointing to the conclusion that on 4 July 1776 no signatures were appended to any document. But even if they were, it is most likely that only two, those of the president and secretary of the Congress, were signed at the bottom of the text following the standard format for all the documents that were issued by Congress at the time. As we have already seen, the discussion on the 4th resulted in an instruction given to John Dunlap to print the words that were now agreed, but it has never been claimed that this material document (such as it may have been) or any of its copies is the Declaration. That honour belongs to a subsequent artefact, the piece of parchment on which the words were inscribed as per the resolution Congress made on 19 July. And we know for certain that this document was subsequently signed since it survives to the present day and may be inspected in the National Archives. But even this may not be the original or first signed document. The *Journals of Congress* refer to a 'comparison' of the parchment copy, but to what is not recorded.

On 6 August 1822, Jefferson, having just received a copy of the printed *Journals of Congress* (they had remained confidential until that year), added a marginal comment to his copy of a letter he had sent S.A. Wells three years before. Jefferson, as is well known, was fastidious in his correspondence, having invented a copying machine which allowed him to keep multiple copies of letters he penned, and kept not only the replies to his letters but also copies of his own. In this addendum to the original letter sent to Wells on 12 May 1819, prompted by what he had just read in the record of Congress's meetings, Jefferson claimed that the 'comparison' mentioned in the *Journals* was between the parchment and a paper version of the same document. Furthermore, there is an implication that both included the signatures of the delegates. Unfortunately there is no corroborating evidence for what Jefferson referred to as the 'original signed on paper' anywhere in the substantial archive of letters, papers, minutes, or journals of any of the key players of 4 July 1776.

And in point of fact, already by the turn of the century, as the story of the nation was being refined and remade, the veracity of the account in the printed *Journals of Congress* of what happened on 4 July in the State House in Philadelphia had been questioned. One of the delegates to the Congress, Thomas McKean from Delaware, was first to raise the alarm in a letter to Alexander James Dallas of 26 September 1796. In the course of this correspondence he questions whether the public record does, in fact, get the matter right. He wrote: 'By the printed publications referred to it would appear as if the fifty-five Gentlemen, whose names are there printed and none other, were on that day personally present in Congress and assenting the declaration: Whereas the truth is otherwise.' It has been suggested that the origin of this inaccuracy lays in the misreading of both the printed *Journals* and Jefferson's own notes, taken during the meeting and subsequently written up. But a careful reading of the printed Congress *Journals* indicates that a blank space was left at the time of writing up the meeting of 4 July so that at a later date the full text of the Declaration, with signatures, could be inserted. When it came to printing up the *Journals*, the document, which by then had been in the public domain for over forty years—the vellum with its impressive looking legal handwriting—provided the text complete with signatures. And we know that the vellum document was made following the resolution passed on 19 July 1776 by the Second Continental Congress which indicates that it was to be signed by all the delegates. If, as Jefferson claimed, a different paper version was also signed the Journals are silent on the matter.

As for the misreading of Jefferson's note it has been claimed that Jefferson did not mean to imply that the document was signed at the conclusion of the debate, on the evening of 4 July. Rather, so it is said, his last clause indicating that it was signed 'by every member except Mr Dickinson' gives no indication as to *when* those signatures were appended. Whatever we make of these corrections and counter-claims it remains the case that the common understanding of the events of 4 July has it that the document was signed by the fifty-five assenting delegates that day. This we know to be false. As Thomas McKean's letter continues, 'The following Gentlemen were not Members of Congress on the 4th day of July, 1776, namely, Mathew Thornton, Benjamin Rush, George Clymer, James Smith, George Taylor and George Ross: the last five named were not chosen Delegates until the 20th day of the Month, the first not until the 12th day of September following, nor did he take his seat in Congress until the 4th of November, which was four Months after.'

These are correct statements. Although each of the five Pennsylvania delegates voted into Congress on 20 July were proud to sign the document after they took their seats, the record indicates that they were not present for the debate which concluded with the order to print the document we know as The Declaration of Independence. And, to make matters worse, at least for Thomas McKean, the relevant volume of the printed Journals of Congress was also inaccurate in its omissions. As McKean writes:

> Modesty should not rob any man of his just honour, when by that honour his modesty cannot be offended. My name is not in the printed Journals of Congress as party to the declaration of Independence, and this, like an error in the first concoction, has vitiated most of the subsequent publications; and yet the fact is, that I was then a member of Congress for the State of Delaware, was personally present in Congress and voted in favour of independence on the 4th day of July 1776, and signed the declaration after it had been engrossed on parchment, where my name in my own hand writing still appears.

Of course McKean's correction, made as it was at the end of the eighteenth century, could easily have fallen into the inner recesses of the archive where it may have languished forever more. But in 1922 Carl Becker published a book that was to become a standard source for the history of the era—*The Declaration of Independence: A Study in the History of Political Ideas*—in which he pointed out in very direct language that 'Contrary to a tradition early established and long held, the Declaration was not signed by the members of Congress on July 4th'. Becker was himself drawing on the work of John Hazelton, published as *The Declaration of Independence: its History* in 1904; it is a curious fact, however, that from 1922 until 1978, when Garry Wills published *Inventing America: Jefferson's Declaration of Independence*, scholarship by and large turned a blind eye to the intricate history of the nation's founding document. And even though one would have imagined that the story about the events of 4 July 1776 would by now have come closer to the facts exhibited in this scholarship, it nevertheless remains the case that Jefferson's version of events—or at least one interpretation of his version—holds sway.

If one consults what might be regarded as the official site of the nation, the White House website, the current administration makes no mention of the signing, preferring to make a different claim about the significance of the day. It reads: 'On 4th July, 1776, we claimed our independence from Britain and Democracy was born.' There are other stories in this brief sketch of what happened in 1776 with piles just as deeply driven into the sea bed of the nation's founding ideology: the notion of right compacted within the formulation 'we claimed', for example, or that Democracy was born on 4 July 1776. But it is out of step with the 130 million websites which contain 'July 4th' on their pages, many of them devoted to telling the story of the nation's founding. One, entitled 'Happy Birthday America' states:

> Welcome to Independence Day on the Net.
> Independence day celebrates the birthday of the United States of America. Founded July 4th 1776, with the signing of the Declaration of Independence America is celebrating its 230th birthday this year (2006).

So why does this myth of the Fourth continue to have currency? Why, even in the face of good clear evidence to the contrary, does it seem attractive to believe that on 4 July 1776 America was born? Of course, nations do not have singular moments of origin any more than any other complex political events do. The answer to that question can only be understood in the context of the history of the tradition of celebration that makes the Fourth of July a present and continuing act with political significance. An act with deep and continuing connections to the project that is America. Even if the selection of the day itself, the 4th, cannot sustain the weight that has subsequently been placed upon it one should nevertheless hold on to the fact that *something* took place that day which now symbolically stands for a punctual moment that never was. Furthermore, it is salutary to remember that the aspirations given voice in the act of declaring independence, whenever that transpired, are not only noble—they have also yet to be fully achieved. And this—America's destiny—announced by those who count themselves among the number making a declaration of intent, to hold certain truths self-evident, is worth celebrating.

Declarations of Independence

Sometime in June 1775 Captain James Jack set out from Charlotte, North Carolina, for Philadelphia. He was riding 'express', as quickly as he could, since he had been instructed to carry news of the Declaration of Independence made by the citizens of Mecklenburg County on 20 May to the Second Continental Congress that was then meeting in Philadelphia. The town he had left could not, in today's terms, be called substantial. Fewer than one hundred people lived within the town limits. Only one of the houses was painted and almost all of the others were little more than log cabins. The courthouse, which stood on pillars twelve feet above the marketplace, was also of log construction, and it had a porch at the front entrance which was approached up a flight of steps.

There were some rudimentary amenities around the central square. Nicholson's was a tavern, as was Pat Jack's. There was a general store and a jail but not much else. Charlotte was, however, the centre for the community in the county of Mecklenburg which was home to seven Presbyterian congregations scattered around the outlying country. Their names evoke the local scenery: Sugaw Creek, Poplar Tent, Rocky River, Steele Creek. In all around 7,000 people inhabited the county and the homes of many were to be found on small plantations. The roads were narrow and most of the countryside remained uncultivated with thick woods dominating the landscape.

By far the greater number of the local families had their origins in Northern Ireland, from where the Ulster-Scottish Presbyterian community had begun emigrating to the colonies around 1684. They were proud of their heritage and reluctant to bow to thedictates arriving at regular intervals from London. One recent aggravation had been caused by the Vestry and Marriage Acts passed in 1769. This had imposed fines of five pounds on Presbyterian ministers if they chose to conduct marriage ceremonies. By the time of the Mecklenburg convention in 1775 most of the town elders—almost exclusively ministers in the Scottish church—were implacably set against the governor, William Tyron, and his political masters back in England.

On the day set aside for the meeting—19 May—an express rider arrived in Charlotte bringing news of the engagements between British forces and the colonists at Lexington and Concord that had occurred a month earlier. The meeting was scheduled for the evening, and had been called by Colonel Thomas Polk, the founder of Charlotte. Twenty-six men convened, two delegates from every militia company in the county supplemented by a few other dignitaries. It was chaired by Abraham Alexander, and John McKnitt Alexander, a 42-year-old planter and surveyor, acted as clerk. They met through the night, finally coming to a resolution at 2 a.m. on Saturday 20 May. Later that day, at noon, the town's founder stood on the courthouse steps and read aloud the resolutions they had made. He began: 'That whosoever directly or indirectly abetted or in any way, form or manner countenanced the unchartered & dangerous invasion of our rights as claimed by G. Britain is an enemy to this County—to

America & to the inherent & inalienable rights of man.' These words were undoubtedly prompted by the extreme indignation the citizens of Mecklenburg felt for their fellow colonists in Massachusetts who had, just one month before, suffered an invasion from His Majesty's troops. And having been prompted to their declaration of solidarity they began to warm to the theme of independence. The second resolve began, 'We the Citizens of Mecklenburg Country do hereby dissolve the political bands which have connected us to the Mother Country' and then, in the third resolution, the principle upon which the colonies were to stake their future was declared:

> That we do hereby declare ourselves a free and independent people; are, and of right ought to be, a sovereign and self-governing Association, under the control of no power other than that of our God and the general government of the Congress; to the maintenance of which independence, we solemnly pledge to each other our mutual co-operation, our lives, our fortunes, and our most sacred honor.

Among those who had been charged with the responsibility of drafting the document was William Kennon, a lawyer from the town of Salisbury, forty miles to the north. Kennon had been born in Virginia, where he also received his legal training, before moving to Rowan county. And it was Kennon who greeted Captain Jack when he arrived in Salisbury sometime in early June on his way to deliver the news of Mecklenburg's declaration of independence to the Second Continental Congress. After a brief delay Jack continued his express ride northwards, arriving in Philadelphia sometime before 23 June when Washington left the city to take command of the army, then outside Boston. And at some point in the days immediately preceding the 23rd Jack delivered his document to at least two of the three North Carolina delegates, Richard Caswell, Joseph Hewes and William

Hooper, who had been in Philadelphia all summer.

For forty-five years this obscure event in colonial American history lay buried in the memories of its protagonists. The course of history had not seen fit to include the story of how the citizens of Mecklenburg County had pre-empted the declaration announced on 4 July 1776 by over a year. But then, on 5 June 1819, the *Essex Register*, a local Massachusetts paper, reprinted an account of the Mecklenburg resolves which had appeared two months earlier in the 30 April edition of the *Raleigh Register* and *North Carolina Gazette*. The ageing John Adams read his copy of the *Essex Register* with amazement and wrote promptly to his old rival Thomas Jefferson with whom, in late life, he had become reconciled: 'How is it possible that this paper should have been concealed from me to this day?' he asked, continuing, 'Had it been communicated to me in the time of it, I know, if you do not know, that it would have been printed in every Whig News-paper upon this Continent.' Adams then has some fun by suggesting that if such a declaration had been known about at the time he would have capitalised on the fact: 'You know if I had possessed it, I would have made the Hall of Congress Echo and re-echo, with it fifteen Months before your Declaration of Independence.'

In reply Jefferson was adamant that the Mecklenburg story was just that, a story put about by proud North Carolinians: 'what has attracted my peculiar notice, is the paper from Mecklenburg county, of North Carolina, published in the Essex Register ... you seem to think it genuine. I believe it spurious.' By the second decade of the nineteenth century the revolutionary war was far enough in the past, and the sense of future security sufficient for various rivalries to emerge in relation to the respective roles individual colonies had played in the founding of the nation. And few were as proud of their history of resistance and independence as North Carolina. Jefferson, the proud Virginian, had his own loyalties. He may have felt the way he did about North Carolina on account of his opinion of the three delegates from the colony at the Second Continental Congress, none of whom played a significant role in the proceedings of that body. But within the local context of the colony and subsequent state there were many heroes who had stood firm for the rights of the colonists. And their number included both Thomas Polk and John McKnitt Alexander.

It may have been the case that Adams also remained sceptical about the Mecklenburg initiative, for he too had a reputation and a proud colonial affiliation to protect. He did, after all, give Jefferson a get-out by suggesting that such intelligence could never have been concealed from the two most prominent members of the drafting committee for Congress's own declaration. But, even so, in letters to other correspondents he—perhaps mischievously—countenanced the possibility that the Mecklenburg resolves were known to at least some delegates at the time. Jefferson, for his part, would have none of it. His reply to Adams continues: 'I deem it to be a very unjustifiable quiz. ... It appeals to an original book, which is burnt, to Mr Alexander, who is dead, to a joint letter from Caswell, Hughes, and Hooper, all dead, to a copy sent to the dead Caswell, and another sent to Doctor Williamson, now probably dead, whose memory, now probably dead, did not recollect, in the history he has written of North Carolina, this gigantic step of its county of Mecklenburg'. And then, in appealing to Adams's own, considerable, ego, he opines: 'Armed with this bold example, would not you have addressed our timid brethren in peals of thunder, on their tardy fears?' Furthermore, he writes, 'Would not every advocate of independence have rung the glories of Mecklenburg county in North Carolina in the ears of the doubting Dickinson and others, who hung so heavily on us?' 'Yet', he notes by way of hopefully sealing the fate of this scurrilous rumour, 'the example of independent Mecklenburg county, in North Carolina, was never once quoted.'

It seems very likely that Jefferson, the 'author of the Declaration of Independence', went to his grave convinced that the Mecklenburg resolves were a hoax. And many Jeffersonians took the same view. But the citizens of Charlotte, North Carolina, were not so easily persuaded. So, in 1830, the governor of the state, Montfort Stokes, set up a commission to inquire into the veracity of this story and to 'examine, collate, and arrange' all the documentary evidence that could be obtained. They faced one very significant problem: there was no written record extant of the meeting allegedly held through the night of 19 May 1775 and into the early hours of the morning of the 20th. The minutes taken at this meeting in Charlotte's courthouse, attended by twenty-six delegates, had been destroyed in a fire in April 1800 at the house of John McKnitt Alexander who had acted as secretary on the occasion. The members of the commission were aware of the claim that copies of these minutes had been made and sent to Hugh Williamson in New York who, at the time, had been writing a history of North Carolina. And that a further second set of the same notes were also supposed to have been sent to General W.R. Davie. None of these documents seemed to have survived.

Not to be disheartened by this lack of hard evidence they set about locating all those still alive who had played a part in the alleged activities. Once a surviving protagonist had been found they dispatched attorneys—some as far as Georgia—to take depositions from them. The number of survivors was not great. And they were, of course, by this time mostly aged men whose memories, at least according to some, were far from reliable. But all of those deposed corroborated the story that in May 1775 the citizens of Mecklenburg County resolved to separate from the mother country. It is true that the longest and perhaps most important deposition, given by the 88-year-old Captain Jack—the person instrumental in delivering the resolves to the delegates meeting in Philadelphia—has inconsistencies. He was, after all, well into his dotage. But the concluding text of his sworn testimony is completely unambiguous. It states that he 'delivered the Mecklenburg Declaration of Independence of May, 1775, to Richard Caswell and William Hooper, the Delegates to Congress from the State of North Carolina'.

Delivering their report in 1831, Governor Stokes's commission came to the same conclusion. The long report, complete with notarised depositions which to this day may be consulted, states that

> By the publication of these papers, it will be fully verified, that as early as the month of May, 1775, a portion of the people of North Carolina, sensible that their wrongs could no longer be borne, without sacrificing both safety and honor, and that redress so often sought, so patiently waited for, and so cruelly delayed, was no longer to be expected, did, by a public and solemn act, declare the dissolution of ties which bound them to the crown and people of Great Britain, and did establish an independent, though temporary government for their own control and direction.

If this is an accurate record of what transpired in Mecklenburg County during 1775 why did Caswell and Hooper fail to make much impression on their congressional colleagues? According to one version of events they reported the resolves but, it is claimed, at that moment in 1775 the colonists were not ready to act in concert and go all the way with a declaration of independence. According to another version the delegates from North Carolina decided not to communicate the resolves taken by their compatriots in Charlotte because they believed them to be too inflammatory. Or, in another, perhaps more credible hypothesis, given that such language and the intention expressed by it would have alerted the agents of the king to treasonable acts, Caswell and Hooper informally discussed these resolutions with colleagues and made sure that any open debate in Congress took place under the usual rules which placed an embargo on the taking of minutes or notes. And since there are no minutes of these meetings, we will never know what happened to the intelligence Captain Jack delivered to the members of the Second Continental Congress. Or if he ever did deliver anything at all from the townsfolk of Mecklenburg County.

Historians of our own time have mostly been sceptical of this story, finding in it a series of contestable claims and shaky hypotheses. Most have concluded that the so-called resolves printed in the *Raleigh Register* and *North Carolina Gazette* must have been fabricated sometime long after the text of the Declaration had been agreed by the Second Continental Congress, and indeed far from providing the form of words for sections of that document it was precisely the other way around. The 'fake' Mecklenburg declaration simply copied the wording of the Philadelphia text. This argument, however, has a fatal flaw. If the so-called Mecklenburg resolves were taken from the Philadelphia Declaration the clause which appears in the allegedly fake document 'endowed by their creator with inherent and inalienable rights' ought to echo that in the officially adopted version of Congress. For, although Jefferson had written 'inherent and inalienable' in his draft, the final, printed version of the text has 'endowed by their creator with certain unalienable rights'. It has never been claimed, and indeed seems unlikely, that whoever wrote the 'fraudulent' Mecklenburg text had access to Jefferson's drafts.

Does any of this matter? If it is factually correct that the good citizens of Mecklenburg resolved to separate from Britain a year or so before the thirteen colonies acted in concert, what difference did this make to the course of history? Any more difference than the similar 'declarations' which were made in a number of colonies in the year or so before the Declaration was published? And how does this, albeit brief, piece of forensic historical analysis help us understand something about the force and power of the story of the Fourth? In order to answer those questions we need to look elsewhere, away from an incidental event in the history of the colonial period, for the real curiosity of this piece of local detail lies in the reaction the third president had to hearing the news from his erstwhile colleague Adams. Why did Jefferson dismiss the story with such dispatch? Why did he protect his 'authorship' of the Declaration so vociferously? In doing so he was cultivating and protecting the narrative of the punctual moment. The story which claims that the colonies cut their ties to the mother country in a *single declaratory act*. As we have seen, although in retrospect it may have come to feel as if it had been like that to the actors in the drama playing throughout the summer of 1776 in Philadelphia, in point of fact, as their letters and journals indicate, at the time of its unfolding matters were rather more murky. Furthermore, in promoting this notion of the single declaratory act which lead to the 'birth of the nation' another claim may also be entered: that an individual, or group of individuals, *made* that act. Call them the 'Signers' or even the 'Founding Fathers'. Or, in the case of Thomas Jefferson, *the author* of the Declaration of Independence.

The significance that proprietorial rights were to assume over this act can be traced by focusing on the particular status accorded to the words which were adopted by the Second Continental Congress and subsequently published as the Declaration of Independence. For, as will become evident, the question of property rights in words was not a matter of indifference to those closely involved in the drafting of the document, prime amongst them Thomas Jefferson. One can begin by noting that title to the words in the document has been subject to variation over time. For those who literally made the declaration in July 1776, the delegates to the Second Continental Congress, the words were held as common property, within collective ownership, even if the delegates never, so far as we know, formally 'made' the declaration in the sense of speaking out loud the words of the text they had finally agreed to.

This was for a very good reason: the words of the document printed on instruction from the Congress and issued on 4 July performed a very specific task. They were to indict the monarch on a large number of counts of negligence and improper action. These, the colonists held, were proof of the fact that George III had abdicated his role as sovereign. This is why the document has the air and formality of a legal writ. In drafting the text the delegates—nearly half of whom were practising lawyers—very clearly had in mind legal precedents for their case but they were far from secure in regard to the protection the prevailing law might have offered them. Consequently no single person, at the time of its making, would have even felt it appropriate, still less comfortable, to claim for himself ownership of the words which comprise the document. For we must remember that at the time of its being made public those words provided ample cause for a charge of treason to levied on whosoever declared them. It was not merely the practical advantage of combining resources which motivated the colonists towards seeking unanimity over the issue of separation. Strength in numbers was seen as one of the few protective measures within their reach—something they learnt from both the history books and legal treatises which were their guides in constitutional matters.

But once separation from the mother country had been effected, once Washington had begun his campaign to successfully defend and protect the colonies from their oppressors, the document's significance and meaning altered. Then, once the new nation had been fully established, the moment at which Congress had publicly declared its independence from British oppression began to take on the trappings of an heroic act, performed by the courageous men who were to become the nation's 'Founding Fathers'.

It might be said that rivalry and amour-propre were no strangers to this constellation of strong-willed and in many cases visionary revolutionaries. Within this later context the Declaration began to be understood not as a significant document but as the founding act of the new republic. And here rivalry began to become apparent—all the more so since the two beasts in this particular jungle, the second and third presidents, were to end up on opposing sides of the emerging party political structure of the now United States of America. There was, then, considerable political capital to be made out of the claim that one had 'authored' the text of the nation's founding.

So let us return to Jefferson's reply to the letter of 19 July 1819 he received from his then reconciled revolutionary colleague, John Adams. Does this now look like a case of special pleading? Was he really unaware of the Mecklenburg resolves? Here, once again, is the third of the 22 May Mecklenburg resolves, which states:

> That we do hereby declare ourselves a free and independent people; are, and of right ought to be, a sovereign and self-governing Association, under the control of no power other than that of our God and the general government of the Congress; to the maintenance of which independence, we solemnly pledge to each other our mutual co-operation, our lives, our fortunes, and our most sacred honor.

If we read this sentence alongside the last paragraph of the 4 July Declaration the similarity in phrasing and diction is so close that one must wonder whether Caswell and Hooper did in fact give some airing to the document delivered to them by Captain Jack. Here is the later text:

> That these United Colonies are, and of right ought to be Free and Independent States; that they are absolved from all allegiance to the British Crown, and that all political connection between them and the State of Great Britain is and ought to be totally dissolved; and

> that as Free and Independent States they have full power to levy war, conclude peace, contract alliances, establish commerce, and to do all other acts and things which independent States may of right do. And for the support of this declaration, with a firm reliance on the protection of Divine Providence, we mutually pledge to each other our lives, our fortunes and our sacred honor.

Late in life Jefferson was both too grand and too fêted for the charge of plagiarism to stick, but he did, nevertheless, commit himself to paper on this issue in such a way as to leave the door open as to whether or not 'his' words were really his. Writing to Henry Lee on 8 May 1825 he admitted that 'When forced, therefore, to resort to arms for redress, an appeal to the tribunal of the world was deemed proper for our justification. This was the object of the Declaration of Independence.' It was not, he said 'to find out new principles, or new arguments, never before thought of, not merely to say things which had never been said before; but to place before mankind the common sense of the subject, in terms so plain and firm as to command their assent, and to justify ourselves in the independent stand we are compelled to take.' In other words he saw himself more as a conduit or mouthpiece for the general views all around him in Philadelphia than as the author of a document which would bear his own name.

In words which have become renowned he continues to explain to Lee how he understood his commission from the Congress. 'Neither aiming at originality of principle or sentiment', he continues, 'nor yet copied from any particular and previous writing, it was intended to be an expression of the American mind, and to give to that expression the proper tone and spirit called for by the occasion.' In the extensive literature on this extraordinary architect of the nation the success of Jefferson's endeavours in this regard is, quite rightly, repeatedly emphasised and the brilliance with which he managed to convey 'the American mind' often remarked upon. There's no sense that the third president 'owned' the words of the Declaration, or that only he was equipped to make a claim of this kind. Indeed Jefferson himself made the point in his letter to Lee that 'All its [the declaration's] authority rests then on the harmonizing sentiments of the day, whether expressed in conversation, in letters, printed essays, or in the elementary books of public right, as Aristotle, Cicero, Locke, Sidney, &.' Furthermore, as we know from the exhaustive work that has uncovered the archaeological texture of the document, the accepted revisions made by Congress to Jefferson's draft meant that words he had never even penned made it into the final document. And we also know that even if the Mecklenburg resolves never came to light in Philadelphia that summer, even if they are in fact fictitious, there are other examples of resolutions adopted around the colonies in the period leading up to the declaration on the 4th in which similar or even identical phrases are used. The Ulster-Scottish community of Palmer, Massachusetts, for example, sent word on 17 June to Congress that they supported a move for separation. Their resolve closed: 'we do unanimously determine and declare we will support them with our lives and fortunes'. This only strengthens Jefferson's admission that he saw his main task as harmonising 'the sentiments of the day'.

It is all the more strange, then, that Jefferson allowed, even encouraged, the idea to be put about that he was 'the statesman who drew the memorable Declaration of Independence', as democratic-republicans called him in the early nineteenth century in their toasts to the Fourth. And as he honed and refined the self-image that he wished to give to posterity he became increasingly in thrall to the myth that the founding document had a singular origin. And so he fabricated the person who would be known to history from the words he wrote down in 1826 intended to convey his life's accomplishments. Words he deemed appropriate for his tombstone. They read:

Here was buried
Thomas Jefferson
Author of the Declaration of American Independence
Of the Statute of Virginia for religious freedom
& Father of the University of Virginia

This identification with the 'author' of the Declaration became so complete, so compelling, that he was able to forget that in at least one conspicuous detail he had never been the author of *all* the words of that now famous document. He had never even copied these words into his drafts of the document that Congress was to debate. For the phrase in the last paragraph of the document that reads 'that these united colonies are and of right ought to be free and independent states', words which echo the Mecklenburg resolves, were adopted by Congress in place of Jefferson's rather more pointed 'reject and renounce all allegiance and subjection to the kings of Great Britain'. And Congress was using its own earlier 7 June resolution where these words appear, words which had been penned by another Virginian, Richard Henry Lee. Since Jefferson was far from comfortable with the process by which the Committee of the Whole amended and altered his original draft, it must have taken an act of extreme will to forget that one of the most resounding phrases of the document's last paragraph had been borrowed from his Virginian compatriot's motion of 7 June.

It is easy enough to grant to Jefferson the fiction that he had 'authored' the text that is now celebrated, for his accomplishments were indeed on a superhuman scale. We are happy to buy into this small departure from the facts because it corresponds with what we believe at the level of self-evident truth. Someone went off and drafted the document that would subsequently be revised, and that person was incontestably Thomas Jefferson. Even if all the words of the final text were not his—and in what sense are words one's own property in any case?—it hardly matters since they convey a set of aspirations and ideals we continue to subscribe to. But, more importantly, allowing that the Declaration of Independence has *an* author contains the same architecture of belief as the proposition that America has *a* birthday: July 4th.

The following chapters set out to show how that architecture was established and maintained. And, in coming to understand that, it is to be hoped that the chances of building noble and enduring edifices with it will be improved.

3

Making Independence Day

The first anniversary of the Fourth fell on a Friday. No one—at least no one in the Second Continental Congress—had given much thought to the notion that something might be done to mark the occasion, precisely a year earlier, when the intention to separate from the mother country had become public. This ought not surprise us since the future of the colonies—still at war in early July 1777—was at the time very uncertain. Although some of the delegates to Congress may have predicted an outcome which effectively sealed the fate of a new confederation of states there was still much discussion and debate ahead on matters of great significance—on the constitution of what would become a single republic, the relations between its constituent states and the nature of government itself in a republican confederation. Put simply, there was not much—yet—to celebrate.

Nevertheless on Wednesday 2 July 1777 Congress turned its collective attention to the matter of what, if anything, ought to be done in Philadelphia on Friday the 4th. As with so many of its decisions nothing was agreed then and there, postponing until the following day the discussion at which it was proposed and agreed that on the 4th, Congress would adjourn for the day. Most, if not all of the delegates were in favour of asking someone to give a sermon but it was too late to organise this for the following day. Instead it was agreed that the delegates would have dinner together.

As it turned out, rather more noise was made that day than might occur at a simple repast. John Adams wrote to his daughter on 5 July that he had gone on board a frigate, the *Delaware*, accompanied by the president of the council and 'several gentlemen of the Marine Committee'. A salute of thirteen guns was fired off followed by a response from thirteen further ships in the river. Adams, who was rather boosterish about the matter of celebrating the separation, recounts: 'The wharves and shores were lined with a vast concourse of people, all shouting and hurrahing in a manner which gave great joy to every friend to this country and the utmost terror and dismay to every lurking tory.'

This reference to 'lurking tories' reminds us that one year on, in 1777, there were still serious voices of dissent to be heard in the colonies over the matter of the 'rebellion', as His Majesty referred to the War of Independence that was ongoing at the time. And indeed for the following thirty years the Fourth was marked by a severe division in party and political allegiance all over the former colonies. Far from celebrating the founding of the nation, the Fourth—at least in the immediate years following the declaration—provided a locale and occasion for the continuing battle over the history and future of the confederation. Over its allegiance to a past that tied it to the mother country and a future that might or might not seek to reconfigure that relation as one of economic and diplomatic dependence. And it is this—the sense of facing both the past and the future—which provides the structure of the ritual of observance embedded in the Fourth to this day. For as long as the republic endures it is, above all else, this structural configuration of the rites of observance for the Fourth that will enable the nation simultaneously to both commemorate and instantiate, as if for the first time, its origin. It is this which makes America's signature legible: poised between a commemorative right that is widely understood to honour the signing of the Declaration and an enactment of independence in the vocal declaration of the words Congress published to the world. A signature whose form is the belief that the many speak as one.

Adams may well have embellished his account of the festivities in Philadelphia on that first anniversary just a little since he, like Jefferson, was committed to the fiction of a punctual moment for the origin of the nation. But even if he did, his account was to prove prescient in the longer term, at least, since 'bonfires in the streets and fireworks' were to become defining features of celebrations on the Fourth. In the immediate aftermath of the declaration, however, more pressing and local, political priorities were uppermost in the minds of celebrants. Even so, before the second anniversary rolled around, Congress determined that the Fourth would, henceforth, be honoured with a 'public celebration of the anniversary of independence at Philadelphia' in a vote of 24 June 1778.

The fate of the Fourth as a nationally respected day of commemoration and celebration was not yet sealed; in fact it was not until 1870 that federal legislation was passed making the day into an official national holiday. Nevertheless, local customs were already being codified into legislation from the early 1780s. Massachusetts was first to enshrine the celebration as an official event in the yearly calendar in a resolve asking the governor to 'direct that suitable preparation be made for the celebration of the Anniversary of the United States of America'. This formulation of the focus of the celebrations was to prove to be deeply satisfying and, in time, almost universally adopted. In this regard Massachusetts was a trailblazer: the drift towards national acceptance of the purpose and utility of a day devoted to the celebration of 'the Anniversary of the United States' was mired in the long struggle over the precise nature of the political bonds of the Union and the role that federal government was to play in the delicate set of relations between the constituent parts of the new nation.

Notwithstanding the long process of national adoption, the vote passed by Congress on 24 June 1778 did determine a second extremely important feature of the character of celebration that to this day persists in the honouring of the Fourth. The vote reads: 'Resolved that Congress will, in a body, attend divine worship on Sunday, the 5th day of July next, to return thanks for the divine mercy in supporting the independence of these States and that the chaplains be requested to officiate and to preach sermons suited to the occasion.' Although these two moments of observance—the public celebration of the Fourth and the collective attendance of church the following day—were distinct in 1778, they became almost instantaneously fused together. For what characterises the structure of celebration for the anniversary of the declaration from 1778 and thereafter is a strange hybridisation of the public and private, the political and the devotional: a kind of sacralisation of the political.

All over the emerging new republic the predominant feature of the celebration which could be said to contain a manifest content was an oration. In most cases this was given by a preacher from the community, but important townsfolk—the mayor or a well-known attorney—also had their turn. And these orations, at least in the first half-century following independence, took a shared template that was supposed to recall and invoke those beliefs which had led to the separation of the colonies from the mother country. In particular the orator was to consider the feelings, manners and principles appropriate to the occasion and to move through five topics. The first was the causes of the revolution, the second the 'distinguished characters' who played a role in the event, followed by an explicit recognition of the role France played in bringing a successful conclusion to the process of independence. The fourth topic, the 'superior advantages ' of a republican government, no doubt played differently to politically partisan audiences, while the fifth, the supreme importance of public and private virtue, was less contentious (even if its basis in a particular version of republican ideology may have also been rebarbative to some).

Orations were not the only common feature of 4 July celebrations. Other rites, less obviously connected to the fusion of church and state but still very much enacting a bridge between the public and private, were also quickly established. Dinners, for example, were almost universally adopted as a way of bringing people together in celebration, although the timing of these meals was determined by local climate—July in the southern states was not conducive to open-air feasts at almost any time of the day or night. And dinners were frequently punctuated by toasts. From the very first celebrations, fireworks or the firing of cannon or muskets were a feature of the day, as were military parades of one sort or another. Both can, of course, be read as political acts or as participating in the domain of political representation.

These two sentiments contained in the 24 June vote of Congress in 1778—on the one hand the directive to hold a public celebration and on the other the resolution to gather together in divine worship—provide the germ for all subsequent 4 July celebrations. One might say that the hinge which articulates these two distinct features of the Fourth, the public manifestation of belonging to a common cause and the private observance of faith, provides the very genetic imprint for this new body politic, the first modern republic. Which is not say that the celebratory practices of 4 July comprise a singular politics. Far from it, as the history of the first fifty or so years demonstrates. But what may well turn out to be the most impressive and enduring strength of this combination of the devotional and the secular celebration is its elasticity. Adaptation and inclusion are seamlessly woven into the traditions of the Fourth which has enabled many different constituencies to speak in the language of origins and with the rhetoric of authenticity. One, the individual about his or her private devotions, is gathered up into the heterodox celebrations of the many.

What I mean by this hinge can be understood from the discussions in Congress around the third anniversary. In 1779 the 4th fell on a Sunday, and this caused some consternation in a constituency which, although not entirely comprised of devout Protestants, many of whom belonged to what today would be called 'low church' congregations, nevertheless recognised the Sabbath as not only culturally or devotionally significant but also politically so. Consequently, following a discussion which had divided the delegates, a vote was passed seven to three—New Hampshire, Connecticut and New Jersey voting against—'that the Chaplain of Congress be requested to prepare a sermon suitable to the occasion' and this was to be the only mark of observance of the anniversary on that day, Sunday the 4th. But then 'a further motion was made that the President cause an entertainment to be prepared on the 5 July in celebration of the independence of these United States'. And since that day every year in which the Fourth falls on a Sunday, celebration of Independence Day in most places around the country has been postponed to Monday the 5th (although some towns opted to go a day earlier, on Saturday 3rd).

Once again the hinge between the private devotional and the public celebratory is revealed in descriptions of the Fourth as the 'Sabbath of our Freedom' an expression used by the *Independent Gazeteer*, on 11 July 1789, or 'a sabbath in the calendar of liberty' by another local newspaper of the time. One can also see it in the quickly established form of the oration on the Fourth which was in effect a secular version of the Sabbath day service and often held in church buildings. During the early nineteenth century there was no embarrassment in openly referring to the Fourth in religious terms. A Boston newspaper of 1810, the *Columbian Centinel*, remarked of that year's celebrations in the city as having proceeded with 'more religious rites and with greater festive pomp than for many years past'. And by the jubilee in 1826 the orator for the occasion in Boston, Mayor Josiah Quincy, described the observance of the rituals of the Fourth as 'a solemn and somewhat religious duty'. Such overt religiosity casts a long shadow that is still perceivable in many contemporary versions of the American Project even if for many the practices of everyday life are resolutely secular. Here once more we can see the strength of a hinge: it allows for both secular and devotional forms of commemoration.

Although the first ten or so years following 1776 saw mainly local traditions being established, some of which were focused on events specific to the region such as the Boston Massacre of 5 March 1770, the general trend was to give way to the significance of the Fourth. Indeed, as we have seen above, the first 'official' state recognition of the 4th as a day of celebration, referring to the festivities held in Massachusetts in 1781, introduced one form for the phrase—'the Anniversary of the United States of America'—which right to the present time encapsulates the 'meaning' or purpose of the day. And in that gesture of origination it was almost as if the prehistory of the nation, the history of colonial dependence, was to be erased. The birth of this new entity brought into the world a new polis comprising citizens each and every one of whom embodied a set of virtues that defined the future for the new republic, and expressed their consent to be governed in their willing inclusion in the 'we' who spoke for it. Those virtues can be gathered together and symbolically represented in one word: independence.

This word was, of course, in the years immediately following the Declaration, freighted with political meanings articulating the desire to gain and maintain freedom from what had previously been seen to keep the colonists in bondage. Where His Majesty sought to maintain their subservience and bind them to the corruptions of colonial rule, Americans now claimed rights and freedoms that belonged to them in their own right. Independence, to the generation of '76 was a virtue on behalf of the fact of being a citizen. But to later generations the capacity of the term to attract and hold within itself more capacious and circumstantial meanings—ethical as well as political—allowed it to become associated with the myth of origin that was so firmly promoted by those early celebrants who feared for the continuation of the new republic and strenuously sought to create an identity for it. Independence, to these men and women, was not only a political fact. It was at the core of a new kind of person, a citizen claiming universal rights. And the birth of the nation is the crucible within which this new citizen comes into being. It is a story of biblical proportions in which virtue, freedom and independence are fused together in a new dawn that almost has the capacity to rewrite the fall from grace undergone in the garden of Eden.

We can detect the biblical rhetoric which pushes celebration of the Fourth in this direction from the wording of the 1783 resolution passed in Boston. This vote states that the city resolved to honour the 'Fourth of July, A.D. 1776' as a day 'ever memorable in the Annals of this country for the Declaration of our Independence' and it went on to prescribe the nature of the observance stipulated for celebrations from that time forward. Each 4 July, for ever more, there was to be a 'Publick Oration' delivered in a location deemed proper by the town officials. And in the course of this speech 'the Orator shall consider the feelings, manners and principles which led to this great National Event as well as the important and happy effects whether general or domestick which already have and will forever continue to flow from the Auspicious Epoch'. Although this directive was specific to Bostonians it nevertheless captures the form of countless Independence Day orations all over the new nation. Even so, the content of such speeches was not immune to political contingencies, so by 1788, when the country was locked into battle over the adoption of the Federal Constitution, the Fourth and its traditions of celebration were marshalled into a party political conflict that was to endure for a number of years.

Prior to this internecine battle around the final decade of the century—in the years immediately following the Declaration—the meanings of the Fourth were closely tied to the requirement to maintain morale in the face of an uncertain future. The longevity of the new republic was at that time still to be determined. Consequently any celebrations that took place on the Fourth were coloured by the necessities of war and the need to keep morale high. This explains the frequent exposition of the 'spirit of '76' and the almost obsessive reiteration of the virtues of the founders (albeit inflected by party political loyalties) and of republicanism in general. And the same impetus gave rise to the sense that it was crucial to re-imagine, even re-experience, the state of bondage which had been the immediate cause of the revolution. These inflections of the rituals of the Fourth played a vital part in the process of founding a new identity since it was a matter of survival for the nation that its citizens continued to hold a vivid picture of the war in their heads, and that they *felt* the honourable gift of the lives of those citizens who had perished at the hands of the oppressors. While veterans from the war continued to live, this sense of linking the present of remembrance each Fourth of July to the real of the revolution was a significant feature of the celebratory practices observed on the day. And although the last few veterans lived beyond the jubilee, the fact that two of the principal architects of the new nation died within hours of each other on that day, 4 July 1826, was widely taken to signal a new phase in the practice and meanings of celebration.

Intervening between then and the end of the War of Independence we find a different set of partisan political interests asserting themselves around the observance of the Fourth. From the late 1780s what one did and said on the Fourth became a hot potato. In the years of heated discussion leading to the Philadelphia Convention of 1787 which was to thrash out the adoption of the Constitution two factions had emerged. On the one hand 'federalists' supported Madison's scheme which gave significant powers to a federal government, while on the other 'anti-federalists' who later became known as 'democratic-republicans' vainly fought for the maintenance of the pre-eminent power of state legislatures. Many of the provisions of Madison's Constitution sought to bring the individual states into a collective political entity which had the power to direct and drive the country forward through the interlocking institutions of the bicameral federal legislature and the offices of state, most especially that of the president. Those, like Jefferson, who wished to preserve what they saw as the indispensable architecture of a true republic and the principles upon which the revolution had been based, namely the autonomy of its constituent parts, each state's legislature, opposed the moves towards Madison's blueprint for the new nation. As far as the anti-federalists were concerned he was merely proposing to re-institute the monarch under a different guise.

These opposing political groups in the now firmly established republic sought to reclaim independence for their own specific party political purposes. Republicanism now had another set of meanings, resonating with another struggle that erupted in Europe at the century's end. This, within the context of the fierce battle that had been entered into over the precise terms and structure of a federal constitution, led to a deeply divisive view about the recent past and the future direction for the infant new nation. If the years immediately following the Declaration in '76 had managed to instil a sense of common purpose—had in effect created a common past for the citizens who came into being with the declarative act itself—the years following the adoption of the Constitution witnessed a bifurcation of allegiance and the promotion of a contested collection of identifications. Now, it appeared, there were contrasting views about what the revolution had been about, what it had been for, and whether or not it had ended.

Federalists abhorred the events in France and saw their opponents, the 'anti-federalists', as promoting a set of values that were inimical to the purposes of the revolution and that would, if adopted, lead to nothing less than the destruction of what they considered to be the American republican experiment. From the other side, anti-federalists saw their opponents as nothing more than rebranded monarchists. And each side in this partisan political struggle sought to claim the Fourth for its own purposes.

In some cities, like Boston, the fight between opposing ideologies was brought to a indelicate climax each Fourth of July. Federalists and anti-federalists each met in their own locations and co-opted the symbols of the day—the flag, orations, the liberty cap and so forth—for their own ends. Militia from each side paraded through particular parts of the city and dinners became the occasion for expressing loyalty to a specific party cause. To make matters more fraught, the Society of the Cincinnati, comprising almost exclusively Federalist supporters, chose the Fourth for the date of their annual meeting and dinner, thereby exacerbating the intense rivalry that surrounded the battle for the future of the nation. Furthermore, the federalists, at least in Boston and Philadelphia, almost held a monopoly over the rites which characterised the celebrations. The official orators chosen to speak were almost always federalist, and the toasts at the dinners were almost exclusively designed to ennoble federalist heroes of the cause—Washington, Hancock, John and Samuel Adams. The record indicates that for forty years following the Declaration the name of Jefferson was not uttered in a formal toast at any federalist dinner in Boston. Perhaps this should not surprise us since anti-federalists were equally inattentive to Jefferson's role in drafting the Declaration until he became vice-president in 1797.

The following year a Boston anti-federalist newspaper was referring to the 'immortal Jefferson' which only served to highlight the deep divisions that now ran through party politics. Bostonians began to feel the wounds very keenly so that by the Fourth of July 1799 the *Independent Chronicle* was counselling the suspension of hostilities, urging that 'we lay aside the divisions which disgrace us when the glory of our country calls us to unite in the celebration of her honour and independence ... Let the spirit of 1776 prevent us, when established as a sovereign power, from crumbling into parties.' But that same year federalist celebrants in Philadelphia continued to toast their heroes Washington and Adams and to neglect Jefferson. In riposte their opponents toasted Vice-President Jefferson as the 'statesman who drew the memorable Declaration of Independence—may his virtue and patriotism live forever in the hearts of the freemen of America', and from this time on, the indissoluble association of Jefferson's name with the text of the Declaration began to gain ground.

As Jefferson's stock began to rise in the third presidential race, those who continued to oppose his election began to find ways of criticising what had by now become the traditional forms for celebrating the Fourth. Where until now the general festivities and commotion—firing off muskets, fireworks, parades and so forth—had been indulged in by both sides in the political firmament, these practices began to become targets for those who wished to minimise any association between the recently constituted republic and revolutionary fervour across the Atlantic. The link between the American and French revolutions had been an element in 'democratic' anti-federal celebrations from the early 1790s. The Democratic Society of Philadelphia, for example, held its first Fourth celebration in 1794, to which it invited 'other patriotic citizens', and its supporters also celebrated ten days later, on the 14th, to mark the occasion of the fall of the Bastille. Such open embrace of what, to some, were dangerous—even anarchic—political beliefs and sympathies ran the risk of corrupting the orderly development of the United States and of dangerously making common cause with revolutionaries around the world. A sentiment that anti-federalist republicans in Boston, for example, abhorred—and they lost little time in showing it by flying the French and Dutch flags alongside the colours of the

Unites States on Independence Day in 1796.

A similar motivation prompted 'democratic-republicans' in Philadelphia to fly the American and French flags joined together at the top under a French liberty cap which had been augmented with an American cockade. These and other 'inflammatory' interpretations of the rituals and symbols of the Fourth prompted a Philadelphia newspaper to note that: 'It is said that some Federalists begin to think that the celebration of the 4th of July is not a matter of most importance, that it frequently creates riot and disturbance and that is would be more productive of good order to discontinue in future any particular attachment to the Anniversary.' And, perhaps unsurprisingly, the tone of reproach very quickly began to sound moralising. Good citizens, those who supported the federal cause, would not condone the riotous behaviour or loose talk which characterised the dinners held on the Fourth by anti-federalists who were by now commonly known as 'democrats'. According to them the toasts proposed were 'seditious and treasonable and flagrantly immoral and flagitious', as the Philadelphian *Gazette of the United States* of 14 July 1800 put it. Moreover, if the 'sentiments exhibited in the drunken revels of democrats were realised and acted upon, the State would topple headlong and all the bands of morality would be unloosed'.

During these last years of the century, party political skirmishes aside, the gradual acceptance of the Fourth as a national holiday to be substantially spent away from the workplace became widespread. Even so, in 1793 a French visitor to Philadelphia could still note that while the celebrations on the Fourth were marked by the ringing of church bells and the firing of cannon, nevertheless 'more than three fourths of the stores remain open'. A year later the *Gazette of the United States* asked its readers, especially those who had the power to act, to 'let the hand of industry be suspended'. And so it became. Banks began to close, turning the day into a bank holiday. By 1802 in Philadelphia virtually all business was suspended for the day and observing the anniversary was deemed to be a correct way of demonstrating one's patriotism—no matter which party one supported. This pattern is echoed across the country and, as momentum for a public holiday gained ground, the nature of the celebration began to evolve.

In the years immediately following 1776, whether or not the Fourth was observed as a punctual moment in the young history of the nation, the future still seemed inextricably tied to the act of declaration. And while the principal players in the Second Continental Congress were still alive, the *commemorative* function of observance on the day was likely to be uppermost in the minds of celebrants wherever they were located. But inevitably, as the generation of '76 died, the ties to Philadelphia's State House and the act of declaration began to loosen. Anti-federalists in the 1790s remade those ties in a very striking fashion—they started the tradition of reading the Declaration each Fourth. And since they were committed to supporting the person who now became widely known as the 'author' of that document, anything that revived the true republican spirit of '76 was grist to the mill of their partisan politics. For the same reasons, for fifteen years in the early nineteenth century Boston's *Independent Chronicle* reprinted the text of the Declaration on its front page every 4 July.

But alongside these politically opportunistic uses of the Fourth there also developed a more open-ended sense of how the celebrations of the day might be adapted and enlisted in projects of a very varied kind. In fact the party political uses of the celebration throughout the 1790s helped create a feeling for the plasticity of the day's significations. Civic projects of different sorts suddenly became 'sanctified' by their being tied to Fourth celebrations. In 1795, for example, the foundation stone of Massachusetts's new State House in Boston was laid by two heroes of the revolution, Samuel Adams and Paul Revere. In 1818 the same city officially began the building of its General Hospital on Independence Day. If one wanted to launch a new initiative—say a contest to find a new national patriotic song, as the Philadelphia Military Association did—then the Fourth was the day to do it. And so to this day all manner of events have been bundled into the extraordinarily capacious girth of the Fourth of July—the laying of a railroad, opening a civic institution, the construction of a canal, the dedication of a monument, the naturalisation of immigrants, the defeat of tyrants. It is this openness, the symbolic generosity of the Fourth which gives it such potency and longevity. The genius of the formulation in the Declaration—not to diminish the Herculean labours of the great artificer of the Constitution, Madison—lies in precisely its openness. For what is held to be self-evident truth is not prescribed: it states that 'among these truths...'. Herein lies America's magnificent power of self fashioning.

By the time of the jubilee in 1826 most aspects of the public celebrations which were not tied to specific local traditions had hardened into an institution. Although not all of these elements persist to the present day, many are recognisable even if our daily lives are significantly altered in shape from those of citizens of the late eighteenth century. First up is the ringing of bells and the firing of cannon. The latter may no longer be common but modern equivalents have certainly played and continue to play their role. In the early days the bells would ring for half an hour following sunrise on the Fourth and then again at noon and sunset. The most obvious near connection to this practice was muster day or certain church occasions.

Second up was the military parade. Again in the early days the local militia paraded through the town or city, watched by the children and wives of the menfolk who served as the protectors of the municipality. This practice seamlessly evolved into the military parade of the armed forces familiar from more recent experience. Following the militiamen in the parade came functionaries such as the governor, mayor, members of the Society of Cincinnati or simply the resident men of power or distinction. The destination was usually a large civic building or space, failing that, a church. The parade almost always ended with a fired salute—the number of shots growing as the Union itself grew.

Once inside the building or standing in a town square the order of observance was most obviously modelled on that of a Protestant church service. A clergyman might initiate proceedings with a prayer, to be followed by a patriotic song and then the reading of a poem or some patriotic text, frequently penned for the occasion by a local writer. Towards the final years of the century the Declaration was invariably read in republican-leaning observance and into the nineteenth century this became a feature of almost all celebrations. By 1825, the year of Lafayette's celebratory tour around the country, the Frenchman, who held honorary status as one of the revolutionary generation, noted that the custom of reading the Declaration aloud had spread into the home itself. Having concluded this part of the ritual, ears were pricked up for the real heart of the matter: the oration by a minister or municipal functionary.

Following the oration the company made its way to another location—most commonly a large square or green out of doors, but where a hall large enough existed it might be inside—for a communal but exclusively masculine dinner. Dignitaries were placed around the tables and the food was often prepared by a local tavern keeper. Although there is no enduring tradition of food served from the eighteenth century to today—Independence Day does not retain a significant role for the equivalent of, say, a Thanksgiving turkey—nevertheless at different times and in particular regions traditions did emerge. In the early years the most widely adopted was the consumption of turtle soup and ice cream. No matter what food was served, copious quantities of refreshment were provided, including beer, cider and spirits. A second oration at the dinner might be given but the universal activity which accompanied eating was the proposal of toasts.

The practice of toasting was deeply embedded in eighteenth-century British culture. Almost any occasion, public or familial, might provide an opportunity to raise a glass to the monarch or some auspicious figure, dead or alive. In colonial America this practice was continued but unsurprisingly toast to the king or mother country became increasingly fraught around the time of the Stamp Act and its subsequent reverberations. Immediately after the revolution the first toast, which by British tradition was always to the monarch, became replaced by one to 'the Nation'. The number of toasts proposed on the Fourth was symbolically tied to the commemorative function of the day: thirteen, for the thirteen colonies which had signed the Declaration. But frequently, as spirits became more lively, those attending the meal were moved to propose further toasts, most often as a way of indicating agreement with a particular regional issue or allegiance to a local cause or person. Even the 'official' toasts, to the heroes of '76, say, were subject to the vagaries of party political pressures. As the nation settled into its mature identity the toasts became less partisan in tone and sympathy, but they never lost their capacity to respond to immediate concerns and regional identities, a feature that persists in current celebrations of the day. One can get a sense of the flavour of these encomia from some examples, such as that of the celebrants in Georgia who in 1789 proposed a toast to 'the principle of patriotism, and the spirit of union, to pervade the states of North Carolina and Rhode Island' in the hope of encouraging those two states to ratify the constitution. More barbed was the toast proposed by federalists in Springfield, Massachusetts, in 1808 while Jefferson was entering the last year of his presidency.

These disgruntled folk proposed a toast to 'The President of the United States—to ruin a country, govern it by a French Philosopher—we hail the fourth of March 1809', the date upon which a new president was to be inaugurated. But even taking account of local incidental loyalties or enthusiasms the conformity of the sequence of toasts across the country by 1826 was quite remarkable. What by then had become the initial toast 'to the Day' or 'the ever memorable 4th July, 1776' was almost universally respected. As was the second, to the 'patriots and sages' or the 'departed heroes'. The name of Washington seems to have been usually attached to this toast or to the third which was either to 'the president of the United States' or to 'the Constitution of the United States'. From here on, more narrowly defined custom and political allegiance began to assert themselves, as toasts to a state figure or proximate militia company might be proposed, and so on down to the symbolically resonant thirteenth.

If these activities provide the core of the structure of celebration for the Fourth, a very wide range of additional entertainments could be indulged in. At various times in the history of the Fourth between 1777 and today these have included theatrical performances, concerts, hot-air ballooning, horse racing, parades dedicated to many different causes, and increasingly in more recent times demonstrations mounted by those disaffected with some aspect of contemporary American life and politics. But whatever inflection might be given to the day its conclusion has been, at least in aspiration, unwavering and almost universally applauded: fireworks.

Alas—to many aficionados of the entertainment—pyrotechnic displays have also had their ups and downs. In the early twentieth century a campaign to make the day's events 'safe and sane' led to the attempt to restrict the sale of fireworks since the casualty rate from improperly ignited or carelessly aimed rockets and crackers had been deemed to be unacceptable. As the print from 1878 shows [illustration 3], boys having fun with horns may be one thing, firing pistols another. A century earlier, in 1778 and indeed in the war years following the Declaration, gunpowder was a valuable commodity whose use was directed at more pressing matters. Nevertheless, the first celebrations included 'illuminations'—usually candles set up in windows and in public places. Given the

3. A late nineteenth-century depiction of Fourth celebrations.

absence of street lighting such illuminated scenes often struck contemporary observers with delight and amazement. But candles are nowhere near as exciting as the thunderclap and sparkle of fireworks. Once they became relatively inexpensive and widely available no Fourth celebration was complete without a firework display, no matter how modest. And some, like the mock re-creation of an atomic bomb exploding in the harbour at Baltimore in 1951, must have been truly mind-blowing.

Freedom's Jubilee

By the 1820s the intense partisan political rivalry of the early decades of the century had become less pronounced and observance of the Fourth's rites slowly began to be more inclusive. Women, for example, began to take a full part in the celebrations, organising their own versions of the by now standard elements of the day. Where the menfolk continued to hold their drink-fuelled suppers, women gathered together at tea parties, or, like the 'Sabbath School Unions' formed in New England, gathered for picnics that day. Dancing and socialising as the evening wore on became a socially mixed affair and diversions for children began to comprise an increasingly large part of the celebrations. As 1826 loomed on the horizon thoughts turned to the fiftieth anniversary of the Declaration and once again the proclaimed punctuality of the historical event began to exert its considerable powers of bewitchment. Interest in the early years of the nation had intensified as the decade of the 1820s arrived, perhaps nowhere more tellingly indicated than by the popularity of the nine-volume *Biography of the Signers of the Declaration of Independence* which Joseph Sanderson began to publish in 1823 (and only completed it the year following the jubilee). Amazingly, by the turn of 1826 three of its subjects were still alive. John Adams, at 91 years, was living in his family home at Quincy. Charles Carroll of Carrollton, one of the signatories to the Declaration from Maryland was 89. And Thomas Jefferson, though in poor health at 83, was still occasionally receiving visitors at Monticello.

Congress appointed thirteen members to its Committee of Arrangements and charged it with the responsibility of organising the Capitol's celebrations. Their first thought was to invite all the living Signers of the Declaration along with all surviving former presidents to Washington for the festivities. It turned out that none of these men of '76 were able to attend but they all sent elegant letters of regret which were reprinted in the newspapers.

Jefferson, as one might expect, though close to his final weeks, wrote in terms which encapsulate the enduring quality of the Fourth: its combination of the retrospective, commemorative preservation of the past with the prospective pledge of allegiance to a future always yet-to-come. His letter is worth citing at length since it conveys so well the intricately wound strands of the fabric of Jefferson's self-fashioning, his sense of his own role in the founding of the nation and of the nation's role in the promotion of a universal brotherhood of man. He wrote:

> Respected Sir:
> The kind invitation I received from you, on the part of the citizens of the city of Washington, to be present with them at their celebration of the Fiftieth Anniversary of American Independence, as one of the surviving signers of an instrument, pregnant with our own and with the fate of the world, is most flattering to myself.

There is Jefferson's always coyly gauche self-aggrandisement: 'is most flattering to myself'. It occurs as if by surprise to the writer himself and comes embedded in the deftly pointed albeit understated political rallying call: the 'instrument, pregnant with ... the fate of the world' has work yet to do. The powers of this man, ailing, months before his death, are still formidable and the incandescence of his desire to shape the course of human history continues to burn within his soul even if that revolutionary flame now appears to finally dim with age. But his pen, to the very end, never gave up its eloquence. As his apology continues, he writes:

> It adds sensibly to the sufferings of sickness to be deprived by it of a personal participation in the rejoicings of that day, ... I should, indeed, with peculiar delight, have met and exchanged there congratulations, personally, with the small band, the remnant of that host of worthies who joined with us on that day; in the bold and doubtful

> election we were to make, for our country, between submission and the sword; and to have enjoyed with them the consolatory fact that our fellow citizens, after half a century of experience and prosperity, continue to approve the choice we made.

The cadences of the scriptures are so deftly overlaid upon the rhetoric of democratic inclusiveness, perhaps beyond compare in the voluminous archive of public speaking in America, that a casual reading might overlook the millennial force of Jefferson's will to posterity. And while that will is, inevitably, focused upon his own standing in the history of the nation it nevertheless takes into its orbit the fate and continuing endurance of the republic itself. Not one to miss an opportunity for ennobling the actions of the revolutionary generation and his own participation in the course of human events, Jefferson brings the letter to a rousing climax:

> May it be to the world, what I believe it will be, (to some parts sooner, to others later, but finally to all,) the signal of arousing men to burst the chains under which monkish ignorance and superstition had persuaded them to bind themselves, and to assume the blessings and security of self-government ... All eyes are opened or opening to the rights of man. The general spread of the light of science has already laid open to every view the palpable truth, that the mass of mankind has not been born with saddles on their backs, nor a favoured few, booted and spurred, ready to ride them legitimately by the grace of God. These are the grounds of hope for others; for ourselves, let the annual return of this day forever refresh our recollections of these rights, and an undiminished devotion to them.

By the time Jefferson wrote these magnificent sentences they would have summoned up a set of associations—sounds, smells, the unbidden guests allowed in by the visceral somatic senses—that reeked of a distant far-off place, a time that was another century. And while some people, though not many, one suspects, might have picked up the fact that the author had, once again, not striven for originality in expression—borrowing the words of one of Cromwell's soldiers, Richard Rumbold, who had proclaimed from the scaffold: 'I never could believe that Providence had sent a few men into the world, ready booted and spurred to ride, and millions ready saddled and bridled to be ridden'—this served only to underscore the fact that an era had passed. For Jefferson was, of course, a son of the Enlightenment, as deeply versed in its rhythms of conceptualisation and attuned to its pace as he wassubmerged in its learning. He was from that other century. But America in 1826 was another country.

All over the Union, jubilee celebrations were planned with the same Janus-like motivations. The day was to be both commemorative, proudly exhibiting what it now had enshrined as the 'spirit of '76' and, at the same time, looking forwards, prospective, tentatively embracing what many thought or hoped would be a bright shining future for the first modern democratic republic.

The events that took place in Newark, New Jersey, that day are typical of Fourth celebrations all over the Union. Dawn brought the jangling resonances of clanging bells and the bursts of cannon fire. Sixty war veterans headed up the parade, many of them dressed in what they had preserved from their uniforms of the time. They carried muskets, powder horns or cartridge boxes from the same revolutionary campaign. Behind came the current young men who comprised the militia. And following their footsteps were the resident tailors, blacksmiths, carpenters, stone masons, cabinet makers, saddlers, shoe makers. Bringing up the rear, the Committee of Arrangements proudly wore their caps of liberty and included within their ranks the orator and the person selected to read the Declaration. The procession made its way to a church which was to host the official speeches. On leaving the church the revolutionary veterans headed up a second procession which included teams of oxen dragging a fifty-foot obelisk that was to be erected as a monument to 'Independence and Government'. A second civic monument, called the 'Temple of Independence', was also dedicated that day on the town common. This structure comprised thirteen columns supporting a domed roof. The words 'Independence', 'Fourth of July', '1776', and 'Liberty and Equality' were inscribed around the top, and slightly lower, around the outer ring of the dome, ran a list of names of revolutionary war generals.

By 1826 Washington had become firmly established as the seat of the national government and it was fitting for the jubilee to be celebrated with considerable pomp in that city. No such plans were laid by the local representatives of the city which could stake a claim for being at the epicentre of the revolution, the city in which the nation's independence had been set in motion: Philadelphia. That year, one of the most prominent Philadelphian newspapers reported that 'all was quiet' on the Fourth, and it went on to remark the 'apathy of the citizens'. Perhaps all eyes and ears were on the Capitol, where the second of the Adams family presidents was efficiently going about the business of government. On the morning of the celebrated day John Quincy Adams met with his secretaries of War and of the Treasury at nine, without heed to the final preparations for the procession which were being made outside. The parade set off with cavalry, the militia and a military band, followed by the mayor and the orator for the day. The president joined the procession in a carriage which he shared with the members of the Committee of Arrangements. His vice-president, John C. Calhoun, from whom he was now politically estranged, rode behind in a second carriage. As had become customary, the parade included the great and the good and, bringing up the rear, the 'citizens and strangers' who were allowed in to the executive mansion following the official ceremonies. Perhaps the gesture that was to have most enduring significance, made by the sixth president on this day, was the planting of various trees—acorn, hickory and chestnut—in public spaces around the capital.

The real legacy of the jubilee, what it gave and continues to give to the story of the nation and what, even at the time, was understood as its enormous symbolic weight, is wound up in the interlocking lives and punctual deaths of two of the architects of the revolution, John Adams and Thomas Jefferson. Although both were facing their imminent decease each nevertheless strenuously gave his distinctive stamp to the story that was to emerge from the celebrations of the nation's jubilee. For what history has remembered is the romance, the breathtakingly apposite, punctual coincidence which saw these two grand men of '76 die on the very day of the nation's fiftieth birthday. And around that fact history has burnished and embellished what little we know about the final days and hours of these two presidents. It is this story, the interlinked narratives which comprise the lives and deaths of these two men, which enhances the symbolic power of the Fourth.

One should begin by recalling that these two men who had sat on the committee charged with the responsibility of drafting the Declaration, and seen it through the cut and thrust of congressional collective editing, had ended up on different sides of a political divide. Adams, the second president, had become a figurehead of sorts for the federalists, while his successor to the presidency was one of the leading lights in the democratic-republican opposition. But in the last fourteen years of their lives they had repaired bridges and in the considerable volume of correspondence that flowed back and forth between them recovered a friendship that ran into the foundations of the nation's history. Although the public at large was, of course, not privy to that correspondence, both sides in the political landscape could, by 1826, respect each other's grand old man. It would be fair to say, then, that both were held in considerable affection by the time the jubilee was celebrated. All the more so given the ailing health of both men.

By 1818 the palsy from which Adams suffered had become acute enough to prevent him from writing with any regularity. He had been blessed with good health for most of his life, give or take minor ailments, but now, entering his last eight years, the wear and tear of advancing age became far more evident. By the time the jubilee year kicked off he was almost blind, toothless and pretty much confined to the family home in Quincy. Notwithstanding the slow decrepitude he was experiencing, visitors during these last months spoke of his lively conversation and sharp mind, not to say occasionally sharp tongue for which he had become renowned as a young man promoting the cause of independence sixty years earlier. He had reason to be entering his final months and weeks in an equable state of mind: his first son was holding the pre-eminent office of the nation and he was surrounded by his extended, loyal and loving family.

Jefferson, now bankrupt, was still atop his hill at Monticello but also ailing. He too had been fortunate to live a life free from major illness but now the three or four hours a day in the saddle—a custom he had observed until his early seventies—were becoming very rare occurrences, all the more so since breaking his left arm at the age of sixty-eight. Now, entering his last year, he was suffering with chronic and debilitating digestive problems which prevented him from receiving visitors.

But both men were determined to see their lives through to the day which loomed as the fitting terminus to their individual and collaborative odysseys. 'Argonauts', as Jefferson called the men of '76 in the last letter he wrote to Adams in March of the jubilee year, who had weathered the storm of 'our Argosy', the foundation of the first modern republic. Many alive in 1826 regarded the fact that both did, in fact, prevail until the day itself as the result of divine intervention. And from here on history takes over: all that follows from the remarkable coincidence that these two signatories to the Declaration, the second and third presidents of the country, died within hours of each other on the day of the fiftieth anniversary of the nation's birth is now part of the story that is America.

Jefferson, according to one of the strands in this story, died the same hour on the same day that the Declaration had first been read in Congress: 1 p.m. And on the day itself, 4 July 1826, only a few miles from his beloved Monticello, as he was taking his final gasps of air, the Declaration was, once more, being read aloud in Charlottesville. Although the veracity of this story was far from universally credited—the *Albany Argus & Daily City Gazette*, for example, qualified the story, pointing out that the Declaration had been 'promulgated in the halls of Congress' at that hour, while it had first been read aloud at 'about a quarter before five o'clock' [10 July 1826]—it is the punctuality of the story of Jefferson's demise that so bewitched the nation. It was no secret that Jefferson had been very close to death for weeks—during the second half of June his doctor, a young Englishman named Robley Dunglison, had been summoned to help him through what appeared to be the final stretch of his life. By 2 July his digestive system was unable to deal with much in the way of sustenance. Laudanum helped alleviate the pain. But on the 3rd, Jefferson roused from a delirium, agitated about the Committee of Safety—'Warn the Committee to be on the alert', he is supposed to have said. And all through that night, when he roused from fitful sleep, he inquired: 'This is the Fourth?'

In a variant of this story Jefferson asks more than once if the day has arrived, enquiring of his interlocutor, Nicholas P. Trist, husband of his granddaughter, Virginia Randolph Trist, 'Is it the Fourth?' Trist, not wanting to distress the dying man, is supposed to have replied in the affirmative even though he knew that the hour had not yet come. And then, with grace and resignation, the third president is claimed to have said, 'Just as I wished.' So, to his dying words, whatever they were, this most self-fashioned man of the Enlightenment managed to arrange history the way he wanted. Thomas Jefferson, the Author of the Declaration of Independence, willed his demise to coincide precisely within the very hour that marked the fiftieth anniversary of the nation he had been instrumental in bringing into existence.

Adams's legacy to history is no less characterised by the romance of the Fourth. By June that year he had become so weak that he rarely left the family home, even though his mental faculties remained in good order. On 3 July, for example, he is supposed to have been visited by Daniel Webster who inquired, 'How do you do this morning, Mr Adams?' to which the second president replied, 'Not very well. I am living in a very old house, Mr Webster, and, from all that I can learn, the landlord does not intend to repair.' As the day approached it became very clear that he would be lucky to survive and to be granted his wish of seeing it through to the day of the nation's jubilee. Although lucid right up through the first days of July, his strength was diminishing almost hourly. On the night of the 3rd he appeared to be suffering and close to the end.

He awoke on the morning of the Fourth to the sound of cannon firing off their salutes and a servant is supposed to have asked him if he knew what day it was. Adams, so history tells us, replied, 'O yes, it is the glorious fourth of July—God bless it—God bless you all.' Later in the morning the orator for the celebrations in Quincy, the Reverend John Whitney, paid this most illustrious citizen of the town a visit and asked the 91-year-old patriot if he had a 'sentiment' that might be conveyed to the massed audience who would be gathering for the oration. 'I will give it to you,' Adams said, 'Independence forever.' The old man's granddaughter, Susan B. Clark, asked if he had anything to add to this. 'Not a syllable,' he replied.

According to another source, Judge William Cranch, a classmate of Adams's son, John Quincy, the grand old man was fully cognisant of the day's unfolding. Cranch's story—he wrote a biography of Adams shortly after his death—was based on his acquaintance with those who were close to the family or indeed a part of it. In the account that Cranch published, at one point during the course of the day Adams proclaimed, 'It is a great and good day', indicating that 'his thoughts were dwelling on the scenes of 1776'. Then, as life ebbed away from one of the architects of the nation, Cranch gives us the punctual moment that has fallen into history. He claimed that 'the last words he uttered ... were "Jefferson survives"'. It is not known who recorded these words—Cranch does not reveal his source—but the symbolic power of the story is such that it seems to compel belief anyway. Certainly Adams's son, John Quincy, wanted to believe it since he recorded in his diary entry for 21 July of that year that his father had spoken the words 'Thomas Jefferson survives' at 1 p.m. on the 4th.

Seen this way, an incredible accident of history occurred that day in 1826. At the precise moment when his old ally and venerable friend Thomas Jefferson, having for the last time refused the laudanum offered by his physician, was painfully taking his last gasps 450 or so miles away at his home in Monticello, John Adams uttered his very name. And these were the last words he, Adams, was himself to speak.

It is unlikely that events transpired according to such perfect symmetry. It may well be that Adams's last words were these, but if so the coincidence of his speaking them at precisely the moment (or very close to it) that Jefferson died is hard to credit. We do not know if Adams sank into semi-consciousness following this last flickering of his powerful mind, but we do know that the time of his decease was around 5.30 p.m. It might be said that the precise detail really did not matter since the will to have it so, for the jubilee to be touched by a kind of divine providence, was in the ascendant. All over the country, as the news slowly spread, citizens were touched by the extraordinary finale to the lives of these remarkable men. And immediately on its tails the siren voice of history began to whisper in low seductive tones. Already by 16 July the story had become embellished with detail that people wanted to believe. In a sermon given that day in Washington by the former chaplain to the senate, William Staughton, we can find the building blocks of the legend already in place. 'Mr Jefferson', he claimed, 'expressed his wish to live until the day of Jubilee; his desire was granted him.' His friend 'Mr Adams, on hearing the voice of the cannon, and being informed that it announced the Jubilee of our Independence said, "O it is a great, a glorious day"; and spake no more.' Another account, this time put about by Samuel Smith in Baltimore, claimed that 'The last words of the venerable Adams were "Independence forever". The last words of our beloved Jefferson (let not his country forget them) were "I resign my Soul to my God, and My daughter to my country. And I humbly hope that this country will watch over and guard her, aid and cherish her"'.

And so, perhaps for all time, the strange conjunction in which two former presidents died within hours of each other on the day of the jubilee will cast its strange spell. Many Americans, from that day to this, have chosen to see in this unlikely fact the hand of something more than human. As Abraham Lincoln remarked in 1863 about the near simultaneous decease of the two great men, 'This extraordinary coincidence we can understand to be a dispensation of the Almighty Ruler of Events.' Whether one subscribes to this or not, it remains the case that the legacy of the jubilee has been to reinforce the sense that the Fourth marks a singular moment in time, the punctuality of the birth of the nation.

4

The Symbols of the Fourth:

The Flag

History is full of accidents—small events prompted by the efforts of mainly insignificant actors which, by chance, may gain an importance undreamt of by their perpetrators. The spring day in March 1870 when a certain William Canby rose to his feet and addressed the Pennsylvania Historical Society is one such accident of history. 'Mr President, and gentlemen of the Historical Society of Pennsylvania,' he began, 'A number of persons, who, like yourselves are impressed with the importance of preserving every item of history relating to the origin of our beautiful national standard ...' And what then followed was to provide in both outline and detail the basis of a story that for generations has cast its compelling spell. A story which encapsulates the heroism of the founding of the nation. A story that *feels* right even if the evidence for its detail is far from secure. In fact, according to the strictest protocols of historical inquiry, there is no evidence for the central claim made by Canby's lecture about the 'origin of our beautiful national standard'. It is a myth. It is, therefore, all the more intriguing that what has come down to us, the narrative that has been told and retold, has the air of a true story. It appears to makes a claim on history. Why and how this came about is the subject of the first part of this chapter.

Canby was well aware of the difficulties he was about to encounter in his attempt to convince his audience that what he had to say was historically accurate. This is why he began his talk almost immediately with an account of the thorough archival research he had undertaken, demonstrating his bona fides as an amateur historian. Even so, he was nevertheless forced to conclude with the admission that 'It is quite needless to detail the labors of this search, or to enumerate the works examined; suffice it to say that the result was as anticipated—the printed official record was found to stand, where it had been alleged to stand, bare and unsatisfying, involved in a mass of conjecture, with but one central point.' That one point lies within John Dunlap's *Journal of Congress*, dated 14 June 1777, where a record of the following resolution may be found: 'Resolved that the flag of the thirteen United States be thirteen stripes, alternate red and white; that the union be thirteen stars, white in a blue field, representing a new constellation.' This much is history. But it is the other material, the 'mass of conjecture' that has played the more significant role in the story of the nation's founding.

For in the remainder of his paper Canby spun a tale that has become familiar to millions of Americans over the intervening 140 years. A story that he claimed he had heard from its source, his grandmother, Betsy Ross. But, standing in front of his historian peers that day in March 1870, he knew that questions would be raised about the accuracy of his own memory. It was bound to pointed out, for example, that he had only been eleven years of age at the time of his conversation with his grandmother. So, being an enthusiastic amateur historian, he had set about gathering sworn affidavits from those surviving family members who had recollections of Betsy's story. All of them told, roughly, the same story. The story Canby had now come to deliver as fact, that his grandmother, Betsy Ross, had been approached by a secret committee comprising George Washington, Robert Morris and George Ross and asked to 'make the first star spangled banner that was ever made', as his aunt, Margaret Boggs, put it in her sworn affidavit.

Canby knew that parts of this story were going to be hard to sell. In the first place, as he had admitted in his preamble to the paper he presented, there is no record of a secret committee of three charged with responsibility for commissioning a flag in any documents relating to the Second Continental Congress. This in itself is not particularly noteworthy since, as we have seen, written records for those proceedings are very rudimentary. For good reason, of course, since the colonists were meeting to discuss matters that could lead to the charge of treasonable offences. There is also the minor problem of chronology. According to Canby's relatives Washington et al. called on Betsy some time before the Second Continental Congress had issued its Declaration of Independence. Why, then, would it have need of a flag? This is further complicated by the fact that we do have documentary evidence for the resolution made by Congress on 14 June 1777 in which a new flag for the then fledgling nation was proposed. And, to make matters worse, there is no record whatsoever of Washington having been appointed to any committee of the Congress, secret or otherwise—this can be explained by the simple fact that he was not a member of that body; he was, rather, beholden to it.

Canby, however, was not to be thrown off his track. He had, after all, heard the story told in its variants by many family members, and there was one version, sworn to under oath in June 1870 as testimony by another aunt, Rachel Fletcher, which seemed to convey an undeniable truth. It was so full of colour, detail, lived experience. And, given that it was Betsy's own daughter speaking, how could one raise a sceptical eyebrow to such an authoritative source? Fletcher, referring to her mother by her last married name, Claypoole, swore that 'I remember having heard my mother Elizabeth Claypoole say frequently that she, with her own hands (while she was the widow of John

Ross), made the first Star-spangled Banner that ever was made. I remember to have heard her also say that it was made on the order of a Committee, of whom Col. Ross was one, and that Robert Morris was also one of the Committee.'

Fletcher's testimony essentially covers the same ground as that sworn to by Margaret Boggs, but it is fuller, pungently smelling of historical veracity. And much of the detail in it provides seed for the later flowering of the full-blown Betsy Ross story. Fletcher, for example, introduces the fact that Betsy was connected to the congressional committee by marriage—her husband was the nephew of Colonel George Ross. This innocuous-looking detail will later prove to be one of the supports for the credibility of the story since it helps explain how it came to pass the Betsy, rather than anyone else in Philadelphia, had been given the historic commission to make the first flag.

Fletcher herself seemed to be sensitive to the objection that the connection between her mother and some of the prominent leaders of the revolution—indeed with the first president—was far fetched. In order to head off such qualms she stated that Betsy 'was previously well acquainted with Washington, and that he had often been in her house in friendly visits, as well as on business'. It turned out that her mother 'had embroidered ruffles for his shirt bosoms and cuffs, and that it was partly owing to his friendship for her that she was chosen to make the flag'. How this came about is revealed in the following account of Washington's visit to Betsy's modest parlour, a story which has captured the imagination of generations of Americans and is familiar from countless grade-school lessons. According to Fletcher, Washington and his colleagues 'showed [Betsy] a drawing roughly executed, of the flag as it was proposed to be made by the committee', but her mother 'saw in it some defects in its proportions and the arrangement and shape of the stars'. Betsy opined that 'it was square and a flag should be one third longer than its width'; furthermore, 'the stars were scattered promiscuously over the field, and she said they should be either in lines or in some adopted form as a circle, or a star, and ... the stars were six-pointed in the drawing, and she said they should be five-pointed'. Washington and his colleagues were grateful for the suggestions 'and acted upon them, General Washington seating himself at a table with a pencil and paper, altered the drawing and then made a new one according to the suggestions of my mother'. Fletcher adds that 'General Washington seemed to her to be the active one in making the design, the others having little or nothing to do with it'.

As this story has been handed down it has attracted incidental elements or slightly different emphases. In one version, for example, Betsy had already had some experience in flag making—but according to her daughter this was, in fact, a new departure. This is why Washington and his two colleagues suggested that Betsy call on another member of the Congress, a shipping merchant in the city, who, they said, would be able to supply her with a flag that she could imitate. Betsy duly visited the merchant—Fletcher adds the colourful detail that her mother had been 'punctual to her appointment'—and he 'drew out of a chest an old ship's color which he loaned her to show her how the sewing was done'.

In the meantime Washington's design, now approved by Betsy and Congress, had been supplied to a local artist so that a watercolour could be painted and then worked from in the manufacture of the flag. Fletcher adds another significant detail to this part of the story, noting that William Barrett, the commissioned artist, 'lived on the North side of Cherry Street above Third Street, a large three story brick house on the West side of an alley which ran back to the Pennsylvania Academy for Young Ladies kept by James A. Neal, the best school of the kind in the city at that time'.

Perhaps at this point in his lecture Canby noticed his audience becoming restive. He was almost certainly aware of a problem looming on the horizon, since even if his aunt's testimony was accurate how could one be sure that the design for the eventual flag was in fact his grandmother's and not the artist William Barrett's? So it was with some relief that he was able to provide from his aunt's affidavit evidence that this potentially damaging alternative hypothesis about the source of the nation's most potent symbol was insecure. For Rachel Fletcher swore that 'Barrett only did the painting, and had nothing to do with the design'—adding for good measure that 'he was often employed by mother afterwards to paint the coats of arms of the United States and of the States on silk flags'.

Why is Betsy's story, in all its incidental colour, so tightly woven into the fabric of the larger narrative that is the history of the nation's founding? What is the character of its form or structure which enables it to be tied so comfortably to the other narrative strands which collectively tell the story of the birth of the nation? Does each of these discrete elements—the story of the Liberty Bell, the signing of the Declaration, the manufacture of the first flag—have a common narrative imprint which helps build the larger story that is 'America's birthday'? Although it would be wrong to suggest that the Betsy Ross legend provides the template for all of the different stories about the founding of the nation—some of them pre-date the account of the flag rehearsed above by nearly a century—it does, nevertheless, enable us to see quite clearly how they all share a common narrative shape. How they all bear the imprint of a single storyline about origination and innovation, about the creation of something from scratch. Let's call it the ideology of 'America'.

Motivating the narrative grammar of Betsy's story is a desire to describe or establish a single, unique founding moment, a singular event which brings together various strands of her story—key players in the history of the new republic, local (and unknown) tradespeople, the skills of a single seamstress—into a punctual moment: the creation of the symbol that will speak for the nation: its flag. Like many of the individual narratives which comprise the larger story of the nation, it has an heroic individual—Betsy—at its heart. Much of the incidental detail in the Betsy Ross legend is there in order to help us form a picture of this hero, to both humanise her and venerate her achievement. And it is, of course, of signal importance that our hero is merely a representative of the common weal, not a member of the ruling elite or the professional class. She is testament to the fact that each citizen has equal opportunity, equal rights, equal potential for becoming a significant player in the history of the nation. This is what William Canby wanted to believe and why his story about his grandmother feels credible: it is one example of what the narrative code driving all stories of American exceptionalism can produce. It was the same code, deeply embedded in the third president's capacious learning and intelligence, which gave a shape and form to the story he fashioned of his own life and the part it played in the nation's founding. And like any generative grammar it has the capacity to produce both stories which help bring about the fruition of universal aspirations as well as those which prevent them from being realised.

To this day there are those who insist that the Betsy Ross story is not a myth, that although the historical record cannot provide enough material to corroborate it according to the standards of professional historians, there is nevertheless the 'grain of truth' within it. And in a curious way they are right. For it hardly matters if it is true or not, since common sense dictates that *someone* must have run up the first standard that was adopted by the new nation, and some person, or group of persons, must have designed the flag that was subsequently manufactured. What harm can there be in accepting this story as the moment of origin for the national standard since no other makes a similar claim?

In fact, there *is* a rival account. One of the Signers of the Declaration, Francis Hopkinson, who designed the seal for the Board of Admiralty, claimed in a letter of 25 May 1780 that he also supplied designs for 'The Flag of the United States of America'. Hopkinson had provided these gratis—referring to them as 'labours of fancy'—but now, in 1780, he was inquiring whether or not Congress might see fit to express its gratitude in the form of some pecuniary gesture. But this story hardly even gets to flicker across the screen of history. Almost from the day Canby stood up to address his audience in Philadelphia, Betsy's story is the one that has been accepted as fact, or if not exactly fact, at least a fable that is as good as fact.

In the July 1873 issue of *Harper's Monthly* the story was told again and soon after it began to appear in textbooks used in schools all over the country. Today one can visit Betsy's house in Philadelphia and see the rooms in which she supposedly cut her five-pointed star. Or, if only a virtual visit is possible, there is a web site devoted to maintaining the fable—indeed, it is devoted to dispelling the cruel slander that it *is* a fable. Others have also corroborated parts of the story. Samuel Wetherill, a good friend of Betsy and along with her one of the last two members of the Free Quaker Meeting House which closed in 1834, had his own story to tell. This, a tale also passed down like an heirloom through the generations, has it that the original five-pointed star which Betsy had cut out of paper in front of George Washington survives. According to Wetherill family lore, Samuel visited Betsy shortly after she had been commissioned by the secret congressional committee to make the flag. She told him what had just transpired. Wetherill, recognising the historic import of that meeting, asked if he could keep the five-pointed star which she had cut and she complied with his request. Then, just short of 150 years later, in 1925, the family safe belonging to the Wetherill family was opened and inside was found a five-pointed star. One can still see it today exhibited at the Free Quaker Meeting House, a few blocks away from the Betsy Ross House.

The veneration of such objects and the stories woven about them has parallels with the narratives we find in another important area of human experience: religious observance. Trees that shed blood, shrouds bearing the image of Christ, relics of dozens of saints and holy people have all, at various times, become talismanic objects for observers of various religious faiths. And why should it not be so for the continuing belief in the ideals of the revolutionary generation? In one sense the Betsy Ross story is part of a larger fabric which renews and sustains Americans' commitment to the lofty humanistic principles which were embedded in the Declaration of Independence. The Founding Fathers, Jefferson the principal among them, were deeply suspicious of any state interference in religious observance and sought to maintain a clear separation between government and church. But they were not averse to the ideals of their revolution being revered as if they constituted articles of faith. Indeed, in the long struggle to create and prolong into futurity a new kind of nation, a state founded on the principle of inalienable human rights, something like a religious fervour was and is required. And it is this, above all else, that survives to this day: the commitment to an ideal that is as deeply humanistic as any that has ever been articulated. It is hardly surprising, then, that in the spirit of the Enlightenment that moved the Founding Fathers, stories have been used to memorialise the heroic actions of those who played a part in the founding of the nation. And each year, on 4 July, all citizens are given the opportunity to express their consent to the grand project initiated in Philadelphia in 1776.

It is also hardly surprising, given the role that the flag plays in the founding myths of the nation, that over time this object more than any other has aroused passions. At the time of the revolution flags were, of course, a common feature of social and political life. They were especially evident on the battlefield or at sea, as they had been for centuries. But in the development of the modern state they have taken on wider significance. And during the bitter struggle of the Civil War the flag became the primary means of identification for one's political allegiance. But it was not until the early twentieth century that measures were adopted by Congress to give special prominence to the national flag.

June 14th, 'Flag Day', had been observed by communities across the United States for decades prior to 1916, but on 30 May that year President Wilson proposed that it become a punctual moment in the calendar of the nation. He said:

> It has seemed to me fitting that I should call your attention to the approach of the anniversary of the day upon which the Flag of the United States was adopted by the Congress as the emblem of the Union, and to suggest to you that it should this year and the years to come be given special significance ... I therefore suggest and request that throughout the nation, and, if possible, in every community, the fourteenth day of June be observed as FLAG DAY, with special patriotic exercises, at which means shall be taken to give significant expression to our thoughtful love of America ... our determination to make it greater and purer ...

Seven years later the first National Flag Conference was held in Washington, DC, on, appropriately enough, 14 June, Flag Day. Part of the business of the conference was to adopt a National Flag Code, a set of prescriptions pertaining to the use of the national emblem. Representatives of both the navy and the army attended, as did delegates from some sixty-six other national groups. The aim was to agree upon a common code of conduct for the flag. A year later a few minor changes were made to this code at the second National Flag Conference. Eighteen years later, on 22 June 1942, Congress passed a joint resolution, subsequently amended on 22 December 1942, which now comprises Public Law 829; Chapter 806, 77th Congress, 2nd session. Exact rules for use and display of the flag (36 U.S.C. 173–178) as well as associated sections (36 U.S.C. 171) covering the Conduct during Playing of the National Anthem (36 U.S.C.

172), the Pledge of Allegiance to the Flag, and its Manner of Delivery. The preamble to this document reads:

> This code is the guide for all handling and display of the Stars and Stripes. It does not impose penalties for misuse of the United States Flag. That is left to the states and to the federal government for the District of Columbia. Each state has its own flag law.

Of course, one of the cherished political instruments of the United States is the the separation of federal from state legislatures; for many it is precisely this separation which keeps the Union together, precisely this devolution of legislative power which keeps the Union strong. So it should be no surprise that each state has evolved its own flag law. There are, nevertheless, criminal penalties for certain acts of desecration to the flag which are upheld by federal law and are contained in Title 18 of the United States Code. In 1989 a challenge was made to this statute and ruled upon by the Supreme Court in its decision *Texas v. Johnson* by which it held the statute unconstitutional. This led the legislature to amend the statute on 28 October 1989 in its Flag Protection Act of 1989. According to this redrawn legislation a fine and/or up to one year in prison could be imposed for 'knowingly mutilating, defacing, physically defiling, maintaining on the floor or trampling upon any flag of the United States'. Less than a year later the Flag Protection Act of 1989 was struck down by the Supreme Court decision, *United States v. Eichman*, decided on 11 June 1990. It was stated in this ruling that, 'While the Code empowers the President of the United States to alter, modify, repeal or prescribe additional rules regarding the Flag, no federal agency has the authority to issue "official" rulings legally binding on civilians or civilian groups.' It is for this reason that 'different interpretations of various provisions of the Code may continue to be made' and that 'The Flag Code may be fairly tested'. In conclusion it noted that 'actions not specifically included in the Code may be deemed acceptable as long as proper respect is shown.'

In spite of this ruling, since 1995 the House of Representatives has periodically—in fact every two years—proposed an amendment to the Constitution 'authorizing the Congress to prohibit the physical desecration of the flag of the United States'. Each time—at least up until the time of this writing—the proposal has come before the Senate it has been defeated. Why should this issue continue to raise such heated debate in a mature democracy? Why, indeed, is it felt necessary to protect a piece of cloth? The answer to these questions can be found in the common narrative architecture which supports the various stories told about the founding of America. For that architecture seeks to encourage if not produce a particular form of address—call it an attitude or stance—to objects, ideals or even stories which, on account of their quasi-sacred status, require one to demonstrate good manners in their company. Ideals such as 'truths held to be sacred and undeniable', as Jefferson had first written in his draft of the Declaration. And the flag has become one of these strange secular objects. In the words of the cultural historian Wilbur Zelinsky, it has 'pre-empted the place, visually and otherwise, of the crucifix in older Christian lands'. Such a view was explicitly encouraged by a number of protest groups around the turn of the nineteenth century who took it upon themselves to mount a campaign to protect the flag. According to Charles Kingsbury Miller, one of the most prominent campaigners and author of a book entitled *The Crime of the Century: Desecration of the American Flag* published in 1900, the nation needed to look out for 'those three sacred jewels, the Bible, the Cross and the Flag'. The last most especially since unscrupulous businessmen had 'polluted' the flag 'whose sacred folds were never designed to be defaced with advertisements of beer, sauerkraut, candy, itch ointment, pile remedies and patent nostrums'. One of his colleagues even went so far as to claim that the flag could be compared to the 'Holy of Holies'. Lest this be thought of as a peculiar idiosyncrasy of early twentieth-century Americans, a more recent expression of the same view was uttered by the Louisiana Democratic representative Hale Boggs in 1967 when he described flag desecration as 'outrageous acts which go beyond protest and violate things which the overwhelming majority of Americans hold sacred'. No wonder, then, that acts of disrespect to the flag cause deep distress to so many people.

For the same reason the United States has developed a far more elaborate set of 'Guidelines for Displaying the Flag' than any other modern nation. These guidelines run as follows:

> The flag of the United States should be flown daily from sunrise to sunset in good weather from public buildings, schools, permanent staffs, and in or near polling places on election days. The flag may be displayed 24 hours a day on patriotic holidays or if properly illuminated.
>
> The flag should not be displayed on days when the weather is bad, except when an all-weather flag is used.
>
> The flag should always be flown on national and state holidays and on those occasions proclaimed by the President. On Memorial Day, the flag should be half staffed until noon.
>
> The flag should be hoisted briskly and lowered ceremoniously. It should never be dipped to any person nor should it ever be displayed with the union down, except as a signal of great distress.
>
> The flag should never touch anything beneath it, nor should it ever be carried flat or horizontally.
>
> It should never be used as wearing apparel, bedding, drapery, or decoration, nor for carrying or holding

anything.

The flag should never be fastened, displayed, used, or stored in such a manner as to be easily torn, soiled, or damaged. It should never be used as a covering for a ceiling.

The flag should not be draped over the hood, top, sides, or back of a vehicle. When a flag is displayed on a car, the flag's staff should be fixed firmly to the chassis or clamped to the right fender.

The flag or its staff should never be used for advertising purposes in any manner whatsoever. Not should any picture, drawing, insignia or other decoration be placed on or attached to the flag, its staff or halyard.

The flag should not be embroidered on cushions, handkerchiefs, or other personal items nor printed on anything designed for temporary use and discarded. However, a flag patch may be affixed to the uniform of military personnel, firemen, policemen, or members of other patriotic organisations.

When the flag is so worn or soiled that it is no longer suitable for display, it should be destroyed in a dignified manner, preferably by burning.

It makes sense to see these provisions in a slightly longer historical perspective since from the late nineteenth century Americans have been pledging allegiance to the flag in a ritual that performs one's citizenship. The words which comprise the pledge were originally published in 1892, in the 8 September issue of *The Youth's Companion*, the then leading family magazine. Its author was Francis Bellamy, a Baptist minister. Bellamy had been a chairman of a committee of state superintendents of education in the National Education Association and had been in charge of designing the programme for the public schools' quadricentennial celebration of Columbus Day in 1892. He created a flag-raising ceremony for this occasion and wrote the pledge as a salute to be given the flag as it was raised. His original read:

> I pledge allegiance to my Flag and the Republic for which it stands, one Nation, indivisible, with Liberty and Justice for all.

His initial impulse had been to use word 'equality' as well as liberty and justice but he was keenly aware that many of the state superintendents of education were opposed to equality for women and African-Americans. In October 1892 the word 'to' was inserted between 'and the' so that it read: 'and to the republic for which it stands'.

In 1923, on the occasion of the first National Flag Conference held in Washington, DC, the wording was again altered so that it read: 'I pledge allegiance to the Flag of the United States'. This alteration was against the wishes of Bellamy. The following year a further alteration was made so that it then read: 'I pledge allegiance to the flag of the United States of America'. In this form the pledge became an unofficial daily ritual in schools across America for over fifty years before Congress included it in the United States Flag Code (Title 36) on 22 June 1942. The year following the Supreme Court ruled that schoolchildren could not be forced to recite the pledge as part of their daily routine. Two years after this, in 1945, it was officially designated as 'The Pledge of Allegiance'.

In 1954 a campaign initiated by the Roman Catholic Knights of Columbus brought a bill to amend the pledge to Congress. Senator Homer Ferguson of Michigan sponsored the bill claiming that the proposed addition of the words 'under God' would officially distinguish the United States from the atheist

Soviet Union, and at the same time would remove any ambiguity that the pledge was instrumental in encouraging flag or nation worship. Congress assented to this proposal and on 14 June 1954 President Dwight D. Eisenhower passed into law the formula which now reads: 'I pledge allegiance to the Flag of the United States of America, and to the Republic for which it stands: one Nation under God, indivisible, with Liberty and Justice for all.'

Since then it has not all been plain sailing: in 2002 the California ninth circuit appellate court upheld a ruling that the words 'under God' were unconstitutional. This particular interpretation of constitutional rights provoked a reaction in Congress which sought to reverse the decision by unanimously calling for a further test of the case. Senator Bob Smith of New Hampshire had, after all, only as recently as 1999 sponsored a resolution which was duly passed in the Senate that the Pledge be recited before each day's session of the House. Consequently, following the 2002 ruling in the appellate court the case was indeed brought before the Supreme Court. It is important to note that the original case had come to the California court in a slightly unusual manner: it was claimed that the rights of the young girl who had been required to recite the pledge had been infringed. The case was founded on the observation that it was unconstitutional to induct this girl into any form of religious observance and not that the words 'under God' were in themselves a breach of constitutional rights. The claim, however, was not made by the girl but by her father who brought it on her behalf. The subsequent Supreme Court decision ducked its responsibilities in respect of the soundness of the law regarding the pledge by—rather disingenuously—throwing the case out on a technical ground. During the proceedings it was revealed that the individual who had brought the case on behalf of his daughter was in fact not the legal guardian of the girl—her parents had divorced and she now lived with her mother and stepfather. Given this the court ruled that her biological father could not, therefore, bring the case on her behalf. This leaves in suspension, as of 2024, whether or not there may be subsequent actions brought against the inclusion of the words which were said to be contra constitutional rights.

It is, perhaps, unsurprising that others, holding more mainstream political views, have proposed their own amendments to the pledge so that it might become more in keeping with their beliefs. One such unofficial pledge has it thus: 'I pledge allegiance to the Flag of the United States, and to the Republic for which it stands, one nation under God, indivisible, with liberty and justice for all, born and unborn', while another seeks to return to Bellamy's original intentions by reciting: 'I pledge allegiance to the Flag of the United States, and to the Republic for which it stands, one nation, indivisible, with equality, liberty and justice for all.' And of course the internet is clogged up with all manner of alternative suggestions which chime with whatever current injustice or curtailment of freedom seems to animate particular interest groups. But in what may often feel to some extent like opportunistic petitioning there remains a conceptual knot, a curious feature of the pledge and its symbolic ritual, that is brought out when one attends very closely to the words. For what is stated is that the flag *stands for* the republic.

What does this mean? How should we understand that a flag *stands for* a political entity? It is clearly not a representation of that entity, but nor is it, strictly speaking, a symbol of the first modern republic. Flags are counters in the languages which animate collective activities of many kinds: they have semiotic functions, encoded in the visual presentation of their design, which are precisely legible within the communicative contexts in which they are used—ship to ship, for example. Regiments march to flags, friendly societies advertise their existence by hoisting flags, nations adopt flags, and impartial observers in war seek the protection of flags. But in all these cases the material out of which the flag is made does not have a peculiar immaterial status. Again, in all these cases the flag is symbolic, it stands for something else. But in the ritual of the pledge and enshrined in the Flag Code there is something else at work, a kind of sacralisation process which raises the flag from mere symbol to something beyond the symbolic. For the flag does not merely *stand for* the republic. In some strange way, it *is* the republic. It is the nation. Both a unique object—the official flag whose form is designated in law, whose manufacture requires the use of a unique dye (called O.G. red where 'O.G.' stands for 'Old Glory')—and at the same time a common property. As the Dallas County Assistant DA, Kathi Drew, claimed in the case Texas brought against Gregory Lee Johnson for the desecration of a 'venerated object' (the flag) and which was to lead to the Supreme Court's overruling of the conviction, the flag 'was public property in which every American had a stake'. She went on to claim that it 'is simply different from anything else, it is unique' and 'really belongs to the nation as a whole'. In her view this is why a constitutional amendment is required in order to protect such a 'unique entity'. It is also why there has been such careful attention paid to the correct way to physically address the flag while making the pledge.

Before the Second World War the pledge was initiated with the right hand over the heart while the phrase 'I pledge allegiance' was uttered. The arm was then extended toward the flag at the moment when the phrase 'to the flag' was said, and then it remained outstretched throughout the rest of the recitation, with the palm facing upward, as if to lift the flag. An earlier version of this salute, called the Bellamy salute, began with the right hand in a military salute, not over the heart. But during the war the outstretched arm became associated with the Nazi and fascist salutes so the physical orientation was altered. Thereafter and continuing to this day, the pledge has been made with the hand over the heart from beginning to end. There are, however, other provisions. US Customs, 36, Section 172 states that persons are expected, though not legally required, to recite the pledge 'By standing at attention facing the flag with the right hand over the heart'. It adds that 'When not in uniform men should remove their headdress with their right hand and hold it at the left shoulder, the hand being over the heart.' Those in uniform 'should remain silent, face the flag, and render the military salute'.

No matter how one understands these various protocols and provisions, it remains the case that the words of the pledge give a particular prominence to the flag itself. They begin: 'I pledge allegiance to the flag of the United States', not 'I pledge allegiance to the republic and its flag' or some such other formulation. *First* to the flag, *and then* to the republic for which it stands. *First* to the thing itself, *and then* to its symbolic designator. Perhaps this is why, over the last two hundred years or so, US citizens have, from time to time, become concerned with the sanctity of the material of the flag itself.

There are many Stars and Stripes. Not only has the design of the flag been altered frequently—as every schoolchild knows, the number of stars has been increased each time another state has been admitted to the Union—there are also a significant number of flags which have had starring roles in moments of the nation's history: the flag, for example, that was used to rest Lincoln's head following the shot which killed him. The man who grabbed this makeshift cushion, Thomas Gourlay, kept the flag throughout his life and bequeathed it to his daughter, who in turn passed it on to her son, V. Paul Stuthers of Pike Country, Pennsylvania. And he donated this sacred object to the Pike Country Historical Society whose museum, The Columns, displays it to the present day. A flag with a more sentimental aura is that believed to be the first 'Old Glory' which sits protected under glass in the Smithsonian in Washington, DC. This flag originally belonged to William Driver, a sea captain, who had been given it by his mother and a group of girls from his home town of Salem. Driver is said to have exclaimed on opening his present 'I name her Old Glory!' and thereby another singular material example of the common property of the nation was born.

But perhaps the single most venerated piece of cloth in the nation's repository of sacred objects is the flag deemed to be *the* Star-spangled Banner. This flag has a long and curious pedigree that is entwined in the story of how the words that were to become the national anthem came to be written. The author of this text, Francis Scott Key, had been kept prisoner on board a vessel outside Baltimore during the war with Britain in 1814. He had observed from afar the British attempt to take Fort McHenry, which had flown an enormous flag, 32 feet by 43, throughout the battle. Key anxiously looked on, every so often remarking that the Stars and Stripes continued to fly above the fort, and his experience provided the material for a poem whose words were later sung to a tune. That flag, made by Mary Pickersgill and her daughter Caroline, has since been designated as the first example of an American flag which can claim to be a Star-spangled Banner. It is held in such veneration, indeed it is the most popular exhibit in the Smithsonian Museum, that it is currently undergoing a restoration programme costing millions of dollars.

Just as the Fourth celebrates the birth of the nation, so Flag Day celebrates the birth of the flag. As we have seen, we do not know when the flag that has evolved into the pre-eminent symbol for the nation was first made, or by whom. But there is a story, a good one, with elements of other stories of founding, that conveys why this strange combination of a material thing, the weave of stained and sewn cloth, and an idea, an expression of the American mind, ought to be venerated. As President Woodrow Wilson eloquently conveyed to the nation on Flag Day in 1917, the symbolic power of the flag lies in its openness, its capaciousness. Just as the rituals of the Fourth are open to each generation's inflections of their meanings, so the flag and the republic for which it stands is a work in progress. This, at least, was Wilson's message, which began: 'We meet to celebrate Flag

Day because this flag which we honor and under which we serve is the emblem of our unity, our power, our thought and purpose as a nation.' And he went on to make the explicit point that 'it has no other character than that which we give it from generation to generation. The choices are ours. It floats in majestic silence above the hosts that execute those choices, whether in peace or in war.'

Then, conveying something of the affection, even the affective power of an attachment to this common expression of identity, he said: 'And yet, though silent, it speaks to us—speaks to us of the past, of the men and women who went before us and of the records they wrote upon it. We celebrate the day of its birth...' These sentiments are deeply held and they lie deep within the senses of being American. They are part of the foundations for the architecture of belief given expression in the declaration made each Fourth of July. This is why the story of the flag is caught up in a larger narrative of origination, why, for example, it becomes significant that the first flag ever explicitly designed for a nation (as distinguished from a monarch or other ruler) was the Stars and Stripes. America, seen from within the matrix of these founding stories is the first modern nation. And that is worth celebration.

One very prominent effect of the story of the flag is the strange extra-symbolic power it seems to grant to the material itself, creating an ability to bring comfort in times of great distress. Although there are many reasons behind the unprecedented surge in sales of Stars and Stripes following the September 11th attacks of 2001—in a single day following the event Wal-Mart sold 118,000 flags—one of them is the lived and living experience of the motto stamped on the nation's seal: *e pluribus unum*. One of the largest manufacturers of American flags, Annin & Co., reported that following September 11th 'People were calling us almost in a panic'. The company's head of customer services, Carolyn Albanese, said: 'They didn't just *want* to buy flags, they *needed* flags.' As if to help assuage such a national craving the US Postal Service provided one billion stamps with the flag on them to its post offices by 1 November 2001.

The story of the flag, of its origin, how it was made and who ran up the first example helps us to understand how it came about that a piece of cloth may be beyond meaning. In a secular world it provides evidence for—and often is the occasion for—a kind of veneration that comes into existence with the founding of the republic. When one takes up this attitude of respect or veneration, demanded by something that has gone beyond the sacred, one in effect performs something—call it a pledge or a declaratory act—which indicates a subscription to the notion that some truths are self-evident. And that is why the myth of Betsy Ross's first flag continues to be told and retold.

The Liberty Bell

While there are countless material examples of the Stars and Stripes, millions of American flags, there is only one Liberty Bell. In this case the material that is the bell—the cast iron and copper which comprises its material form—has, through the strange process of symbolisation, taken on quasi-mystical properties. Over the centuries it has become venerated as a sacred object—in fact it already had acquired the symbolic value of the Ark of the Covenant by 1777 when the British occupied Philadelphia. In September of that year the bell was taken down from its tower and removed in a train comprising several hundred wagons and over 200 Virginian and North Carolinian soldiers to Allentown, PA, for safe keeping. How did a very heavy lump of cast metal become the object of such veneration?

The bell was originally cast by one of the period's celebrated foundrymen, Thomas Lester of Whitechapel, whose foundry would also cast the bell that sits atop the bell tower in the Palace of Westminster, known affectionately as Big Ben. The foundry in East London operated until 2017. Lester was instructed by Robert Charles, the colonial agent for the province of Pennsylvania in London. And Charles had received his instruction from the three superintendents—Isaac Norris, Thomas Leech and Edward Warner—of the Philadelphia State House who had written to him in late 1751. A year or so earlier, in January 1750, two years after the completion of the State House, the Assembly decided that the building needed a tower with a bell that might be rung on significant occasions as well as on those days when the town meetings took place. Work on the tower was almost complete when, on 15 October 1751, another assembly meeting discussed the final touches for the tower and the possibility of commissioning the casting of a bell. The speaker of the Assembly was Isaac Norris and he, along with the other two superintendents, was delegated with the task of ordering 'a bell of such weight and dimensions as they shall think suitable'. Since, at that time, no large bell had been cast anywhere in the colonies the three superintendents were obliged to arrange for a bell to be made back in the mother country. A letter was duly dispatched to the province's agent, requesting that he procure 'a good bell of about 2,000 pounds weight'.

During the year 1751 the residents of Philadelphia were celebrating the fiftieth anniversary of William Penn's Charter of Privileges to the Province of Pennsylvania, so when it came to designing the bell it is possible that Norris, who was a scholarly man with sound knowledge of both Hebrew and Latin, was drawn to the verse in the Bible in which the people of Israel are encouraged to hold a jubilee every fifty years to celebrate their liberation from Egypt. The text of Leviticus reads: 'And ye shall hallow the fiftieth year, and proclaim liberty throughout all the land unto all the inhabitants thereof'. Whether or not the local celebrations were the prompt, it is the case that the last clause of this sentence was chosen as a fitting inscription for the bell. In the letter of instruction sent to Robert Charles the superintendents requested that the following words 'well shaped in large letters' be inscribed around the crown of the bell: PROCLAIM LIBERTY THROUGHOUT THE LAND UNTO ALL THE INHABITANTS THEREOF. LEV.XXV.

The power of words to move people, to raise aspirations or commemorate great acts, does not only lie in the words themselves. Context is of course a significant contributor to the force and energy conveyed by any saying, and such contexts need not be originary. As is indeed the case with the Liberty Bell. The good people of Philadelphia could not have known, in 1751, that twenty-five years later the thirteen colonies would rise up and with a clear voice declare themselves free citizens. Nor that the city of Philadelphia would host the Congress at which the Declaration of Independence would be agreed. But history is perforated with contingency. The power and force of the Liberty Bell, its *symbolic* power, is not, however, an accident of history. It is the result of a set of narrative strategies which have invested the material object with a form of ahistorical force, a meaning that is not bound to a singular historical event or period. A set of narratives which removed it from its historical location, thereby transforming the object into a symbol encapsulating the ideals of the revolution.

We can follow those narrative strategies quite closely. It all began with the story of a flaxen-haired youth whose role in the proceedings on 4 July 1776 could not, at the time, have been predicted as particularly significant. This unknown boy, so the story goes, was discharged with the responsibility of conveying the message that independence had been declared by the delegates to the Second Continental Congress to the people at large. And he was to do this by running from the chamber and shouting up to an old man who stood next to the bell in the bell tower: 'Ring! Ring!' And with that the Liberty Bell became a kind of narrative envelope into which the real thing, the bell itself, would be retroactively inserted. And once there, within the curtilage of its narrative form, it would be cut free from its own historical location and turned into something far more enduring: a symbolic marker conveying for all time the aspiration for freedom. This fictional enclave or narrative envelope, in slightly fuller detail, first came to public notice in the Philadelphia *Saturday Courier* of 1847 which published a short story entitled 'Fourth of July, 1776' by George Lippard, at the time a popular Philadelphia writer. And it was subsequently collected in his *Legends of the Revolution*. Not long after, the historian Beson J. Lossing began compiling his authoritative *The Pictorial Field Book of the Revolution*, in which he gathered together salient facts about the revolutionary period. And, ever since, the story made up by Lippard has assumed an air of authenticity, told and retold in school primers, handed down as lore from generation to generation.

In its more embellished form it goes like this. The moment the Second Continental Congress had resolved to declare independence from the mother country, John Hancock, the president of that Congress, ordered that the bell in the tower of what is now called Independence Hall be rung and the articles of the Declaration be read aloud. His message was delivered by an unnamed flaxen-haired boy to an old man who stood at the top of the tower, next to the bell, awaiting his instruction: 'Ring!' It was this same boy who had, earlier in the afternoon, mounted the stairs to the bell tower and read aloud the inscription on the bell to the old man who had found it difficult to discern the words. The young boy had obliged the elder townsman by reading: 'Proclaim liberty throughout all the land and unto all the inhabitants thereof'. And from here the transformation of the bell struck in Whitechapel into the Liberty Bell began. But a curious aspect to the story is that the bell on which the words had been inscribed was not the one cast by Thomas Lester in East London. It was not the original or 'authentic' Liberty Bell at all.

This fact introduces an important feature of the process of symbolisation, which cuts the material form of the bell loose from its moorings in the real. The Liberty Bell, we must bear in mind, is a symbolic form. It conveys the aspirational power of the will to liberty. And it is partly on account of its immaterial symbolic status that, paradoxically, such a high premium is placed upon the authenticity of the actual bell. This is why the object to this day attracts an air of devotion, as if the thing itself were capable of working some strange magic. In common with other objects that have their origin at the time of the revolution—clothes, pistols and muskets, even chairs—the bell has come to be venerated as a relic from the heroic past with the power to move one and encourage subscription to the great ideals which the Founding Fathers espoused. It is almost as if the subscription to political individualism in a secular state comes hand in hand with a need or desire for something in the realm of collective symbolism. Where once the church, certainly in its Catholic guise, provided many objects for collective veneration, now the state builds its authority on a set of commemorative rituals which create secular symbols out of material objects, or even individuals.

But the real history of the bell goes like this. When Lester's bell finally arrived in Philadelphia in August 1752 it was taken from Captain Budden's ship and set up in the State House yard. Its eventual home, the belfry up in the tower, had not yet been completed. But the townsfolk were impatient to test their new acquisition, so the bell was struck. Immediately 'the bell was cracked by a stroke of the clapper without any other violence'. The first plan was to send it back across the ocean and wait for a replacement, but it turned out that Budden already had a full load. At this point two local ironworkers stepped forward, John Pass and his friend Charles Stow, and offered to recast the bell even though they had never done such a thing before. They opined that something in the manufacture of the bell had made it 'too high and brittle' and that the addition of an ounce and a half of copper to the mix of ore would remedy the problem. The bell was duly smashed to pieces and then melted down, some further copper was then added before casting it afresh.

For a second time the bell was hung up in the yard and struck. No crack appeared but the sound was tinny and unimpressive. It is recorded that the two novice foundry men were 'so teased by the witticisms of the town' that they were stung into having a second attempt. Once again the metal was molten and then poured into the cast. This time the result was more successful, even though the sound of the bell was said to be rather unusual. It was this bell that was hung up in the completed bell tower in June of 1753.

For the first eighty or so years the bell was referred to as the 'Old State House Bell' or the 'Bell of the Revolution' or 'Old Independence Bell'; but in 1839 an anti-slavery pamphlet was published entitled 'The Liberty Bell' and this name was thereafter used to refer to the bell in Philadelphia. For a similar length of time the inscription on the bell was hardly remarked, but when Lippard's story appeared in 1847 the time was ripe for the final steps in the symbolic transformation of the material Pass and Stow had recast a century before. It is perhaps ironic that the year before Lippard's story was published the bell was struck for the last time.

From early on the bell had developed problems. A crack appeared, and various attempts to close it (or even, curiously, widen it, as in 1846) were made. On this last occasion it was hoped that the bell might ring out in celebration of the day on which Washington had been born. But every attempt to heal the crack failed. And since 1846 the bell has been silent. But other bells have rung out, simulacra of the sound of the Liberty Bell have been heard on countless significant occasions, while the real bell, or rather the simulacrum of the original bell, has been seen, if not heard, by millions of Americans, either in its current home in Philadelphia or on one of its many travels around the country.

4. A young child is held as to touch the Liberty Bell on one of its journeys via rail car around the country during the late nineteenth century. The crack, even at this resolution, is clearly visible.

For thirty years, between 1885 and 1915, the bell was frequently loaded onto a rail car and shipped around the United States. To New Orleans for the World's Industrial and Cotton Centennial in 1885, to Chicago for the World's Columbian Exposition in 1893, to Atlanta, Boston, Charleston, St Louis in the following years. On each occasion the trip would slowly wind its way through towns and cities, stopping along the way for the crowds to cheer, participate in parades and, on many occasions, kiss the bell which was hung from its original cross-beam, a single piece of hand-hewn black walnut (illustration 4).

The last time the bell was moved from its home town, Philadelphia, was in 1915 at the urging of 200,000 schoolchildren who expressed the wish that it be displayed at an exposition in San Francisco. But twenty-two years earlier in Chicago it had been decided to cast a 'new' Liberty Bell during the World's Fair so that once again its profound ring could be heard. This was not the first 'replacement' for the old bell whose crack prevented it from being struck. On the occasion of the centennial celebrations, Henry Seybert, a wealthy merchant, paid for a new bell to be installed in the tower of Independence Hall. It weighed 13,000 pounds—a thousand for each of the thirteen colonies—and was made from the molten metal of four Civil War cannons.

On 4 July 1876 at 12.01 a.m. it rang out for the first time. Yet another bell was cast, this time on the instruction of Queen Elizabeth II, and presented to the American people on the occasion of the bicentenary. It was made in the same foundry as the original bell, the Whitechapel Foundry, London. And its bears the inscription 'Let Freedom Ring!' Today this bell hangs in a simple belfry that is part of the Independence Park Visitors Center in Philadelphia where, every day at 11 a.m. and 3 p.m. it is rung.

Holy relics have power on account of their presumed authenticity. Thus, even though these replicas and substitutes for the original bell exist and are struck in symbolic recognition of the mythic moment when the first bell rang out marking the Declaration on 4 July 1776, it is still the object itself which has the strange power of symbolisation. From New Year's Eve in 1976 the original bell, not the one cast in Whitechapel but its recasting (twice) by John Stow and John Pass—this 'original bell' was hung in a modern pavilion on the grassy mall below Independence Hall. A project to construct another home for it began in 2001. Visitors to this shrine—around one and a half million each year—are encouraged by the guides to touch its smooth surface and read the inscription which has inspired so many generations of Americans. When asked what they remember of their visit most people mention two things: that the bell is cracked and the name of what is now the state of Pennsylvania is spelt 'Pensylvania'. No one forgets the name by which the bell is known.

Uncle Sam

Proudly marching at the head of countless Fourth of July parades is a man, or sometimes a boy, wearing a tailcoat, striped trousers and a beard. On his head there is a tall top hat that has been decorated with the stars and stripes. How did this figure—instantaneously recognisable as 'Uncle Sam'—become the symbolic figure for the nation? How did someone who would look more at home in a circus or on the stage become the person in whom all the passion and pride of patriotism would be invested?

It is commonly believed that Uncle Sam is hardly more than a comic-book invention, a relic of earlier times when periodicals frequently containing caricatures or cartoons were distributed across the United States. But in fact Uncle Sam was a real person, about whom we know quite a good deal. This is his story. He was born Samuel Wilson on 13 September 1766 in Menotomy, Massachusetts (now known as Arlington), the seventh child in a family of thirteen children, two of whom died in infancy. The family home was located in the triangle of land bounded by Massachusetts Avenue, Mystic Street and Russell Street. The title deed for this modest house indicates that a certain Robert Wilson purchased the property on 27 October 1665. It is not known where he hailed from, but it has been suggested that he had arrived in the United States from Scotland.

Samuel's father, Edward Wilson, married Lucy Francis of Medford on 23 November 1758. When Samuel was nine years old, in April 1775, news of the English action in the colonies was brought to Menotomy by Paul Revere on his now celebrated ride from Boston to Lexington. In 1780 the Wilson family sold up and moved to a hundred-acre farm near the hamlet of Mason,

New Hampshire, just north of the Massachusetts line. Here Sam met his future wife, the daughter of Captain Benjamin Mann, a veteran of Bunker Hill and the proprietor of the local store and tavern. Nine years later Sam and his brother Ebenezer set out on foot, traveling west towards a town called Naderheyden, about 150 miles distant. This village was well situated, seven miles north of Albany on the east side of the Hudson river. In January 1789 the freeholders in the village decided they needed a less cumbersome name and chose Troy, perfectly in keeping with the names of towns close by, which were drawn from the classical tradition—like Syracuse, Rome, Ithaca or Delphi. When the Wilson brothers arrived the village had just accepted this alteration in its nomenclature, and the new arrivals, Sam, now twenty-two years of age, and his brother Ebenezer, twenty-seven, found work as brick makers. They were successful enough at this enterprise to form their own company making bricks and then in 1793 they decided to diversify by entering the meat-packing business. This involved the purchase of land on which to situate a slaughterhouse and a dock for loading sloops with barrels of beef and pork destined for points south down the Hudson. A large farm was also started to provide the meat for their expanding business which went by the name of E & S Wilson.

It turned out that their choice of location, Troy, was a good one since it rapidly began to expand in the early years of the nineteenth century, as did its enterprises. This was partly fuelled by the fact that the US government bought 300 acres of land in Greenbush, New York, just south of Troy, where it established barracks for 6,000 soldiers. By 1812 when the war came, E & S Wilson had grown into a substantial enough company to allow the brothers to bid for government contracts supplying barrelled meat to the army. In fact, as early as 1805 they had claimed that they were able to butcher and pack 150 head of cattle a day. Their bid was successful, as was Sam's application to be become an inspector of beef and pork for the northern army. All this is a matter of the historical record, but it hardly makes for a gripping story. For that we need to reach another narrative form, to the legend that is Uncle Sam.

Here is how that legend got started. It appeared in the *New York Gazette* of 12 May 1830:

> Immediately after the declaration of the last war with England, Elbert Anderson, of New York, a contractor, visited Troy on the Hudson, where was concentrated, and where he purchased, a large quantity of provisions—beef, pork etc. The inspectors of these articles at that place were Messrs. Ebenezer and Samuel Wilson. The latter gentleman (invariably known as "Uncle Sam") generally superintended in person a large number of workmen, who, on this occasion, were employed in overhauling the provisions purchased by the contractor for the Army. The casks were marked E.A—U.S. This work fell to the lot of a facetious fellow in the employ of Messrs. Wilson, who, on being asked by some of his fellow workmen the meaning of the mark (for the letters U.S. for United States, were almost entirely new to them) said that he did not know unless it meant Elbert Anderson and Uncle Sam—alluding exclusively then, to the said "Uncle Sam" Wilson. The joke took among the workmen, passed currently and, "Uncle Sam" himself being present, was occasionally rallied by them on the increasing extent of his possessions.

Very quickly thereafter around the town of Troy all government property—everything, from wagons to arms or payrolls—was referred to as 'Uncle Sam's'. Although the legend did not at first travel that far away from the Hudson Valley, the use of the term 'Uncle Sam' to refer to the government gradually gained ground in the popular literature of the time. Seventy or so years later, in 1917, one of Sam's great nephews, Lucius E. Wilson, who was by then eighty-one, noted that the usage had become ubiquitous. Remembering his youth he said: 'I was about 18 when Uncle Sam passed away. He was the old original Uncle Sam that gave the name to the United States.'

What had happened in those intervening years was the transformation of a fact, a life, into a myth. Leaving behind the real person and his story based in lived experience, the Uncle Sam legend became part of the symbolic capital of the nation. This is how it happened. Initially Sam was encountered most frequently in cartoon form. The first depiction was published in 1832, in which a man swathed in an American flag is seated and attended by doctors, one of whom is the president, Andrew Jackson, and he is drawing blood form the ailing man. The words 'Uncle Sam in Danger' appear at the bottom—a comment on

5. One of the first images of Uncle Sam, suffering with flu and being administered to by a gleeful president Andrew Jackson who is holding the improbably large syringe.

Jackson's proposal to close down the Bank of the United States. This same ensemble appeared in a subsequent print published five years later [illustration 5], again representing the failure of the banking system. But it was not until the 1850s that the caricature now so firmly associated with the symbolic personification of the nation—an old man dressed in patriotic garb with a tall top hat—began to appear. Two famous American cartoonists, Thomas Nast and Joseph Keppler, are often credited with the addition of long whiskers to the character in the years following the Civil War. But at this time Uncle Sam was in competition with another cartoon figure, 'Brother Jonathan', for the emblematic honour of representing the country. The British magazine *Punch* was firmly committed to this 'Jonathan', as were many French cartoonists of the time.

It was the Civil War, however, that brought together two important figures—Abraham Lincoln and the heretofore mythic representative of the nation—and melded them into a composite that has since come to be the stock imaginative presentation of Uncle Sam. It helped in this regard that *Punch* often dressed their cartoon figure of Lincoln in clothes that echoed the stars and stripes. And Lincoln's beard was, of course, instantly recognisable. Following the Civil War the melded figure of Lincoln and the previous 'Jonathan' or 'Sam' character was a common feature of periodicals and newspapers. And then in the 1870s Thomas Nast began using a cartoon sketch that would prove to be enduring: Uncle Sam, in his flag attire with tall top hat and long whiskers. One of the first was published by *Harper's Weekly* in 1874, captioned 'A foreign and poisonous weed', in which a farmer is about to dig up a mushroom labelled 'communism'. Uncle Sam stands behind the offending fungus looking down with a stern gaze [illustration 6]. Nast's figure often seems to have very elongated legs [illustration 7] which may have entered the popular imagination and given birth to the more recent custom of putting him on stilts at the head of parades on 4 July. Nast never indicated his source for the cartoon, but it is often claimed that he drew inspiration from Dan Rice, the most famous clown in America during the mid nineteenth century. Rice had begun his career in the circus as a trick rider, but he subsequently developed an act with a

6. Uncle Sam looks on as Mr Granger weeds his field. His hoe carries a message on the blade: 'In our noble order there is no communism and no agrarianism'. Appearing at the foot of the cartoon are the words: 'That's right, Mr Granger; I thought you would not have that in your field'.

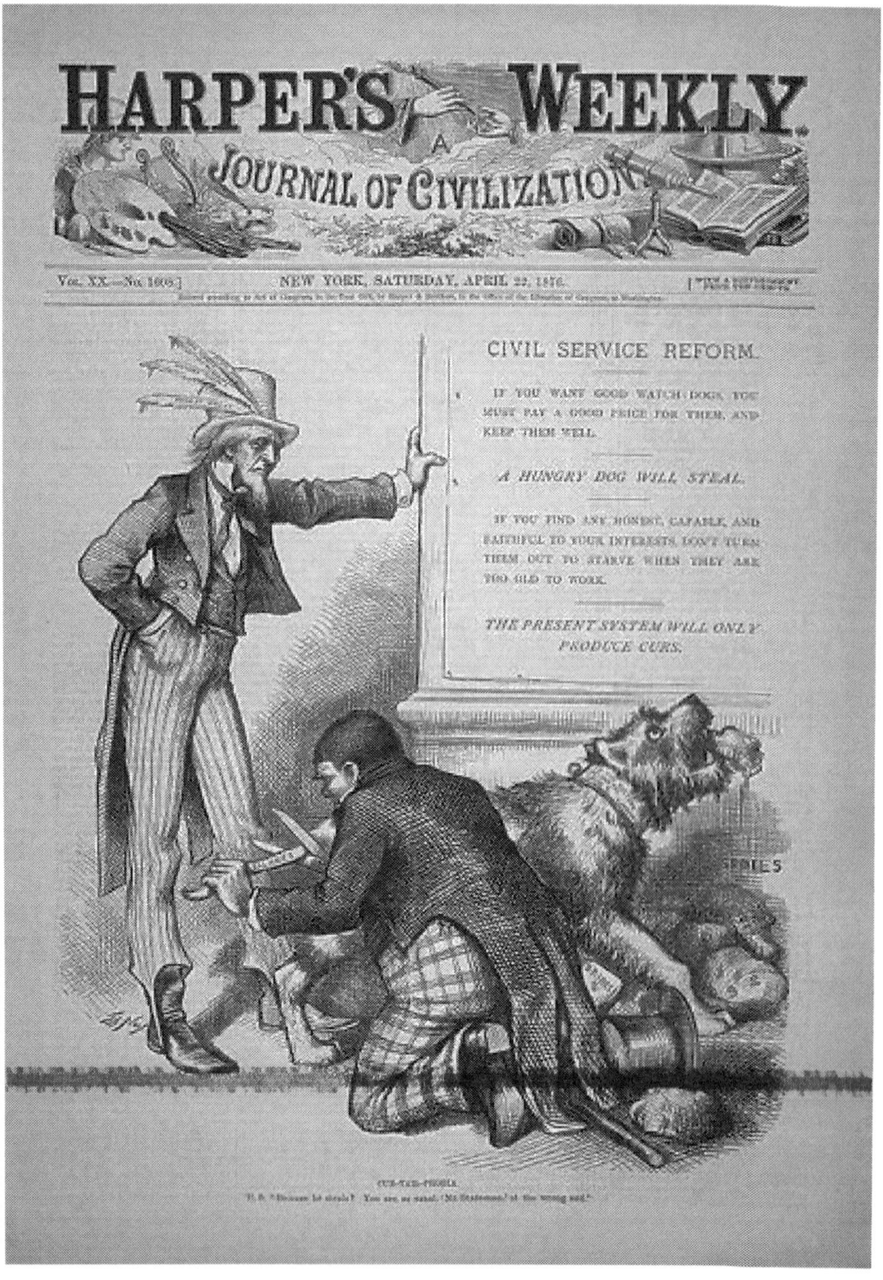

7. Uncle Sam has his rousers fitted alongside a banner announcing civil service reform.

trained pig he called Lord Byron. By the 1850s he had settled on being a clown, styling himself 'America's favorite clown', and dressed in a stars-and-stripes coat with a blue leotard underneath. His trunks were red and white, and he sported long whiskers and a top hat.

There have been variants since Nast's day. Perhaps one of the most popular in its time was Joseph Keppler's, which has Sam as a pot-bellied knockabout comic, recognisable from the music hall of the era. Others depict Sam in rather more sober habit, but in 1916 *Leslie's Weekly* put an image on the cover of its 6 July issue which was to become the most famous depiction of all. The caption read 'What are you doing for preparedness?' and it caught the eye of someone in the War Department who subsequently asked its creator to adapt it for a poster to be used in the war effort. The commissioned image clearly makes reference to the portrayal of General Kitchener on a recruitment poster used in Britain earlier in the First World War, and more than four million copies were printed in 1917 and 1918 [illustration 8]. For many Americans this *is* Uncle Sam, catching the viewer with his stern, beady eye. In a development that could not have been foreseen by Flagg, it is this image, perhaps, which fuels much of the unconscious association of government with surveillance and interference in citizens' private lives in the early twenty-first century. Uncle Sam, with his fixed stare and all-seeing eye.

To this day cartoons continue to make great use of the Uncle Sam figure, and his role in the popular culture of the nation has largely been determined by this form of visual representation. The common figure of speech by which the government is referred to as 'Uncle Sam' has also wielded its own power. But the most ubiquitous use of Uncle Sam in more recent times has been in promotional material. One of the first companies to use Uncle Sam as a means for making a sales pitch was the furniture oil manufacturer Berry Brothers which placed advertisements for their product in many magazines in the early 1900s. The caption

8. Flagg's iconic 1918 depiction of Uncle Sam helping recruitment for the war.

read: 'Uncle Sam supplying the world with Berry Brothers hard oil finish'. He has also been used to help sell tomatoes (the Wapato Fruit and Cold Storage Company), pianos (the Baldwin Piano Company), Cream of Wheat, Campbell's Soup, and Shoes [illustration 9]. In fact almost anything that can be marketed and sold, coffee [illustration 10], say, is susceptible to the same endorsement.

It is likely that the real 'Uncle Sam' would have been surprised by his longevity as a symbol for the government of the nation. He might equally have been perturbed by the uses to which his 'image' has been put: in illustration 11, the use of Flagg's

9 and 10. 'All men are created equal', so Uncle Sam declares, 'Tis true of men, but not of shoes'. To the left, an advertisement for a shoe company; to the right, a coffee supplier gets in on the act.

poster by a political group whose views can hardly be said to command widespread approval demonstrates both the symbolic power attached to the Uncle Sam icon and its adaptability. The following riff on the theme [illustration 12], issued in 1980 when Iran held US citizens hostage, was undoubtedly more sympathetically received. Whatever the historical person Sam Wilson would have made of these images, the inhabitants of Troy, New York, set out to honour their most renowned former resident. A statue at Third and River Streets stands in commemoration of the life of Samuel Wilson, and to make sure

11. Flagg's image put to rather different political purposes.

12. A recent expression of Uncle Sam's patriotism during the 1980 Iranian hostage crisis.

it will never be forgotten that it was this solid citizen and successful entrepreneur who gave birth to the symbolic representation of the United States government, the good folk of the town approached the Senate in 1961. They were hoping to cast in stone, as it were, for all time the fact that 'Uncle Sam' was a real person made from flesh and blood. Their wish was granted when the Senate officially declared that Samuel Wilson of Troy, New York, was the inspiration or progenitor for Uncle Sam.

A flag, a bell and a cartoon character. Symbols which give meaning and expression to the rites of observance of the Fourth. In the cases of the first two, much of what we want to believe about them is based in the sense that stories make of the past. That sense is felt as a truth even if the foundations of the story lie in the playful enjoyment of fabulation. In the last, however, the facts we know to be accurate about a real person, Sam Wilson, hardly grab attention. He might as well have been a myth, a made-up character, since it is the symbol we want to believe in, not the man. But as symbols all three exist in a kind of historically insensitive ether, indifferent to the contingency of event. They are precisely symbolic on account of this strange power to resist alterations in meaning over time. Indeed, the use of these symbols in and around the rituals of the Fourth constitutes in part an act of preservation, maintaining something that has been inherited from the past. But the practice of this celebration could never be entirely symbolic. It lives and breathes in a different ether, the more knockabout world of events and actions. And so, over time the meanings of the Fourth have been prey to the incidental even as its symbolic heart has continued to beat. The following chapter tracks those meanings.

5

The Meanings of the Fourth

A hundred years after Thomas Jefferson had given eloquent expression to the American mind, the document we now take to be the Declaration itself, the parchment with the text carefully transcribed in legal hand which was made on the instruction given by the Second Continental Congress on 19 July 1776, found its way back to its 'birthplace', Philadelphia's Independence Hall, for the centennial celebrations. It was ceremonially placed on the speaker's stand before the expectant audience and read aloud by the Virginian Richard Henry Lee, descendant of the man who had first proposed 'that these United Colonies are, and of right ought to be Free and Independent States'. [illustration 13] For the previous thirty-five years it had been hung opposite a window on an office wall in a government building in Washington—the then recently built Patent Office—perhaps not the optimal position for the long-term preservation of one of the three foundational scriptures of the nation. Rather curiously, during these mid years of the nineteenth century no one gave much thought at all to its darkening yellow surface with the fading signatures at the bottom. Certainly no one proposed to preserve or protect the document as an object of near talismanic power.

13. Richard Henry Lee reads from the Declaration to the celebrants at the Philadelphia centennial of the Fourth.

The Declaration's most recent travels have been to the stage of a global rock concert, Live 8, held simultaneously in a number of locations worldwide to raise consciousness about the plight of the peoples of the African continent. This event, organised by pop stars and hoping to build on the enormous success and importance of a similar event held twenty years earlier called Live Aid, was watched by a global audience of millions. On the Philadelphia stage the actor Will Smith participated by introducing one of the acts, as did many personalities from the worlds of television and cinema in this and the other locations for the concerts. On entering the stage he was accompanied by two Marines in uniform who took their place either side of a display case containing the Declaration of Independence. Smith began his short stint as anchor for this segment of the show by first introducing the world-wide audience to the document.

It was not made clear why the political, let alone the entertainment objectives of the occasion were advanced by this gesture but in a curious way the mere presence of the parchment—introduced in a fashion which seemed to give the venerable document a sense of person, as if one were being introduced to an aged relative—produced its own mysterious and powerful eloquence. It was there as a reminder to the world-wide audience, many of whom were certainly ignorant of the history of the document, perhaps even of the history of the foundation of the United States, that we have it within our power to initiate political acts that can change the world.

Between the mid nineteenth century and today the meanings of the Fourth have been interpreted in many ways, often determined by specific political agendas or coloured by important events, be they national or international. In fact the larger history of the nation can be seen—albeit in either a rather condensed or only outline form—in the changing focus given to the annual celebration of the nation's birth. What happened on that day, the words and actions of so many individuals in many different places, can be extracted from the archive that is the nation's history and help one take the temperature of the times. It is hardly surprising, for example, that in the years immediately following the War of Independence the rites of the Fourth were still strenuously tied to the political and even emotional resonance of the declaratory act itself. And, of course, while survivors from the generation of '76 were still able to attend Fourth celebrations the sense of connection to the events of July 1776 could be made palpable. But as the original event became more distant over time that connection had to be remade or reimagined if the rites of the Fourth were to continue to have a similar significance for later generations. Such attempts at preserving the originary meanings of cultural practices are not likely to succeed, of course, at least in the long term, since the proximate contexts of celebration provide an ever changing set of parameters for understanding the rituals and rites of the day. And these more localised and immediate concerns, crowding in upon observance of the Fourth, are most likely to grab attention, creating meanings for this generation,

14. Uncle Sam contributing to the war effort as 'fireworks' burst in the sky around him.

this moment in time. Here, at a significant moment in world history, is an image [illustration 14] that wonderfully conveys the pressures of the contingent. We must also remember that each year the Fourth rolls around, it has gathered yet one more encrustation to its rites of observance, adding to the stockpile which consists of the many histories of the Fourth.

There are many ways of sampling the variety of this quilted history. One is to look at what the president at any one time chose to do on the Fourth. Although it would be foolish to imagine that the actions of the president on the day are more symptomatic of the nation's mood than other activities we might wish to focus upon, they do, nevertheless, provide a window onto specific moments in the nation's history which can help us begin to assemble the meanings of the Fourth through time. The third president, for example, was the first to open his official home to the public on the Fourth, where he received guests from all walks of life. Most presidents since that time have made a point of attending public events of celebration, though not always in the capital, and to greater or lesser extents have made themselves physically accessible to the citizens of the republic. Eisenhower, however, throughout his two terms as president spent the day at Camp David and invariably played a round of golf. Is this fact too slender to take the weight of a more general observation about the 'comfort zone' of the 1950s in America, the Eisenhower years of corporate expansion as the country evolved into a mature superpower? Is it just a weird irony that in 1970, while President Nixon was meeting at the Western White House in San Clemente, California, to thrash out peace negotiations over Vietnam, on the other side of the country in the capital at 7.30 p.m. his tape-recorded Fourth of July message was played out of speakers along the Mall? Given the role that tape recorders were going to play in the demise of Nixon's presidency, this little snapshot of the Fourth seems to be pregnant with the submerged meanings of contingent historical facts.

Less speculatively, we can gain an insight into the larger history of the nation from certain Fourth celebrations which happened to coincide with significant events. One of the decisive moments of the Civil War, for example, occurred on 4 July 1863, when the Confederate army surrendered at Vicksburg. Although President Lincoln had yet to hear the news of the successful military campaign on the day itself, or of the victory at Gettysburg which had been won the day before, when this information did get to him he rose to the occasion by giving a 'Fourth' address three days later, on 7 July. This speech was widely reprinted in newspapers across the country and can be read as a proleptic oration for the more renowned Gettysburg address of 17 November that year. Lincoln, who had not taken a public role in the actual day's celebrations three days before, spoke as if it was the Fourth. He began: 'Fellow-citizens: I am very glad to see you tonight. But yet I will not say thank you for this call. But I do most sincerely thank Almighty God for the occasion on which you have called. How long ago is it? Eighty odd years since, upon the Fourth of July, for the first time in the world, a union body of representatives was assembled to declare as a self-evident truth that all men were created equal.'

As Gary Wills so deftly points out in his book *Lincoln at Gettsyburg*, the fifteenth president was the great illusionist of political rhetoric, presenting himself as a different person according to the audience he was addressing. So it is difficult to state categorically that he was for this or against that, and this applies as much to the subject of slavery as many other concerns of his presidency. If in saying that 'all men were created equal' he meant to indicate agreement with the emancipation of slaves, he was giving a spin to the words taken from the preamble of the Declaration which would not have been acceptable to many delegates at the Second Continental Congress. For, as we know, the paragraph in Jefferson's draft concerning the iniquities of slavery was removed in the process of Congress's editing of his text. And even if this paragraph had remained in the text, the sense then, in 1776, of who had a claim to equal rights would certainly not have coincided precisely with one way of reading Lincoln's agenda. In 1863, 'all men' could for some public figures comprise the totality of the human race. In 1776, many more would have wavered before committing themselves to such a proposition. And some would have vociferously withheld their support for a political philosophy that did not discriminate between the differences of skin.

The most renowned Fourth oration on the topic of equality is Frederick Douglass's speech to the Rochester Ladies' Anti-Slavery Society on 5 July 1852 (the Fourth falling on a Sunday that year). This speech, commonly referred to by its most famous line 'What to the slave is the Fourth of July?', was published as a pamphlet and had very wide circulation. Douglass actually said 'what to the American slave', and the omission of the qualifying adjective tells us something about the will to universalism that characterises observance of the rites of the Fourth. Notwithstanding such appeals to the transcendental truths embedded in the Declaration which are the staple fare of Fourth orations, Douglass's address was, of course, punctual. It helped maintain pressure to right what many then believed was a wrong in the foundation of the nation: its blindness to the status of citizens of African origin.

In the course of what to us would be a long speech (orations given on the Fourth up through the nineteenth century could last for at least one hour), Douglass made good use of what by then had become conventional tropes of Fourth oratory. But in his hands these rhetorical topoi are given an ideological twist, even a new lease of life, as he sets about his task of chastising the audience for continuing to uphold the inequities of racism. Early on, for example, he refers to the Fourth as 'the birthday of your National Independence' and, in case the point has yet to be heard fully, he adds, 'and of your political freedom'. He has recourse to this use of the second person pronoun throughout the speech as he seeks to distinguish himself from his audience. Indeed, he explicitly makes the point that the nation contains two separate kinds of person. On the one hand there are those who, like Douglass himself, were only in America by dint of their being indentured to a slave plantation, and on the other those who were the descendants of the white colonists—the citizens who comprise his audience. 'The 4th of July is the first great fact of your nation's history', he says, once again assigning the significance of the day to a community of citizens which excludes the speaker. And then, having invoked this trope of origin, he reaches to an image that penetrates to the heart of his message: that fact is, he says, 'the very ring-bolt in the chain of your yet undeveloped destiny'.

With this image another habitual trope of Fourth oratory is introduced. This figure has its roots in Christian millennial rhetoric which gives expression to the future achievement of the promised land. This sense of a destiny, a perpetual future horizon, is a common feature of interpretations of the meaning of the Fourth. One can find it in Bill Clinton's speech of 4 July 1996 when he said: 'America is a work in progress'. The same trope is embedded in President Carter's sentiment, declared on the Fourth in 1977: 'the work of freedom can never be finished, for freedom is not a temple that is completed when the last stone is in place, but a living thing that each generation must create anew'. Once again the narrative grammar of the Fourth produces an account of the American Project which for many citizens is and has been liberatory. It gives full weight to the conceptual invention that is the Constitution in its derivation of legitimacy from those who speak in its name or on its behalf: we the people. But, as the history of the nation shows, such derivation of power may not always lead to universal outcomes. If freedom is an unfinished project, the end of the story has yet to be written.

Both Carter and Clinton spoke in rather elevated terms to the concerns of their era, to issues which today continue to concern us. Douglass, for his part, was addressing the pre-eminent issue of his own time in a language that would have been instantly evocative to his audience: 'I have said that the Declaration of Independence is the ring-bolt to the chain of your nation's destiny'. In fact he had not claimed earlier that the Declaration was a 'ring-bolt'—the image is here being extended by proximity to its first use where 'the fact of the Fourth' was said to be this ring-bolt in the chain of destiny.

But it was the Declaration he wanted his audience to call to mind. As a whole Douglass's speech shows how a small number of themes or common elements may be rearranged in order to speak more compellingly to the immediate context. Hundreds of Fourth orations make reference to the purported 'Declaration' in the sense of a speech act, or to the mythical signing of the document itself on that day. They nearly always include some words from the document (commonly either the preamble or the final few sentences, sometimes both) and often refer to previous explanations of their meaning, pointing up, for example, the rights and obligations of the citizen in a republican state. And many, very many, come to a conclusion by evoking the ultimate (future) realisation of the spirit of '76: the destiny of America. This common stock of rhetorical topoi constitutes a resource of extraordinary symbolic power and it may surprise us, living at a time when the technical arts of rhetoric and oratory are no longer taught in a formal way, that such a small palette can provide enough material for ringing countless changes on a perpetual theme.

Douglass, however, has a more specific agenda. At about ten minutes into the speech this becomes more apparent as he highlights his own position as a representative chosen to speak on this august occasion. For, whom does he represent? 'Fellow citizens,' he starts off, 'pardon me, allow me to ask, why am I called upon to speak here today?' Given the room in which he was standing this can only be taken as a rhetorical question since his hosts were fully attuned to and in agreement with the tenor of his political agenda. Nevertheless, he makes the point assuredly: 'What have I, or those I represent, to do with your national independence? Are the great principles of political freedom and of natural justice, embodied in that Declaration of Independence, extended to us?' It does not matter that later historians and political theorists will question whether or not the Declaration does, in fact, propose something like a Lockean view of natural justice. Here, once again, the plasticity of the sentiments Jefferson so brilliantly distilled allows—even invites—generation after generation to find in the document its own version of 'political freedom' and 'natural justice'. And this is so even when such political goods are said to be timeless and universal. Having, one more time, marked out his exclusion from the lofty ideal of freedom espoused by the Declaration, Douglass turns the screw by cloaking his next question in the unmistakable garb of religious observance: 'and am I, therefore, called upon to bring our humble offering to the national altar, and to confess the benefits and express devout gratitude for the blessings resulting from your independence to us?' Moving to a crescendo in this section of his speech he draws on the familiar millennial imagery of the sun: 'The rich inheritance of justice, liberty, prosperity and independence, bequeathed by your fathers, is shared by you, not by me. The sunlight that brought life and healing to you, has brought stripes and death to me'. And then, once again, he hammers his point home: 'This Fourth of July is yours, not mine'.

Lest his audience fail to recognise the biblical dimension to his oration he next moves into direct quotation: 'By the rivers of Babylon, there we sat down. Yea! We wept when we remembered Zion. We hanged our harps upon willows ...' and so on, culminating with an appeal, 'O Jerusalem, let my right hand not forget her cunning.' It is the same move, albeit routed through a very different historical context, made by Harry S. Truman in his

Fourth speech in 1945. Although on that occasion there was little to celebrate—the war in the Pacific was still a serious threat to the nation—the rhythms and cadences of the Christian liturgy that lie so deeply embedded in the psyche of America are audible in his speech. 'In this year of 1945', he began, 'we have pride in the combined might of this nation which has contributed signally to the defeat of the enemy in Europe. We have confidence that, under Providence, we soon may crush the enemy in the Pacific. We have humility for the guidance that has been given us of God in serving His will as leader of freedom for the world.'

It would be strange if the tenor of the times did not exert some kind of centrifugal force on the meanings associated with observance of the Fourth. Times of war inevitably raise the ghosts of 1776 and the ideals of the revolutionary generation. But they also put enormous pressure on the reinterpretation or reaffirmation of what might be claimed to be the founding creed of the nation. George W. Bush, for example, responding to the most traumatic experience of hostility to those ideals encountered since the Declaration was written, the events of 11 September 2001, spoke of the 'creed of freedom and equality' that underpins the founding of the nation in his Fourth address in 2002. 'This creed draws our friends to us,' he said, speaking from the Courthouse Square in Ripley, West Virginia, 'It sets our enemies against us, and always inspires the best that is within us.' And in keeping with the habitual topoi for the occasion he had recourse to a religious metaphor: 'In this 226th year of our independence, we have seen that American patriotism is still a living faith'. Almost forty years earlier, as the country pursued a war far from its own borders, the faith Bush refers to was tested almost to breaking point in one constituency: the so-called 'counter-culture' which so strenuously voiced its opposition to Vietnam. On the Fourth that year, 1968, anti-war demonstrators made Vice-President Hubert Humphrey's speech in Philadelphia difficult to listen to in a public manifestation of dissent from the leadership of the nation. And for many Americans of that generation the ideals and aspirations embodied in the founding Declaration were shown up in a new and far from favourable light by the prosecution of the war. It was precisely this animus which prompted Ron Kovic to write his memoir, subsequently turned into a film by Oliver Stone, entitled *Born on the Fourth of July*.

That film opens with a scene in which the military parade in a small town celebration of the Fourth is shown to be formative for the young boy who will proudly grow up a patriot, ready and willing to give service to his country even while all those around him—his white schoolmates—evince little enthusiasm for enlisting in the fight against communism. Early on in the screenplay the sacrifice made by the Kovic character in signing up for the Marines is also shown to have repercussions in the family since his younger sibling takes a very different view of the wisdom of the war. But when the young Marine is wounded in action and heroically fights to save his damaged legs in a grim military hospital the realities of the war begin to surface. There is no money to fund sanitary conditions for convalescence. In fact, the wounded are effectively marginalised, deprived of their citizenship. And so the Kovic character begins to alter his views and by the end of the film has become a vocal opponent of the war and the government which sent its young into battle.

Stone's movie does not speak for everyone of the Vietnam generation, nor does Kovic's book, but the simple and effective message—encapsulated in the title—is fully embedded in the structure of celebration of the Fourth. What was 'born on the Fourth of July' is timeless, a set of ideals and aspirations that may be knocked about by specific events, reimagined or refocused, but inevitable as such contingency may be, the obligation to diminish the power of immediate concerns and contexts in order to cherish and preserve, to pass on to future generations of Americans 'these truths ...' is shown to be the very essence of citizenship. No one can argue with that as a founding creed. While some viewers may take a very different position about the country's involvement in Vietnam and the necessity of tackling those who many judged to be mortal enemies of freedom and equality, few would dissent from the account the film both explicitly and implicitly gives of the obligations of citizens to honour the credo of the Fourth.

An unfurled Stars and Stripes proudly ruffles in the wind, the flag fixed to its mast, as is customary, on the left hand side. Behind the flag a landscape stretches out to the horizon. It is a scene of tranquil rural calm. A church occupies pride of place in the small hamlet, painted white with a tall steeple. A road slowly winds its way in serpentine fashion from the foreground through to the rolling hills in the background. Under the image of this bucolic paradise the words 'Land of the Free' are printed, and below these words, in smaller type, 'What price freedom before the election?' And under these words, in parentheses, 'U.S. at War'.

This is the cover of *Time* magazine for 6 July 1942. Following the bombing of Pearl Harbor in 1941 a campaign was launched encouraging magazines the length and breadth of the United States to include the national flag on their cover for the issue published on or around 4 July 1942. The idea was to flood the nation's news-stands and billboards with the patriotic message 'united we stand'. Almost three hundred magazines participated, from *Vogue* to the *New Yorker*, *US Steel News* to *Captain Marvel*. Paul MacNamara, a publicist working for Hearst Magazines, dreamt up the scheme which was also backed by the Secretary of the Treasury at the time, Henry M. Morgenthau Jr, who was keen to raise more cash for the war effort through the 'Buy Bonds and Stamps' initiative.

Of course, each cover was designed with the natural audience for the magazine in mind, but when one looks at them as a group it becomes possible to construct an image of America half-way through the twentieth century. A country then committed to the

Second World War and, in the aftermath of Pearl Harbor, facing for the first time in its history since the War of Independence a very real threat of attack and even invasion by a foreign power. So these images, published to coincide wherever possible with the day celebrating the 'nation's birthday', provide us with a powerful forensic tool for establishing some of the ways the Fourth has been used and represented. Although one cannot but be impressed by the ingenuity brought to the task by many of the designers of the magazines, taken as a whole it its less this spirit of invention that emerges and rather more a vivid image of how America, in 1942, pictured itself to itself. The anniversary (or thereabouts) of the nation provided an opportunity for both small niche market magazines, say *Flower Grower*, and national icons such as *Newsweek* to depict what, from their own corner of the pitch, seemed to them of significance for America's birthday.

Many were, of course, keenly aware of the war situation and the need to keep up the effort in supporting the allied forces. *Boeing News* [illustration 16], for example, included one of the traditional elements of the Fourth in the lower right-hand corner where the word 'fireworks' appears. Given that the military personnel pictured are loading bombs onto what we assume to be a Boeing bomber, it is unclear as to whether the use of this word was intended to be playful or not. While *Infantry Journal* [illustration 17] is rather more appropriately somber in regard to the ongoing war, its companion *Pacific Marine Review* is rather more positive, claiming that 'Ships will win the war!' while managing to include a more traditional up-beat, even celebratory, Fourth of July mood in the image of a ship being launched in the traditional manner. It would be difficult to envisage any outcome except a happy one from this particular presentation of a country at war.

15. *Time.*

16. *Boeing News.*

17. *Infantry Journal.*

18. *Theatre Arts.*

It is, however, those magazines without any military connection whose covers create a patchwork of how America looked and felt to its citizens in 1942. The magazine *Theatre Arts* [illustration 18] had no particular need to make reference to a military theme, but it chose to depict a troupe of players entering an army camp in a motorcade that clearly nods towards the Fourth's tradition of the parade. Each truck carries props and contented-looking players who are busy learning lines from their scripts. The rhetoric of the image is disarming; it says, 'do not panic, we will prevail'. Above all it carries the impression of a young and inexperienced populace dealing with an unusual situation: war. A more serious note is struck by *Photoplay Combined With Movie Mirror* [illustration 19], a journal aimed at the movie industry. This cover presented identity photographs of twelve movie actors who were currently serving the country, reminding readers of the gravity of the situation. Its strip line along the bottom announced 'How Clark Gable is Conquering Loneliness', which one assumes was not a reference to his being marooned on a vessel somewhere in the Atlantic, but rather his efforts at keeping spirits up when so many of his colleagues and friends were doing service. In such a time one can forgive the rhetoric of heroism as displayed on the cover of *Look* [illustration 20]. Here a lone soldier, standing on a promontory and looking out to sea, adopts the at-ease pose next to the flag run up an extremely tall flagpole. The words 'united we stand' take on particular resonance, implying that a lone soldier in a far-off and distant land is just as much a member of the collective as anyone else. This cover seems to picturing the motto the nation adopted on its seal: *e pluribus unum*.

A rather more festive look is given to *Gourmet: The Magazine of Good Living* which does not allow its readership to forget that even in wartime the celebration of the Fourth ought to be graced with appropriately garlanded cookies and deserts in red, white and blue. But it is the covers of magazines such as *Country Gentleman* or *Outdoor Life* [illustration 21] which suggest that the

19. Photoplay.

20. Look.

21. Outdoor Life, July 1942.

22. Capper's Farmer.

rhythms and cadences of American life will prevail no matter what. Indeed, that such habits and customs are hardly touched by the war effort—just as the contented fisherman on the cover of *Outdoors* must have suspected. And one cannot but admire the sheer bravado of *Capper's Farmer* [illustration 22] in its portrayal of the healthy smiling youth of the country making their own contribution by 'lickin' stamps.

This last image brings to the fore the significance of the Fourth in the modern calendar of family life and the place of children in it. For most of the latter half of the twentieth century it would be inconceivable to mark the anniversary of the 'birthday of the nation' without including children in some fashion in the celebrations. To some extent they have always been included as spectators: even in 1777 in Philadelphia the parade and illuminations were enjoyed by those not yet old enough to be enlisted in the local militia or assume household responsibilities. But the primary or most prominent activities of the Fourth only slowly became aligned with those engaged in on other public holidays. It was not, for example, until the middle of the nineteenth century that entertainments such as balloon demonstrations or fairground attractions began to take on a predominant role in Fourth festivities. Even then the social and political meanings of a 'public holiday' were not, as now, so firmly embedded in the culture's promotion of the notion that time away from the workplace is best—and most morally defensibly—spent within the enclave and embrace of the family. For the late twentieth-century American workforce the number of days of 'enforced' holiday—those days designated as officially devoted to activities other than paid work—are far from numerous. Some, like Christmas, maintain their significance as punctual religious rituals, but others, like Thanksgiving, which has its origins in a colonial Puritan observance of a day given over to worship, have been reoriented over time.

The Fourth, as we have seen, does have its feet in the clay

of its colonial cultural origins and, on account of that, its connection to the religious observance of a 'day of rest' has not yet been completely erased. But inevitably over time the senses of celebration change and the activities deemed appropriate for such occasions as public holidays alter. The promotion of competitions for eating the largest number of hot dogs, for example, might not have been approved of, let alone dreamt up, by the generation of '76. And although the grandchildren of the founding generation might have been willing to imagine the development of certain ball games as national obsessions, even they would have been surprised by the prominence that sport has attained in contemporary American life. But they would have been perfectly happy with the idea that the Fourth be celebrated from within the family, marking the day by providing entertainments for children, incorporating them into parades and picnics and, perhaps above all else, sending the day off with spectacular displays of fireworks. So although the Fourth cannot properly be said to be a day of religious observance, it does, nevertheless, embrace its celebrants within a doctrine that is held as sacred as any religious creed: independence.

Happier times produce more contented and certainly less contested celebrations. Here is an image of the morning breaking on 4 July 1876 [illustration 23]—a happy, contented family raising the flag that 'has waved one hundred years'. The centennial was perhaps intended to be the most unifying moment in the nation's history of observance of the Fourth to date. All over the country orations and addresses were given—more than 420 are listed in the database compiled by James R. Heintze—which in their different ways honour the founders while, at the same time, looking forward to the evolution of the country into a mature republic with considerable, even pre-eminent power in the brotherhood of nations. These encomia to the unity of the nation must be seen, however, in the light of the deep divisions which had emerged in the republic between the fiftieth anniversary

23. A family, complete with Afro-American servant, hoist the Stars and Stripes on the centennial.

of the Declaration and the centenary. A civil war had almost destroyed the project of the Founding Fathers, and the bitterness which resulted from that conflict can still, to this day, be seen in the proud traditions of various localities wherever they may be geographically situated across the continent of the Union. But on 4 July 1876 most were prepared to put to one side the animosity which had soured North-South relations and celebrate what one newspaper called 'the permanent establishment of civil and religious liberty'.

Notwithstanding the dampening of such partisan political loyalties, the centennial anniversary was not regarded universally as an occasion for unambiguous celebration. Some were keenly aware of the cost of mounting a big parade—perhaps on the model of the 'World Fair' which had been initiated in 1851 by Queen Victoria at the Hyde Park Crystal Palace; others were disaffected enough to point out that the nation had little to celebrate. It could easily have transpired that the day would go down in history as a damp squib had it not been for the citizens of Philadelphia. Lacking leadership from the federal government, the residents of the 'birthplace' of independence took matters into their own hands by organising an International Centennial Exhibition. Four hundred and fifty acres in Fairmont Park were set aside to house the fair. A private corporation began drawing up plans for the celebrations and the pavilions which were to house them. Most of the money and all the organisation was provided by local citizens. The federal government proved to be indifferent to the proposed jamboree, relenting only in March 1875, when it finally came up with a half-million dollar grant. Throughout 1875 and early 1876 the buildings took shape—the Main Hall was said to be the largest building in the world and the Machinery Hall housed the world's biggest engine. The Horticulture Hall, the smallest of the five principal exhibition halls, measured 380 feet by 193 feet and was made almost entirely out of iron and glass; it contained horticultural specimens from all over the world. The conservatory, or main hall, alone boasted full-grown sago, date and cocoa palms, orange and lemon trees, camphor, eucalyptus, guava, mahogany, India rubber, and banana trees. Plant specimens from the South Sea Islands jostled next to a collection of rare plants sent from a greenhouse in England; a collection of ferns said to be worth $10,000 had been contributed by a collector from Amboy, New Jersey. No one could be in any doubt that here, in the birthplace of the republic, was the largest exhibition of the planet's diversity ever mounted. Here one could witness the fruit of man's most advanced technologies. Here in America.

In spite of all this ingenuity and proud demonstration of the height to which the nation had risen in only a hundred years the population of the federation of states remained largely sceptical. Many opined that the entire project would become a white elephant, perhaps never even to open. Almost at the last hurdle the enterprise seemed to wobble as funds were lacking to complete the preparations; private donations were now exhausted. But in a close vote in Congress a bill was passed authorising a loan of one and a half million dollars. The show proved to be an enormous success with over 100,000 visitors a day crowding into the halls eager to see the marvels on display. In keeping with the ambitions of such 'world fairs', few would leave in any doubt about the superiority of the nation's achievements. Here could be seen the biggest exhibition of photographs ever mounted; 75,000 feet of wall space accommodated paintings from Europe and America. Machinery Hall, at 1,402 feet in length, covered an area of nearly thirteen acres. Objects manufactured from all manner of materials could be purchased—glassware depicting the Liberty Bell was one of the biggest sellers, but not far behind were glass renditions of the Declaration of Independence and of Betsy Ross making a flag.

All this brio—appropriate for a nation eager to present a confident and forward-looking face to the world at large—ought to be seen in the context of the years preceding the centennial which had witnessed a marked indifference, even hostility, to the razzmatazz surrounding the Fourth. Indeed, by 1876 many citizens preferred to celebrate 'Decoration Day', the forerunner of Memorial Day, rather than the Fourth. Notwithstanding the deep divisions which emerged in America's sense of the nation around the issues which led to civil war, the deep seam of patriotism which runs through the observance of the Fourth from its first celebration to today could not be repressed entirely. So, as the nineteenth century drew to a close, the meanings of the Fourth began to be reoriented as the patriotic purpose of its traditions was focused explicitly at children for whom the day became associated with fairground attractions. Their parents, however, were keen to use the day as a means of inculcating the rules and ethos of good citizenry, of making patriots of their charges. Allied to this was a similar innovation designed to bring together the celebration of the nation's birthday with the moment at which new citizens, immigrants to the country, took their first symbolic step as Americans.

The first move in what was to become a campaign to lobby Congress with proposals to change the name of the day was taken in 1915 in Kansas City. On the Fourth that year a number of new citizens took their first oath of allegiance on a day designated by the State officials as 'Americanization Day'. They had taken their lead from the Committee for Immigrants in America, which had been formed following the successful strike of mostly immigrant labour in Lawrence, Massachusetts, in February 1912. This prompted a number of corporate heads to begin to think of ways in which their mostly foreign workforces might be better assimilated into American culture. So they first formed the Committee for Immigrants which then, in 1915, proposed the establishment of another group, the National Americanization Day Committee (NADC), whose purpose was to institute a day for 'a great nationalistic expression of unity and faith in America'. And so was born the 'Americanization movement'. July 4th seemed to be an appropriate day to be co-opted for this purpose, and since 1915 hundreds of thousands of new American citizens have been naturalised on the day that celebrates the birth of the nation. The largest number on any single occasion occurred during the bicentennial celebrations in 1976. And the honour of this distinction falls to Miami, where the beach Convention Center was converted into a federal courtroom in order to naturalise 7,241 persons.

If moments have a particular force in respect to the creation of the ongoing story of the nation, places have no less a power to construct the magical 'fit' between the past and affective relations to it. The iconic sites for the rites of the Fourth are easily identified: the State House in Philadelphia, now called Independence Hall; the sites of important military encounters—foremost among them Lexington and Concord; Faneuil Hall in Boston, scene of so many important meetings which led to independence. But perhaps the place held in greatest affection for many generations of Americans, partly because it opens a window onto the interior life of public office, turning the official into the familial, is the house the third president designed and built in his home state of Virginia. And since 1963 every year on 4 July new citizens have been welcomed into the embrace of the nation in a naturalisation ceremony held on its lawns. The speeches given on that occasion at Monticello also weave a miniaturised history of the more recent past of the nation and, like the orations of the nineteenth century which precede them, they help us make sense of the Fourth, shaping and interpreting its meanings.

In fact, Fourth orations were given from time to time on the steps in front of the portico at Monticello some decades before the tradition of hosting naturalisation ceremonies got started. That given by Harry S. Truman in 1947 is particularly resonant, coming as it did at the conclusion of a world war that many had feared would end in defeat for the Allied powers. On that occasion Truman spoke of Jefferson laying 'the foundation of an independent democracy' and his efforts to form the 'basis for a truly democratic government'. Themes which are, of course, firmly centred in the tradition of Fourth observance even if many of the Signers of the Declaration would have had difficulty in subscribing to the notion of a 'truly democratic government'. But the precise context of his oration also gave a resonance to his remarks which may still be felt today. For Truman and his colleagues were keenly aware that the nation had now accrued responsibilities not only in regard to the citizens of the Union and the abstract principles enshrined in the foundation of the republic but also to those outside its borders where such principles had yet to become holy scripture.

'Two years ago', Truman notes, 'the United States and fifty other nations joined in signing a great Declaration of Independence', only this time, in 1945, at the conclusion to the most traumatic world war yet encountered, that declaration spoke not only for the people of America, it was also intended to speak for a genuine universal, for the peoples of the world. This declaration, Truman points out, is 'known as the Charter of the United Nations'. Reckoning that he ought to provide his reasons for signing up to this document, he continued: we signed 'because we had learned, at staggering cost, that the nations of the world cannot live in peace and prosperity if, at the same time, they try to live in isolation'. And then he moved into the familiar rhetorical territory of the rites of the Fourth: 'We have learned that nations are interdependent, and that recognition of our dependence upon one another is essential to life, liberty, and the pursuit of happiness of all mankind.'

Since 1963 thousands of new citizens have sworn allegiance to the flag for the first time at Monticello on the Fourth in a celebration of its rites that has a very particular feel and flavour. Here, at the house built by the man responsible for most of the words in the Declaration of Independence, presidents, ambassadors, secretaries of state, leading entrepreneurs and chairman of charitable institutions have given their own slant to what it means to become, to be, an American. Gerald Ford, speaking the year of the bicentennial, claimed that 'there is still something wonderful about being an American'. He went on to say that, even if we cannot express it, 'we know what it is'. Addressing his audience of newly minted citizens he said: ' You know what it is or you would not be here today. Why not just call it patriotism?'

It would not be inaccurate to say that patriotism is so firmly embedded in the celebration of the Fourth that the significance of the day could hardly be intelligible without some understanding of what it means to be a patriot. Of course, the word 'patriot' has itself been subject to the immediate contexts in which it has been used: 'patriots' at the time of the revolution sought to distinguish themselves from loyalists, whereas later in the nation's history—once the republic was secure—the senses of patriotism had no need to be distinguished in this manner. Leaving aside the desiderata of party politics, perhaps the most significant and enduring uses of the term bring it firmly into the orbit of what is sometimes thought of as the distinctiveness of the American experiment: its unfolding according to providence. Orators on the Fourth from the early nineteenth century onward made the connection between the Founding Fathers, those patriots who brought into existence the nation, and the will of God. 'It can surely be no disgrace', the Charleston orator Richard Furman declaimed on the Fourth in 1802, 'but a high honor to our patriots, to say "They acted in the cause of God" and that "He smiled on their endeavours"'. Indeed, throughout the nineteenth century Fourth orations returned again and again to the theme of the blessings bestowed upon the nation: God had arranged things so that Adams and Jefferson gave up their lives on the fiftieth anniversary of the Declaration; indeed, it was maintained that he continued to watch over the world's only republic, having in earlier times looked benignly upon the first settlers. Time after time comparisons of a biblical kind were entered into. America, it was claimed, was 'the modern Israel of the Lord'; it had been delivered 'from a second Egypt'. Francis D. Quosh, speaking on the Fourth in 1820, described the heroes of the revolution as putting 'their only trust in Him, who never deserts the faithful', a God who 'as he once led his chosen people from the task masters of Egypt, was able to carry his American Israel through the waves and wilderness of revolution, and to place them in the Canaan of peace and independence.'

These sentiments were far from unusual or aberrant musings of overly portentous orators: many Americans subscribed to the thought that the prosperity of the nation and its continuation as a free republic was in the hands of the divine creator. What else could prevent such a political structure falling into the abuses history demonstrates were inevitable in all earlier attempts at republican government? And, like those miscreant peoples from biblical times, Americans would also find their situation deteriorating if they neglected their Christian duties and obligations. Christianity, observers at the altar of patriotism were told, was the best defence of American liberty. The Bible not only allowed one to espouse patriotic views, it required one to do so. This led to the inevitable conclusion that 'Jesus Christ was a patriot', as George Bethune put it in 1835.

It was not only preachers and Fourth orators who reinforced this story. The very first substantial history of the nation, George Bancroft's ten-volume *History of the United States from the Discovery of the American Continent*, claims that Providence transformed a wilderness into a nation. Providence, then, provided a way of not only understanding the formation of the nation and its pre-history—the era of the Pilgrim Fathers who were seeking refuge from religious persecution—but also the future trajectory of 'America' itself. Just as the Union was the only true free state, cut loose from the tyranny of kings and queens, so its divine calling would lead others into freedom.

It has often been noted that the revolutionaries' ideal of the republic inserted patriotism in the place of religious creed; some have suggested that patriotism became a new kind of religion. But the complex interlocking stories borrowing many narrative structures from Christian texts, which give a sense and shape to the observance of the Fourth as a significant moment in the founding of the nation, create something more potent than a kind of 'secular religion'. For what the rites of the Fourth set loose into the republic is the potential to achieve, one day, the ideals embedded in a few well-chosen words which constitute, precisely, a declaration. They give notice to an intention. These words allow one to *perform*, through the act of speech, one's commitment to an ideal of liberty. As William T. Barry noted of the Fourth, a 'day consecrated to freedom', millions of Americans 'now assemble at the Temple of Liberty, and perform their worship at her shrine; and so long as her genius presides over and controuls [*sic*] the destinies of the Republic, this anniversary will be distinguished with peculiar joy and grandeur'.

While many, if not most, citizens have been content to sign up to the—albeit symbolically mobile—rituals of the Fourth and to assent to its most publicly available meanings, it should be remembered that for some the lofty ideals of the Declaration have never been delivered upon. It is for this reason that many 'alternative' declarations have been proposed. Perhaps the tradition that runs deepest in this vein of political dissent has been developed within the context of working men's and women's associations, within the history of American labour. Not all of these 'declarations' have been issued on the Fourth itself—the first, for example, appeared in December 1829 when George Henry Evans published his 'Working Men's Declaration of Independence' in the *Working Man's Advocate*. Following the text of the Declaration—'we hold these truths to be self-evident...'—

Evans wrote that to secure these rights 'against the undue influence of other classes of society, prudence, as well as the claims of self-defense, dictates the necessity of the organization of a party, who shall, by their representatives, prevent dangerous combinations to subvert these indefeasible and fundamental privileges'. A 'declaration of the rights of the Trades' Union of Boston and Vicinity' was made in June 1834, the 'Anti-Renters' Declaration of Independence' was issued on 4 July 1839, and others in similar vein were made right up to 1902, when the 'Working Class Declaration of Independence' appeared on 4 July. These 'interpretations' of the Fourth's meanings share a concern for the politics of labour and seek to promote a sense of the unfinished project announced by the original document.

On the occasion of the centennial celebrations the National Woman Suffrage Association hoped to expose the government's poor record in respect to universal rights by reading a declaration at the official Fourth party held at the Exposition site in Philadelphia. They were denied access to the centennial park, but the document, containing 'articles of impeachment' against the government, was read aloud by Susan B. Anthony to a large crowd outside Independence Hall on the Fourth in 1876. 'The history of our country the past hundred years', it claimed, 'has been a series of assumptions and usurpations of power over woman, in direct opposition to the principles of just government.' There followed a number of detailed descriptions of aspects of American legislation where discrimination against women was practised and upheld. Here, as with the various declarations made by groups seeking to protect and enhance the rights of working people, the meaning of the Fourth is derived in part from an ironic take on the realisation of the ideals declared in 1776. Thus, when the bicentennial came around, a group styling itself as the People's Bicentennial Commission issued a document—the 'Declaration of Economic Independence'—that could almost be read as a parody of the original. Although there can be no doubting the seriousness of the political aims and objectives of this group of dissenters, the close adoption of the Second Continental Congress's text today reads like a script for an alternative comedy sketch. 'When in the course of human events', it begins in emulation, 'it becomes necessary for one people to dissolve the economic bonds which have tied them to another ...' And, continuing in the same vein: 'that to secure these rights, economic institutions are instituted among people ... it is the right of the people ... to institute a new economic system ... prudence ... will dictate that economic systems long established ...' and so on. This perhaps demonstrates that the standard meanings of the Fourth are so deeply embedded in the unconscious of the nation that when quite legitimate political dissent from established government is garbed in words echoing the founding text its effect is counter-productive. At least counter to the aims of the People's Bicentennial Commission. If the contexts of the Fourth shine new light on the stories the nation lives by, it remains the case that the words of the text itself lay too deep in the foundation of the American psyche to be wrested into new configurations without parody being the result.

The shape and character of Fourth celebrations has always reflected to some extent the wider political, social and economic situation of the time. It is hardly surprising, for example, that the years of the Great Depression were not enlivened by extravagant pageants and costly banquets. And the campaign to make the sale of fireworks illegal, which once again reared its head in 1937 when the National Fire Protection Association attempted to persuade all state legislatures to ban both the sale and use of fireworks, inevitably cast a pall over the traditional way of concluding celebrations on the Fourth. By 1953, twenty-eight states had banned all private use of fireworks and a further fourteen had strict regulations about the size and scope of private firework displays.

In the late twentieth century and early twenty-first the

Fourth has become firmly tied to the 'backyard' tradition of celebration which began to develop in the 1950s. Large-scale public festivities—communal banquets, orations, parades of the great and good—were gradually supplanted by the family get-together. A charcoal grill and hamburger were more likely to feature in most Fourth celebrations than a speech on the spirit of '76. And where parades are still mounted, they more often than not have very local flavours, giving pre-eminence to some event or institution which provides the context for a public celebration. In the era of mass communication the means for creating and promoting a sense of national identity—television, radio and the internet—have firmly replaced earlier forms such as print or the public address. Most people today will only hear the words of the Declaration read aloud on the Fourth if they turn on their televisions. To some extent this represents a significant break with the history of Fourth observance, a reimagining of the significance (or insignificance) of the founding moment. And for some this might suggest that any attempts to recover that history are bound to be prey to the dynamics of nostalgia, of painting arosy past for the purposes of the contingencies of the present. There are, however, continuities which drive deep into the bedrock of the nation's imagination.

One of those continuities, a feature of how the Fourth has been understood since the nineteenth century, is still pretty legible today: the use of the story of the Fourth as a primer for educating children into the first steps of citizenship. It is remarkable that so many books, from the late nineteenth century onwards, designed to help teach reading skills make use of the Fourth story. A survey of those books and others written for young children able to read on their own account demonstrates that the predominant meaning of the Fourth disseminated through this literature is its punctuality as the 'birthday' of the nation. In book after book—with titles like *Doodle Dandy! The Complete Book of Independence Day Words* or *Give Me Liberty: The Story of the Declaration of Independence*—

one encounters the familiar stories of the nation's founding. A typical example can be found in a book which seeks to explain the rationale behind all the public days of celebration observed in contemporary America, fittingly entitled *America Celebrates*. In the chapter devoted to Independence Day, a short piece by Pamela Kennedy gives a particularly vivid account of the deep connection between childhood and the Fourth for contemporary America. She writes: 'Independence Day is about a lot more than freedom from Mother England. For me, it has as much to do with my freedom to be young again, to do silly things, and to enjoy simple pleasures that America has to offer.' And she goes on to characterise some of those 'silly' things that many will recognise, in spirit if not to the letter. The 'World Famous Precision Mower Drill Team', for example, which comprised twenty men dressed in trench coats and fedoras marching in columns, each pushing a lawn mower. Or the 'Largest Kazoo Marching Band in the Entire U.S. of A' which she witnessed in Milwaukee. These examples catch the flavour of countless contemporary Fourth diversions and Kennedy sees it as an almost universal desire on the part of adults across the nation to 'drop the mantle of sophistication and get down to serious silliness on the Fourth'. As she remarks, the day has to do with 'remembering a time when I couldn't see moon dust up close or fly faster than the speed of sound. In short, I can be a kid again on the Fourth of July'. It is unlikely that Kennedy speaks for all adult Americans or that her views have very wide circulation; but the words of President Gerald Ford make a far greater claim for conveying something of the deep connection between current practices of Fourth celebration and childhood. On the eve of the bicentennial celebration in 1976 he said: 'I knew what happiness was when I was a boy. It was the Fourth of July.'

How did the rites of the Fourth become so bound up with the meanings of the Declaration itself? As everyone knows—or believes—the day is set aside to celebrate the signing of the

Declaration. And that act is taken to signify the birth of the nation. Why, in the current era when the pomp and ritual of the day have been largely consigned to history, now replaced by the familial setting of the backyard or the school house, does the celebration of the Fourth transcend region and locality and reach outward to the larger context of state or nation? In answering these questions we need to consider the ways in which the three 'founding' documents of the nation—the Declaration, the Bill of Rights and the Constitution—have become, in the words of historian Pauline Maier, 'American Scripture'. As she wonderfully evokes the conditions in which these documents are now kept, 'encased in massive, bronze-framed, bulletproof glass containers filled with inert helium "to displace damaging oxygen", and with water vapor to keep the parchment from getting brittle', it becomes clearer and clearer that they are now venerated as holy relics. Again, as Maier painstakingly demonstrates, the evolution of the attitude taken to the Declaration is intimately tied to the different ways in which the history, or better still, the ongoing story of the nation, is told.

For what characterises contemporary observance of the Fourth can once again be conveyed by one word: independence. And, perhaps as importantly to the times we now live in, the notion that it might be desirable to 'declare' this independence seems vital to the senses of being American. Independence is so strongly associated with the Fourth in contemporary life that the Declaration's meanings seem to have been distilled into a very modern take on the idea of citizenship and the notion of the individual on which it stands. Independence is synonymous with autonomy, the sanctity of the individual. No longer an expression of common beliefs and ideals, the Declaration today seems more like a performative act which by its very enunciation enacts an individuated independence. But this, as the final chapter sets out to demonstrate, is merely yet one more variation on a theme produced by the narrative grammar that beats deep in the heart of the Fourth.

6

Celebrating Independence

All day the temperature had barely moved below 100 degrees. The local sharps had made a killing selling fifty-cent bags of ice for five dollars a throw. And now, as the hour neared midnight, the guy with the bandanna and the guitar he played as naturally as if it had been an extra limb was surfing the stretched notes, carried onward and inward towards the clear light he felt was home. Eyes tight shut. Lips slightly parted. Kissing the fetid air that was his breath. Hendrix, who would be found dead ten weeks later in London, his body quietened for the last time by the junk that had sustained him, was at this moment supposed to give Alex Cooley a signal. Cooley needed a sign from the stage in order to time the commencement of the fireworks. It had been agreed that on the stroke of midnight, 4 July 1970, Hendrix was to break into 'The Star-Spangled Banner' and, like millions of citizens across the country, wish America 'happy birthday'.

On that day the US Secretary of State, William P. Rogers, had been in Saigon attempting to negotiate a settlement to the increasingly unpopular war in Vietnam. A British airliner crashed into a mountain in Spain, killing 105 passengers. Bob Hope, Jack Benny and the Reverend Billy Graham, among others, had stood in front of thousands of citizens in Washington, DC earlier in the day to 'honor America'. And Hendrix had lost the plot.

Alex Cooley, a promoter from Atlanta, had organised the first

Atlanta International Pop Festival the year before. In its second year, just one year on from Woodstock, it had been promoted as the natural successor to that gorgeous flowering of the counter-culture. It was billed as 'three days of peace, love and music'. The Allmann Brothers, came to play, as did B.B. King, Ravi Shankar, Jethro Tull and Ten Years After. And, topping the bill on 4 July, the counter-culture icon of the moment, Hendrix unfurled his unique quilting of rock, the blues and Afro-American oppression, a musical offering for the 500,000 supplicants who came to witness his devotions. Tickets had been priced at $14.

'It was our Woodstock,' R.Palmer Marsh said. He had driven from Atlanta to the tiny central Georgia town of Byron with friends. The traffic had been backed up the entire 90 miles from the state capital. 'Most of us here didn't go to New York in '69, and Byron brought it south to us. It was a phenomenon, a once-in-a-lifetime event. I didn't really go for the music. The scene was the attraction.' The local law enforcement had been expecting maybe 100,000, but 'there were so darn many of 'em, they ran the alligators and the water moccasins right out of the Echeconnee Creek', claimed the police chief, James Barbour. So, for three days, 500,000 people put up tents in a pecan grove next to the Middle Georgia Raceway. And they had a festival.

Not everyone found it to their taste. Mary Marsh, an artist in the region, had just graduated from high school. She went with a date, perhaps ill prepared for the peace, love and music she was to encounter. When her man pointed to a naked guy in the process of painting himself with the contents of a few cans of Campbell's soup she chose to look away. The heat was unremitting. 'Nobody was selling Coca-Colas,' she said, 'only Kool-Aid with LSD in it.' A number of tents within the festival site were declared 'OD' tents. Hundreds of festival-goers had availed themselves of the services of volunteer doctors who attempted to bring solace to those coming down from bad trips. And there, on stage, in the wet, hot night air was the cheerleader for America's refuseniks. Earlier in the summer the forces of law and order had beaten up those who chose to make their disaffection with the administration's policies public. Kent State was still a gaping wound in the counter-culture's psyche. And Hendrix, smashing into 'All Along the Watchtower', 'Hey Joe', 'Voodoo Chile', and 'Freedom', was providing the soundtrack. Perhaps it was inevitable that the song he was lost in, the soaring trip of a solo he couldn't or didn't want to conclude was 'Stone Free'. So he fluffed his lines and Cooley had to let off his fireworks sometime into Hendrix's irreverent rendition of the national anthem.

As one would expect, the traditions of celebrating the Fourth have evolved over time. In the first half of the nineteenth century the day was suffused with a distinct air of veneration as the palpable sense of connection to the Founding Fathers and the founding moment was still available. Often things were arranged to encourage if not enhance the feeling of being connected to an 'epochal' moment. Thus in 1821, John Quincy Adams, the son of one of the Signers and himself a future president, read from an original copy of the Declaration at a ceremony held in the Capitol. Thirteen years later, in 1834, a man who was at Lexington and Bunker Hill attended the ceremony in New Haven, Connecticut, wearing the coat he had worn in 1775 when the English had opened fire. Five years after that, a student at a Sabbath School in Norwich, Connecticut, read excerpts from the Declaration wearing 'the identical cap' worn by William Williams, a delegate from that state, who had signed the Declaration wearing the said cap.

In fact, for the first fifty or so years following the original declaration there seemed to be a special power attached to any human connection to the original moment. In the early years those who had signed the document—no matter that they had not actually signed it on the 4th—were wheeled out to take leading roles in the celebrations wherever they may have been held. By 1828 only one such person remained alive, Charles

Carroll, and he duly participated in the Baltimore celebrations that year. But as the original Signers became thin on the ground, other, less immediate, connections seemed to emanate similar powers of authenticity. On the fiftieth anniversary, for example, Major John Handy read the declaration in Newport, Rhode Island, 'on the identical spot which he did 50 years ago' and he was accompanied by Isaac Barker of Middletown, 'who was at his side in the same place fifty years before'.

To some extent this reverence for anything making a claim to the punctuality of the event, to authenticity in a very palpable sense, was almost an ethical desideratum. It encouraged an attitude and instilled in the celebrant a feeling of almost religious awe. Even Jefferson—proud architect of Virginia's separation of church and government—was not immune to this strange power of reverence. It can be said that in some sense, towards the end of his life, he promoted it. Writing in a late letter to his granddaughter, Ellen Wayles Randolph, about the 'plain, neat, convenient' writing desk on which he had written the draft of the Declaration, he muses that at some future date this object might be 'carried in the procession of our nation's birthday, as the relics of saints are in those of the church'. Perhaps we should not be surprised at the old man's wish to see the spirit of '76 honoured, even rekindled. As the last letter he wrote puts it, 'let the annual return of this day forever refresh our recollections of these rights, and an undiminished devotion to them'. Certainly early nineteenth-century celebrants of the Fourth would have recognised the tone of religiosity which crept into Jefferson's attempts at myth making. The hardly veiled gestures towards the veneration of iconic objects might, however, strike a Catholic note which is surprising. Indeed, the continuous pressure in the stories of observance of the Fourth to found a myth of incarnation sits awkwardly within the standard conception of the puritan basis for the society in which the revolutionaries came into maturity. Is this a case of making good use of whatever one can in the creation of the belief structures which are to give sense to the founding and history of the nation, or is there some compelling attraction to idolatry deep in the founders' mythopoeia?

As the shadow of the first Fourth of July lengthened, the physical links to that day inevitably began to weaken. But later eras have not been unadventurous in their attempts to re-forge the bonds of connection and authenticity. What strange aura or frisson of excitement was experienced by the 10,000 people who crammed into Independence Hall in 1853, all of whom attempted to sit (thankfully not all at once) in the chair occupied by John Hancock, the president of the Second Continental Congress? What particular privilege might it have been to have heard the 'real' Liberty Bell ring? What were the celebrants packed into the Kennedy Center in Washington DC on the Fourth in 1974 thinking as they listened to a re-enactment of Frederick Douglass's oration 'What to the Slave is the Fourth of July'?

In the attempt to make that connection both resonate with the past and speak to the present, the accidents of history itself have often been enlisted. So, for example, one of the very first sound films ever made was of Calvin Coolidge giving his Fourth of July speech in 1920 before he had been nominated to run for vice-president. In 1941 the day was marked by Chief Justice Harland Fiske Stone leading the nation in a live radio broadcast of the 'Pledge of Allegiance' from Estes Park, Colorado. In 1945 the Stars and Stripes were hoisted over Berlin's Adolph Hitler Barracks in a formal 4 July ceremony and a 48-gun salute was sounded. In 1992 the seven astronauts aboard the space shuttle *Columbia* unfurled the Stars and Stripes and sang 'Happy Birthday, America' from space. In 2003 US troops celebrated the Fourth with a cookout at Saddam Hussein's hometown palace, while in 2004 the cornerstone of the Freedom Tower was laid on the site of the World Trade Center.

It is true that local communities no longer divide into warring party factions holding rival Fourth celebrations, as early nineteenth-century Bostonians did. Orations and celebratory odes penned by local personalities no longer feature in the vast majority of town or city parades. Most Americans will spend their day away from work within the context of the family, perhaps in a park with a picnic, or by the side of a lake, or just in the home's backyard. But the day continues to have significance within the calendar of national events. The president will attend a public occasion—health or more urgent matters permitting—at which a parade, almost certainly military in some degree, will take place. And a speech will be made. Although the gravitational pull of the founding moment is no longer felt, the punctuality of the day continues to be honoured. Thus many local organisers of the celebrations will have an eye out for something that might give a particular, singular flavour to the day—say the opening of a new bridge, or the dedication of a public monument. In Louisville, Kentucky, a new Waterfront Park was dedicated on the Fourth in 1999; Rockford, Illinois, did likewise to a granite war memorial in Veterans Park the same year, and examples like these could be multiplied a thousandfold. And then sometimes, pleasingly, events seems to miraculously conspire to honour the day, as in 1997 when the spacecraft *Pathfinder* landed on Mars.

Every year there are hundreds of such punctual moments which may have only very local association or significance. But notwithstanding these more intimate meanings there is a common feature to them all: they take place on the same day which by rite and history commemorates one thing, America's birthday. Each and every year these celebrations, no matter what their specific focus might be, participate in the ongoing making of the republic. They add another strand to the fabric of the story that is the Fourth of July. And in doing so they bind each celebrant into the larger history of the nation. Even if current modes of public political behaviour are less demonstrative or collective than they were in the nineteenth century, there nevertheless remains a strong sense of adherence to the principle given voice by the single most important word of the document that, sealed under glass in a vacuum, ought now be preserved for ever: independence.

This word conveys both the legacy of the generation of '76 as well as the prospective ideal each citizen commits to in celebrating the declaratory act of founding. An independence which may be located in or claimed by the unique individual but whose guarantor is the collective. That ideal comes clothed in universalism—although George W. Bush was far from the first person to say it, the words he spoke on 4 July 2003 capture a very significant feature of the political act that is the ongoing observance of the Fourth. Speaking at the United States Air Force Museum in Dayton, Ohio, he said: 'The Declaration of Independence holds a promise for all mankind.' And then in explaining why this is so he adverted to the proprietorial rights that come bound up in the declaratory act: 'Because Americans believe that freedom is unalienable right, we value the freedom of every nation.'

Perhaps the most remarkable feature of the Fourth is its capacity to withstand being wrested into many conceivable contexts. Even when that context, as in the scene with which this chapter began, may be hostile to anything like a sense of veneration or good manners in the face of the symbols held dear to the traditions we have been tracking. The great strength of the rituals of the Fourth lies in the capaciousness of its symbols. But even if specific contexts may inflect the core meanings of those rites in new and different ways, something immutable remains deep in the heart of their observance. For each and every time the Fourth rolls around in a kind of Groundhog-Day recursion, a declaration is made that is founded on an architecture of belief that may well endure to the end of time. And the lineaments of that architecture are conveyed in the phrase Jefferson so brilliantly captured: 'we hold these truths to be self-evident'.

Philosophically speaking, the notion of a truth having a quality of 'self-evidence' is not particularly easy to grasp. Those who eventually put their signature to the document were mindful of this, introducing the statement of *their* beliefs—'*we* hold these truths'—thereby indicating they were aware they may have, at least initially, seemed eccentric. Or held views requiring careful justification. But the conceptual muscularity of this formulation, what gives it such enduring power, is not the part about self-evidence. It is the performative act of declaring a commonly held architecture of belief.

If we compare Jefferson's first thoughts for this phrase—he wrote 'truths held to be sacred and undeniable'—to the phrase millions have committed to heart—'we hold these truths to be self-evident'—we can see how this revisionary stroke of genius creates a new kind of belief structure. To say that something 'is held' to be sacred is to subscribe to a theological creed which provides the architecture for one's belief system. And what may be sacred to one theology, say a cow, may well not be so to another. But in saying 'we hold' the speaker is indicating something radically different. Far from subscribing to a theology or a metaphysics, the speaker is deriving the imprimatur to the truths that are self-evident from the act of claiming, in common with others included in the 'we', that 'we hold'. In the very declaratory act of saying 'we hold these truths', such truths are in and by that performance given the necessary support to enable the speaker to claim that he or she believes them to be self-evident. Consequently the basis for the belief is not a metaphysics but what might be called an *apodictic declaratory act*. And it is this act which creates a new architecture of belief. Just as government in the new political system that is the first modern republic is derived from 'we the people' governed, so the belief in the truths that are self-evident is derived from the declaratory act of stating that 'we hold'. It is a fundamentally new conceptual departure, the most daring innovation in the philosophy of government since Machiavelli's *The Prince*. Perhaps—it is devoutly to be wished, since humankind has not bettered it—the most enduring conceptualisation of the authority and legitimacy of government there will ever be. The extraordinary gift of those who have come to be called the Founding Fathers. America's signature.

Each year on 4 July Americans celebrate the birthday of their nation. The rites and rituals of the day have undergone changes of focus and alterations in precise content since the first celebrations in 1777. Although the symbols which continue to play a significant role in the practice and understanding of those rituals are less prey to the forces of change, they too, like the reverence in which the Stars and Stripes is held, inevitably come under pressure as the nation evolves. But one thing remains unchanging and is unchangeable: the power of being included within the 'we'. Both Adams and Jefferson, in their own ways, recognised this and wished to make it clear that what would become their legacy, the legacy of the generation of '76, is also loaded with a burden of responsibility. For the 'we' who give their consent give it on behalf of certain principles.

The story of the Fourth of July presents a supreme fiction. That the nation came into being on a particular day in 1776. It does not matter in terms of the coherence of the story whether or not this has any basis in fact. It does not matter insofar as one subscribes to this story that nations, complex geopolitical organisms, are never founded at a single stroke. For in telling this story something fundamental and very significant occurs: the declaration of a new kind of belief structure. We have it in our power to determine what shall be taken to be a self-evident truth. Each and every Fourth, as if for the first time, a new architecture of belief is both celebrated and instantiated in the many speaking as one. And in that collectively imagined common tongue, 'America', by simple force of a declaration, is founded. In celebrating independence each Fourth may it also be remembered that the birthday of the nation, the declaratory act that founds America, created and continues to create an architecture of belief which, for both good and ill, has power to change the world.

Further Reading

General

Two books on the subject of the Fourth have aided my research significantly: Diana Karter Appelbaum, *The Glorious Fourth: An American Holiday, an American History* (New York, 1989); and Len Travers, *Celebrating the Fourth: Independence Day and the Rites of Nationalism in the Early Republic* (Amherst, 1997). An unpublished PhD, R.P. Hay, 'Freedom's Jubilee: One Hundred Years of the Fourth', submitted to the University of Kentucky in 1967, provides a good amount of material for both of these more recent books and has also been extremely helpful for this study.

Chapter One

The various myths surrounding the Fourth have been the object of scholarly study from time to time. The earliest of substance is Charles Warren, 'Fourth of July Myths', *William and Mary Quarterly*, 3rd Ser., II (1945). Less scholarly accounts are legion; see, for example, Cornel Lengyel, *Four Days in July* (New York, 1958), Donald Barr Chidsey, *July 4th, 1776: The Dramatic Story of the First Four Days of July, 1776* (New York, 1958).

The literature on the Declaration of Independence is now very substantial. The book which can be said to have originated this scholarship and to which my own understanding of the process of making the Declaration is indebted is Carl Becker, *The Declaration of Independence: A Study in the History of Political Ideas* (New York, 1922). This work was made possible by John Hazelton, *The Declaration of Independence: Its History* (New York, 1906). Dumas Malone was the first scholar to put into general circulation the story of the Declaration's genesis; see his *The Story of the Declaration of Independence* (New York, 1954). More recently Pauline Maier's thorough and readable *American Scripture: How America Declared its Independence from Britain* (London, 1999) has been invaluable for my own project. Two further books of outstanding interest are Garry Wills, *Inventing America: Jefferson's Declaration of Independence* (New York, 1978); and Jay Fliegelman, *Declaring Independence: Jefferson, Natural Language, and the Culture of Performance* (Stanford, CA, 1993).

Scholars have been well served by exacting editions of many colonial and revolutionary-era documents. In particular the *Journals of the Continental Congress, 1774–1789,* edited by Worthing Chauncey Ford (Washington, DC, 1904–06); the *Letters of Delegates to Congress, 1774–1789*, edited by Paul H. Smith (Washington, DC, 1976–79); the *Letters of Members of the Continental Congress*, edited by Edmund C. Burnett (Washington, DC, 1921–23); and *A Decent Respect to the Opinions of Mankind: Congressional State Papers, 1774–1776*, edited by James H. Hutson (Washington, DC, 1975) have all been crucial resources.

For an account of the Declaration as a physical document see Verner Clapp, 'The Declaration of Independence: A Case Study in Preservation', *Special Libraries*, LXII (December 1971). The various drafts and revisions are set out in Becker (above) and Julian Boyd, *The Declaration of Independence: The Evolution of the Text as Shown in Facsimiles of Various Drafts by its Author* (Washington,

DC, 1943). The history of the reputation of the document until 1826 is set out in Philip F. Detweiler, 'The Changing Reputation of the Declaration of Independence: The First Fifty Years', *William and Mary Quarterly*, 3rd Ser., IXX (1962).

The most important book on the philosophical underpinning of the revolution is Bernard Bailyn, *Ideological Origins of the American Revolution* (Cambridge, MA, 1967), and this work was built upon the very extensive literature which preceded it. In particular see Louis Hartz, *The Liberal Tradition in America: An Interpretation of American Liberal Thought since the Revolution* (New York, 1955). More recent revisions and qualifications to this monumental tradition can be found in Lance Banning, *The Jeffersonian Persuasion: Evolution of a Party Ideology* (Ithaca, 1978); Joyce Appleby, *Capitalism and a New Social Order: The Republican Vision of the 1790s* (New York, 1984), and an extremely helpful collection of essays, also by Joyce Appleby, *Liberalism and Republicanism in the Historical Imagination* (Cambridge, MA, 1992).

For an account of Jefferson's extraordinary multifaceted intelligence and its deep roots in the culture from which he came see Merrill D. Peterson, *The Jefferson Image in the American Mind* (New York, 1960). A more recent and thoroughly readable re-creation of the relations between the most important Founding Fathers is Joseph J. Ellis, *Founding Brothers: The Revolutionary Generation* (New York, 2000); and for a slightly different emphasis Stuart Leibiger, *Founding Friendship: George Washington, James Madison and the Creation of the American Republic* (Charlottesville, 1999). Jefferson's inventions of writing technologies is the subject of Silvio Bedini, *Thomas Jefferson and his Copying Machines* (Charlottesville, 1984).

For a good overview of the political process which resulted in the creation of the United States see Merrill Jensen, *The Founding of a Nation: A History of the American Revolution, 1763–1776* (New York,

1966); and for the legal context in which the Declaration was made see John Philip Reid, 'The Irrelevance of the Declaration', in Hedrick Hartog, ed., *Law in the American Revolution and the Revolution of the Law* (New York, 1981).

For an exemplary account of the context in which the Declaration was made and the so-called 'other' declarations see the second chapter of Pauline Maier's *American Scripture*. Two books are indispensable for the strange turns in the historiography attached to the Mecklenburg declaration: William Henry Hoyt, *The Mecklenburg Declaration of Independence* (New York, 1907) and V.V. McNitt, *Chain of Error and the Mecklenburg Declarations of Independence* (Palmer, MA, 1960).

Chapter Two

An account of the first observance of the Fourth by legislative enactment, held at Salem, North Carolina, is to be found in *July 4th, 1783: A Day of Thanksgiving* (Winston-Salem, NC, 1966)

The fiftieth celebrations in 1826 is the subject of Andrew Burstein, *America's Jubilee* (New York, 2001), to which my own account is indebted. The first hundred years of orations is the subject of Paul Goetsch and Gerd Hurm, eds., *The Fourth of July: Political Oratory and Literary Reactions* (Tubingen, 1992). The early chapters of Diana Karter Appelbaum, *The Glorious Fourth,* also cover this ground, as do Len Travers, *Celebrating the Fourth,* and R.P. Hay, 'Freedom's Jubilee' (see above).

Orations are the subject of Henry A. Hawken, *Trumpets of Glory: Fourth of July Orations, 1786–1861* (Granby, CT, 1976). Earlier studies include Cedric Larsen, 'Patriotism in Carmine: 162 Years of July 4th Oratory', *Quarterly Journal of Speech*, February 1940; and Howard Martin, 'The Fourth of July Oration', *Quarterly Journal of*

Speech, December 1958. For the Boston context see Gerd Hurm, 'The Rhetoric of Continuity in Early Boston Orations', in Paul Goetsch and Gerd Hurm, eds., *The Fourth of July: Political Oratory and Literary Reactions, 1776–1876* (Tubingen, 1992). Of the many orations published those which give a very good insight into their time include Edward Everett, *Orations and Speeches on Various Occasions* (Boston, 1856); Hugh Henry Brackenridge, 'Oration on the Celebration of the Anniversary of Independence, July 4th, 1793', in *A Hugh Henry Brackenridge Reader, 1770–1815*, ed. Daniel Marder (Pittsburgh, 1970); Daniel Webster, 'Fourth of July Oration' (1802), in *The Writings and Speeches* (Boston, 1903); and Frederick Saunders, ed., *Our National Centennial Jubilee: Orations, Addresses and Poems Delivered in the Fourth of July, 1876, in Several States of the Union* (New York, 1877).

The formula for Boston Fourth speeches is reproduced in many pamphlets of the first half of the nineteenth century. See on this James Spear Loring, *The Hundred Boston Orators Appointed by the Municipal Authorities and Other Public Bodies from 1770 to 1852* (Boston, 1853).

For the tradition of celebration established in North Carolina see Fletcher M. Green, 'Listen to the Eagle Scream: One Hundred Years of the Fourth of July in North Carolina, 1776–1876', in *Democracy in the Old South and Other Essays* (Nashville, 1969).

Toasts and other forms of address occasioned by the celebration of the Fourth have been collected in Philp S. Foner, ed., *The Democratic-Republican Societies, 1790–1800: A Documentary Sourcebook of Constitutions, Declarations, Addresses, Resolutions, and Toasts* (Westport, CT, 1976).

On the last hours of Adams and Jefferson see John E. Ferling, *John Adams: A Life* (Knoxville, 1992); David G. McCullough, *John*

Adams (New York, 2001); W. S. Randall, *Thomas Jefferson: A Life* (New York, 1993); Merrill D. Peterson, *Thomas Jefferson: A Reference Biography* (New York, 1986).

Chapter Three

Canby's paper can be consulted online at http://www.ushistory.org/betsy/more/canby.htm. There are many web pages devoted to the Betsy Ross story; the most efficient means for accessing them is at http://www.ushistory.org/betsy/flagtale.html.

The most substantial account of cultural attitudes to the flag can be found in Scot Guenter, *The American Flag, 1777–1924: Cultural Shifts from Creation to Codification* (Rutherford, NJ, 1990); for more anecdotal histories see James A. Moss, *The Flag of Our United States* (Chicago, 1940); Michael Corcoran, *For Which it Stands: An Anecdotal Biography of the American Flag* (New York, 2002); Richard H. Schneider, *Stars and Stripes Forever: The History, Stories, and Memories of Our American Flag* (New York, 2003). An outstanding illustrated catalogue of the varieties of flags produced from the birth of the republic to today is Boleslaw and Marie-Louise d'Otrange Mastai, *The Stars and Stripes: The American Flag as Art and as History from the Birth of the Republic to the Present* (New York, 1973).

For an immensely detailed and fascinating account of the controversy occasioned by the trials of Gregory Lee Johnson for desecration of the flag see Robert Justin Goldstein, *Burning the Flag: The Great 1989–1990 American Flag Desecration Controversy* (Kent, OH, 1996). For the longer history of desecration see Robert Justin Goldstein, *Desecrating the American Flag: Key Documents of the Controversy from the Civil War to 1995* (Syracuse, NY, 1996).

The pledge of allegiance is the focus of a study by John Baer,

The Pledge of Allegiance, A Centennial History, 1892–1992 (Annapolis, MD, 1992).

The story of the Liberty Bell is told in Olga W. Hall-Quest, *The Bell that Rang for Freedom: The Liberty Bell and Its Place in American History* (New York, 1965); Charles S. Keyser, *The Liberty Bell* (Philadelphia, 1893); Victor Rosewater, *The Liberty Bell: Its History and Significance* (New York, 1926), Charles Michael Boland, *Ring in the Jubilee: The Epic of America's Liberty Bell* (Riverside, CT, 1973); David Kimball, *Venerable Relic: The Story of the Liberty Bell* (Philadelphia, 1989). The story of the building in which it was first housed can be found in Edward M. Riley, *The Story of Independence Hall* (Gettysburg, PA, 1954); and Charlene Mires, *Independence Hall in American Memory* (Philadelphia, 2002). Of the many books for young readers on the bell perhaps the most appealing is Wayne Whipple, *The Story of the Liberty Bell* (Philadelphia, 1910).

For an account of Andrew McNair, the doorkeeper to the Pennsylvania Assembly in 1776, see Mary D. Alexander, *Andrew McNair and the Liberty Bell, 1776* (Chicago, 1929).

An early source for many of the myths surrounding the birth of the nation and its early years is George Lippard, *Legends of the American Revolution* (Philadelphia, 1847).

Materials on Uncle Sam are predominantly anecdotal. The best historical account is to be found in Alton Ketchum, *Uncle Sam: The Man and the Legend* (New York, 1959); a good source of illustrative material is Elinor Lander Horwitz, *The Bird, the Banner, and Uncle Sam: Images of America in Folk and Popular Art* (Philadelphia, 1976).

Chapter Four

On Lincoln and Gettysburg see Gary Wills, *Lincoln at Gettysburg: The Words that Made America* (New York, 1992).

On Frederick Douglass see James A. Colaiaco, *Frederick Douglass and the Fourth of July* (New York, 2006); Bernard W. Bell, 'The African-American Jeremiad and Frederick Douglass' Fourth of July 1852 Speech', in Paul Goetsch and Gerd Hurm, eds., *The Fourth of July: Political Oratory and Literary Reactions, 1776–1876* (Tubingen, 1992).

On the centennial celebrations see John S. Ingram, *The Centennial Exhibition Described and Illustrated* (Philadelphia, 1877); and John D. MacCabe, *The Illustrated History of the Centennial Exhibition* (Philadelphia, 1876).

The tradition of celebration of the Fourth in Bristol, Rhode Island, is the subject of an informative illustrated book by Richard V. Simpson, *Independence Day: How the Day is Celebrated in Bristol, Rhode Island* (Bristol, RI, 1989).

On alternative declarations see Philip S. Foner, ed., *We, the Other People* (Urbana, IL, 1976).

A good illustrated guide to important Fourth celebrations at Monticello is *The Great Birthday of Our Republic: Celebrating Independence Day at Monticello* (Chapel Hill, NC, 2003).

Among the books written for children about the Fourth, those particularly useful to the current study include Alice Dalgliesh, *The Fourth of July Story* (New York, 1987); James Giblin, *Fireworks, Picnics, and Flags* (New York, 1983); Lynda Graham-Barber, *Doodle Dandy! The Complete Book of Independence Day Words* (New

York, 1992); Mary Jo Borrenson, *Let's Go to the First Independence Day* (Toronto, 1962); Barbara Brenner, *If You Were There in 1776* (New York, 1994); Russell Freedman, *Give Me Liberty! The Story of the Declaration of Independence* (New York, 2000); Stan Hoig, *It's The Fourth of July* (New York, 1995); Leslie C. Kaplan, *Independence Day* (New York, 2004); David F. Marx, *Independence Day* (New York, 2001); Cass R. Sandak, *Patriotic Holidays* (New York, 1990); Tom Shachtman, *America's Birthday: The Fourth of July* (New York, 1986); Delno C. West and Jean M. West, *Uncle Sam and Old Glory* (New York, 2000).

PART TWO

THE FOURTEENTH

Christopher Prendergast

[ ]

Louis XVI's diary, 14 July 1789

How much the greatest Event it is that ever happened in the World! & how much the best!

Charles James Fox

But, to the living and the struggling, a new, Fourteenth morning dawns. Under all roofs of this distracted City is the nodus of a drama, not untragical, crowding towards solution. The bustlings and preparings, the tremors and menaces; the tears that fell from old eyes! This day, my sons, ye shall quit you like men. By the memory of your fathers' wrongs, by the hope of your children's rights! Tyranny impends in red wrath: help for you is none, if not in your own right hands. This day ye must do or die.

Thomas Carlyle

1

The Convocation Of The Estates-General

On 5 May 1789 the Estates-General convened at Versailles for the first time since 1614. The meeting came, with hindsight, to be seen as one of the founding moments of the French Revolution and of political modernity, a first step on the road to the creation of a sovereign National Assembly. In reality the occasion was fraught and inconclusive, the king making it abundantly clear that he had no intention of acceding to the more radical demands of the Third Estate.

The myth has it that 14 July 1789 embodied an absolutely new Beginning, but the events of that day did not of course occur *ex nihilo*; in historical reality, the mythical Beginning has its own beginnings, and, if we continue to see it as a uniquely pivotal moment, its intelligibility nevertheless rests on a plethora of antecedents, both regressive (through time) and expansive (across space). For example, the great historian of the taking of the Bastille, Jacques Godechot, has plausibly situated 14 July as a climactic moment in a history of uprisings that goes back to the social disturbances of the Wars of Religion and, in the context of the later eighteenth century, as having precedents and parallels on a large geographical canvas that includes America, Ireland, Belgium, Holland, London and Geneva. Things get even fuzzier when historical context is assimilated to the category of 'causes', which can all too easily spiral into the endlessly regressive.

Ouverture des États généraux à Versailles en 1789 (engraving),
by Isidore Stanislas Helman.
Opening of the Estates-General at Versailles, 5th May 1789.

Yet causal analysis of what produced this extraordinary day is something that exercised even the eyewitnesses of the time, the very people one would have thought far too excited by what had been happening to command the requisite analytical detachment. In August 1789, Elysée Loustalot, one of the most successful journalists of the early years of the Revolution, stated in the newspaper *Révolutions de Paris* that it was not enough 'just to give some arid account of certain facts'; it was also the duty of the contemporary commentator 'to go to the source of the facts and discover the causes of changes'. The following month he returned to this preoccupation, calling for 'a historical and political picture of everything that has happened in France since the first Assembly of Notables' as a basis for understanding 'the astonishing revolution that has just taken place'.

The Assembly of Notables was set up by the king's chief minister, Calonne, in February 1787 as a way out of an impasse in the negotiations between the royal administration and the *parlements* over tax reform. It failed miserably. What happened between then and 14 July 1789 supplies a causal crux with a twofold advantage. On the one hand, it breaks the otherwise unmanageable regress by bringing us as close as one can get to the events of 14 July while still retaining the distinctive character of causal antecedents. On the other hand, it shows how what began as the final spasm of a long-standing dispute between the crown and the nobility over the means of replenishing the depleted coffers of the state erupted into a fully fledged political crisis, involving not just who was to be taxed and by how much, but who had the authority to make these decisions.

The monarchical state, backed by the doctrines of absolutism, claimed that authority. The nobility, on the other hand, anxious to hold on to its privileges, claimed that there were limitations to royal power based on the laws and customary rights enshrined by the judicial institution that best served its own interests, the *parlements*. Had the conflict remained locked in this form, it is certain that, despite its institutional weaknesses at the time, the monarchy would have won, not because of the prestige of absolutism, but from the pressures of modern state-formation (a point magisterially developed by one of the greatest historians of the revolution, Alexis de Tocqueville). The frame of the dispute was, however, massively enlarged and complicated by the intervention of a third factor to which at the time the principal disputing parties had paid relatively little attention. This was what changed everything, with historical consequences that no one foresaw: namely, the increasingly vocal demands of the commoners (or the so-called Third Estate). What began as a traditional relation between taxation and war (the right of the sovereign to levy the former to fund the latter) rapidly evolved into something quite different. The issue of taxation became indissolubly joined to the issue of representation and the question of sovereignty to the idea of a 'national' sovereignty, vested in neither the king nor the privileged orders, but in the People. This was also the formula of the American Revolution, but a more complex version of it. The issue was not just no taxation without representation (this is what the *parlements* had effectively been arguing in their resistance to the monarchy), but also the converse—no representation without taxation (emphatically what, in its more demanding forms, the *parlements* and the nobles did not want to hear).

The whole business started, then, as a problem of national debt, arising from the unsustainable costs of war (the Seven Years' War, followed by France's involvement in the American War of Independence). These ventures were funded mainly by the taking out of loans, but repaying them in peacetime required further loans, thus generating the classic circle of creating new debt to service previous debt. Necker, the Swiss banker, who had been summoned in 1776 to act as director-general of finance, was a past master at manipulating the credit markets. In 1781 he published the first ever national accounts (the *Compte rendu au roi*), a wonderful smoke-and-mirrors job corresponding more or less to what today would be called 'off-balance-sheet financing'. But however adroit, this was no long-term solution to the burgeoning fiscal crisis. The law of no gain without pain could not be indefinitely suspended. Someone was going to have to pick up the tab for the consequences of military-imperial overstretch, and thus at some point the state was going to have to grapple with the thorny question of taxation. Necker resigned in 1781 and bequeathed the problems of squaring the circle to his hapless successors, d'Ormesson, Calonne and Brienne.

Their first move was on the sanctuary of Privilege. The wealthy aristocratic landowners were not only wealthy, they also enjoyed time-honoured exemptions from direct taxes as well as benefitting from equally time-honoured feudal dues from the labouring classes. Although in the course of the eighteenth century direct taxes were levied on many of the nobles, with the pattern of exemption thus becoming increasingly ragged, on the whole the system of imposition and evasion remained scandalously unjust. On the other hand, the fiscal crisis is not to be explained solely by the exemptions of the privileged orders; the chaotic state of the revenues was due as much to maladministration as to an unfair distribution of the tax burden. The economic power of many of the landowning aristocracy was ebbing, as exploitation of the land based on traditional methods became less and less profitable in contrast to the new methods of capitalist agricultural production (to which the more enterprising nobles, however, quickly adapted). Those who refused or failed to do so were in many ways a 'vegetating class', but this only made them altogether more anxious and defensive; the closer they got to ruin, the more they insisted on privilege and mobilised the *parlements* to protect them. In 1787 Calonne delivered an apocalyptic retrospect to the Assembly of Notables on how things stood: 'The coffers were empty, public securities devalued, circulation at a standstill; alarm was widespread and confidence had been destroyed.' This was of course but a prelude to billing himself as saviour. He saved nothing in all the relevant senses of the term, including the fiscal. The deficit he reported to the Assembly as out of control he succeeded only in worsening (he was popularly known as *Monsieur Déficit*).

Dismissed and exiled by Louis XVI in April 1787, Calonne was followed by Loménie de Brienne, who fared no better. In July, the largest and most powerful of the *parlements*, the *parlement de Paris*, refused to 'register' (i.e. confirm) the financial edicts of the royal administration. Brienne at first stood firm, in August suspending and banishing the *parlement* to Troyes. He soon buckled. Six weeks later the *parlement* returned to Paris, amid scenes of jubilation and riot (the *parlements* mistakenly seen as defenders of the 'freedom' of all the king's subjects against the exercise of arbitrary power). Brienne withdrew his two main proposals for tax reform, replacing them with a scheme that was much lighter on the wealthy and much harder on the poor, to be accompanied by the raising of a new loan, which the *parlement* refused to register. By the spring of 1788, Brienne's ministry was blocked and the *parlement* had prevailed, and in the process had convinced large numbers of the common people that its version of 'liberty' was their liberty too (an illusion that had completely evaporated by early 1789).

Brienne's lack of political will was partly offset by the resolution of that much tougher political beast, the keeper of seals (roughly the minister of justice), Chrétien-François de Lamoignon. He was responsible for the framing and enforcement of the so-called May Edicts of 1788, the drift of which was to remove all legislative power from the *parlements* and to forestall resistance by stripping them of any powers whatsoever through the simple expedient of once more suspending them. As a more forceful repeat of Brienne's confrontation with the *parlements* the previous year, this was again interpreted as an assault on established freedoms. But by 1788 much had already changed. In some of the provincial *parlements* and assemblies both a new composition and a new political language were to be seen and heard. Lamoignon's suppressions sparked riots in Rennes, Besançon, Pau and Grenoble throughout the month of June, the most significant being the *journée des Tuiles* in Grenoble, which was followed by the gathering of the Dauphiné Assembly in the village of Vizille demanding a meeting of the Estates-General. What in 1787 had seemed merely fraudulent now began to resemble a genuine political alliance of *parlement* and people (even Robespierre, at the time still a lawyer in Arras, saw it in this way). In Paris there were violent protests against the Lamoignon edicts, along with the burning of effigies of Brienne and Lamoignon (the effigy, destroyed or paraded, was to become one of the leitmotifs of revolutionary demonstration).

Yet if the mood had changed, the notion of an alliance

of interests still rested on a misidentification. The freedoms championed by the nobles and the notables remained basically their freedoms and no one else's, least of all those of the common people. When the *parlements* were reinstated in September, they immediately reverted to form and showed their true face as bastions of privilege. By then, however, both Brienne and Lamoignon were thoroughly discredited, Lamoignon particularly hated as the king's strongman. In August Brienne and in September Lamoignon—though in his case well-upholstered with a gratuity to enhance his pension so lavish as to exceed what actually remained in the exchequer—followed Calonne into the political graveyard (one year later Lamoignon disappeared for good into the real thing, having shot himself, although whether by accident or design is not known).

In many respects, all this was but the ministerial merry-go-round of appointments, resignations and dismissals presided over by a temporising monarch, little more than an extended flurry of futile endeavour. (Carlyle struck just the right note when he wrote of Brienne's fall from grace: 'Let us pity the hapless Loménie; and forgive him; and, as soon as possible, forget him.') An exception should, however, be made for Lamoignon, who is far more important to the story of the Revolution for the reason that he consistently, unambiguously and publicly identified the practical issue of the fiscal crisis with the principled question of political authority and legitimacy. When, in late 1787, the king called on the *parlement de Paris* to endorse further borrowing by the state, Lamoignon addressed the *parlement* in terms linking the issuance of a bond to the doctrine of divine right:

> These principles, universally acknowledged by the entire kingdom, are that the King alone must possess the sovereign power in his kingdom; that He is answerable only to God in the exercise of his power; that the tie which binds the King to the Nation is by nature indissoluble; that the interests and reciprocal obligations between the

> King and his subjects serve only to reassure that union; that the Nation's interest is that the powers of its head not be altered; that the King is the chief sovereign of the Nation and everything he does is with her interests in mind; and that finally the legislative power resides in the person of the King independent of and unshared with all other powers.

In November 1787 Lamoignon was speaking to the appropriate audience. There was, however, another waiting in the wings whose arrival centre-stage he feared but whose historic significance he, like so many others, did not foresee. Where the vacillations of Louis proved fatal to both the *ancien régime* and eventually the monarchy was in respect of the one development that was to produce the greatest irony in the causal skein that precipitated the outbreak of the French Revolution: the convening of the Estates-General. Brienne had reluctantly agreed to the convocation, at first for some unspecified future date (he presumed it would all fizzle out), then, on 8 August, for 1 May the following year. The proposal did not come from the ministry, nor did it originate with the Vizille assembly. It was in fact the nobility's idea, first floated by the Assembly of Notables in 1787. Faced with deadlock in their running dispute with the absolutist state over fiscal reform, they devised what they thought was a smart ruse. Instead of continuing with the futile tactic of refusing to 'register' royal edicts, the *parlements* were to declare themselves 'incompetent' in matters of taxation. The deadlock, they suggested, could be broken by the only body that could properly decide the matter, the Estates-General, which had not met since 1614.

The Estates-General was an institution that had evolved from its origins at the beginning of the fourteenth century into a tripartite assembly in which representatives of each of the 'estates'—what very roughly we would call 'classes'—would convene at the pleasure of the king to discuss royal policy on matters of taxation. The belief of the Notables who argued for summoning it once more was that, if reconvened, it would proceed as in 1614, with the three orders (nobles, clergy and commoners) meeting in separate assemblies and voting as blocs; in this form, the two most powerful estates, the clergy and nobility, could combine electoral forces to frustrate the royal will. It was thus to be game, set and match to Privilege.

Its proponents, however, made one immensely consequential error of political calculation: they assumed the docility of the Third Estate. Little did they know that they were setting in train a sequence of events that would lead from the meeting of the Estates-General in May 1789 to the Third's self-declaration in June as a National Assembly and, after 14 July, both the king's recognition of the new assembly and the formal abolition of 'feudal' rights. Here was a classic case of history as unintended outcomes. For the Third Estate was no longer willing to be docile; if the Estates-General was to be summoned, its forms and terms of representation had to change. While the majority of nobles congratulated themselves on their astuteness, the more far-sighted sounded warning notes. The duc d'Ormesson observed: 'You will get your Estates-General, and you will repent it.' More liberally inclined aristocrats, such as Lafayette, saw an opportunity. In his speech to the Assembly of Notables he described the proposal to convene the Estates-General as holding out the possibility for the 'convocation of a truly national assembly', alarming words to the likes of the reactionary comte d'Artois (the king's younger brother), who sensed that their clever ploy contained the potential for backfiring badly, his apprehensions a (for him rare) sign of political clairvoyance among a company of the blind. After Brienne's confirmation in August 1788 that the meeting would take place, Mirabeau declared: 'The nation has stepped forward a century in twenty-four hours.' But the decisive formulation of what this could and should mean was to be Sieyès' pamphlet of January 1789 *What is the Third Estate?* His own reply to the question of his title was to become the most celebrated formulation of its time: 'Everything. What has it been until now in the public order? Nothing. What does it want to be? Something.'

'Now that daylight is rising' (Sieyès' words), the movement from everything via nothing to something came out as a drastic recasting of the structure of political representation. It turned on three questions. Firstly, what scale of representation was the Third to have in the Estates-General, given that the people it notionally represented formed the bulk of the population? Secondly, how was voting to take place—on the traditional model of separate assemblies for each of the three orders, each voting *en bloc*, or as a common assembly with representatives voting by head (i.e. as individuals)? Thirdly, how were the representatives within each order to be elected? The last question mattered in the sense that the multilayered selection mechanisms governing the system of election within the Third ensured that its representatives were universally drawn from the professional classes, thus keeping workers and peasants at a distance. But this question was subordinate to the first two, which raised the grand issues of authority and legitimacy that were to yield the idea of a National Assembly in which power would be rearranged and redistributed.

The format for the articulation of these demands was the *cahiers de doléance* (grievance books). The input of the liberal professions was all about representation, the basis on which to meet and vote. At parish and district level, however (the level at which the peasant and labouring classes had access to the *cahiers*), the grievances were overwhelmingly about taxes and food prices, especially the price of flour, grains and bread (the staple diet of over three-quarters of the population). Peasant smallholders, agricultural workers and urban artisans had long been caught in an economic pincer movement between traditional privilege and capitalist modernisation, burdened on the one hand with 'feudal' obligations and, on the other, victims of new 'market' forces. The former included seigneurial dues paid to landowning aristocrats (the range was staggering, involving a whole nomenclature: *corvées, banalités, champarts, lods et ventes*) and tithes paid to the Church, deemed by both parties to be natural 'property' rights; the more fundamental 'natural' right—not to die of starvation—does not seem to have figured on the radar screen in quite the same way.

During the 1770s Turgot, as Controller-General of Finances, had tried to rationalise the system by allowing prices to find their own level in a liberalised economy, while at the same time abolishing feudal impositions on incomes. The actual outcome was that the price of grain and bread rose, while incomes remained depressed by the continuing refusal of the nobles and clerics to forfeit their 'rights'. Turgot thus made enemies on all fronts. He dealt ruthlessly with the popular outbreaks of violence in 1775 known as the Flour Wars, while alienating the nobles by his efforts to dictate tax changes through royal decree. The king knew—one of the very few things Louis could be relied upon to understand—when he was on to a loser and dismissed Turgot in 1776, though not without a prescient parting shot from the deposed finance minister: 'Do not forget, Sire, that it was feebleness that placed the head of Charles I on the block.' Necker was recalled, an experience to which he was to grow accustomed.

These social and economic inequities were compounded by natural as well as man-made causes, accidents of the weather and their effect on harvests. In 1770, 1772, 1774 and 1777 the harvest ranged from mediocre to bad. In 1788–9 it was close to catastrophic. The summer of 1788 witnessed the worst drought in living memory, with crops further destroyed by massive hailstorms; the countryside was commonly described as a barren desert. During the winter that followed, the trope shifted from Sahara to Siberia. The rivers and the mills froze. Travelling through Provence, usually blessed by the Mediterranean climate, Mirabeau recorded his impressions:

> One is tempted to say that the exterminating angel has struck the human race from one end of the realm to another. Every scourge has been unleashed. Everywhere I have found men dead of cold and hunger, bread often at five sous a pound, never less than three sous and seven deniers. In fact people are starving to death with wheat all around them, for want of flour. All the mills are frozen.

In the spring of 1789 the thaw finally arrived, flooding the fields. In March, grain and game riots erupted across the countryside. The impact of this triple natural disaster—drought, freeze-up and flooding—was dramatic. Between the summer of 1777 and the early spring of 1789 the price of bread almost doubled. From the point of view of the poor, the question was no longer equity but sheer physical survival. One does not have to subscribe to economic determinism in historical explanation to see that the reality or dread of hunger (what the politician Barnave called 'the bread interest') was a key factor, and explains why food riots were to be a regular feature of the Revolution through to 1795, the issue of subsistence progressively infused with new forms of radical political consciousness; when in 1795 the *sans-culottes* invaded the National Convention, they did so with the slogan 'Bread and the Constitution of 1793'. In the spring of 1789 the marriage of economics and politics was yet to be fully consummated, but the scale of the grain and game riots suggested that grievance had taken hold at a deep level. Meanwhile, in the towns and cities, artisans were threatened with falling wages and rising unemployment, partly as a consequence of a developing free trade in manufacturing equipment, most notably the new spinning machines imported from England (on 14 July, while the Bastille was being stormed in Paris, the spinners of Rouen were destroying the machines that had crossed the Channel; one of the minor ironies of history is that Danton's stepfather, a textile manufacturer, was a substantial importer).

This was the backdrop to the violent Réveillon riot that took place in Paris on 28 April. Réveillon was a 'modern' industrialist and also an Elector for the purpose of determining the city's slate of representatives to the Estates-General. His views were 'enlightened' in the Turgot mode, and at a meeting on 21 April to discuss his district's *cahier de doléance*, he had made a speech arguing that, with the removal of irrational and unproductive levies (most especially the hated customs tolls on goods coming into the city collected by the Farmers-General), both prices and wages would fall in tandem, thus generating the virtuous circle that was capitalism's formula for general prosperity.

Simplified and distorted reports of his speech were circulated, and widely interpreted as recommending a direct attack on wages. The workers at his factory in the faubourg Saint-Antoine reacted by destroying the factory. Although rumour vastly exaggerated the casualty figures, it was nevertheless a bloody affair that was to send shock waves through the city; fired on by troops sent to restore order, the dead and wounded were in the hundreds. Apart from the unprecedented scale of the violence, a further important feature of the incident was that it took place in the faubourg Saint-Antoine, an area of growing working-class militancy that was to be one of the hotbeds of 14 July. Although their concerns were primarily economic, the rioting workers were also heard to shout and chant political slogans; it was a sign that urban riot was about to mutate into insurrection. The first item on the morning agenda of the capital's *lieutenant de police* was to check the daily price of bread.

The second recall of Necker in the autumn of 1788 was supposed to be the magic recipe for defusing these tensions and conflicts. Although he could not be expected to control the weather, he was nevertheless generally perceived (largely on the back of his earlier repudiation of Turgot's draconian measures) as the People's Banker, the man who could be trusted to place controls on the price of grains and flour and dispose of the fiscal deficit by means of another virtuoso juggling the nation's finances (he at least put his own money where his mouth was by lending the French state two million francs from his private fortune). It was also believed that he would further the cause of political reform. One of the first things he did on resuming office was to confirm that the Estates-General would meet the following May and that the representation of the Third Estate would be doubled. When, however, the deputies convened in Versailles, Necker's speech was something of an anticlimax. He uttered not a word on the other two demands of the Third Estate (common assembly and voting by head), less from cowardice, it seems, than from prudential considerations. Necker appears to have believed that a single assembly and individual voting would follow automatically from the concession of a doubling of the Third's deputies; why then provoke by making explicit what would happen naturally? This was to stake a reckless bet on the virtues of common sense. In any case, his speech was badly received ('a mind intoxicated with vanity, displaying an incapacity or unwillingness to explain or illustrate: a composition, indecent, unmanly, out of place, betraying a narrow understanding and a timorous heart', was one uncharitable judgement). As for the king's behaviour, he rejected the demands of the Third outright (speaking of 'a much exaggerated desire for innovations'), while going out of his way to make clear what he thought the proper place of the commoners was in the natural order of things. Here was another confrontation between the king and his subjects, but this time involving a very different constituency, although one equally determined to have its way. From this point on, things start to unravel and to develop an unstoppable momentum. For a month or so not much happened in Versailles, basically a saga of inertia and delaying tactics. Meanwhile, the price of bread in Paris continued to rocket (Necker's reimposition of price controls had not worked in the face of dwindling supply). Then on 17 and 20 June the Third Estate representatives make two declarations, whose performative force was to transform the French (and

European) political landscape. On the 17th they announced their unilateral conversion into a National Assembly, with prerogative on all matters of taxation. On the 20th, locked out from their customary meeting place in the Salle des Menus-Plaisirs, they repaired to the nearby royal Tennis Court, where, with one single abstention, they made the celebrated oath 'never to be separated until we have formed a solid and equitable Constitution as our constituents have asked us to do'.

There was of course something incongruous to the greatest oath of them all, the gesture of political defiance that was to furnish the very ground of modern political legitimacy, occurring in a place of leisure and exercise (much favoured by the comte d'Artois, favourite of the queen and rabidly hostile to reform, who after the 20th made sure of booking the court for a week). But if symbolically incongruous, the mismatch of solemnity and locale was in no way historically odd, but rather an index of the improvised adaptations to contingency that is one of the hallmarks of revolutionary transformation.

Faced with the resoluteness of the Third, in late June the solidarity of the other two orders began to crumble. At first there was a trickle of defections. On 19 June, however, the clergy voted to join *en masse*. Yet the king and his advisers persisted in believing that the tide could indeed be rolled back. A *séance royale* for 23 June was decreed (to which the deputies of all three estates were invited), preceded by a private meeting with his counsellors at which the hard-line views of the party of reaction were adopted. On the following day, the Third Estate was once more reminded of its preordained status (its representatives were herded into the hall through a side door). The king spoke at (for him) considerable, even inordinate, length. He then had read out a set of statements and 'decisions', including the reminder: 'I owe it to the commonweal of my kingdom, I owe it to myself, to make you cease your fatal dissensions.' He then proceeded to exacerbate dissension by flatly rejecting common assembly ('the King desires that the old institution of the three orders in the state be preserved in every particular, as an essential part of the constitution of his realm'). There may perhaps be occasional collective meetings of the Estates-General, but, if so, it was expressly forbidden to discuss both the form of future meetings and the question of 'feudal and seigneurial possessions, and the honorary prerogatives of the first two orders'. In short, everything that had been raised in connection with the twin issues of taxation and representation was to be kicked into touch, and to stay there for ever. The deputies were finally ordered to return to their separate assemblies: 'I command you, gentlemen, to disperse at once and to go tomorrow, each to the chamber intended for your particular order.'

The deputies were stunned, the king leaving the hall enveloped in silence (there was not a single utterance of *Vive le roi*). The self-declared National Assembly refused to disperse; flamboyantly defiant, Mirabeau threw down the gauntlet: 'We are here by the power of the people, and we will not leave except by the force of bayonets.' More ponderously but no less firmly, Sieyès intoned: 'Gentlemen, we are today what we were yesterday. Let us deliberate.' Protests erupt, the crowd entering the courtyard of the royal palace, where—in a first sign of shifting loyalties—the troops refuse to disperse them by force of arms. A text drafted by a number of *gardes françaises* soon enters circulation, *Avis aux grenadiers et soldats du tiers-état* ('Announcement to the grenadiers and soldiers of the Third Estate'), the predicate a bold act of sedition in its own right. Faced with such obduracy and determination, Louis backed off, dithered for several days and, on 27 June, recanted, 'instructing' the clergy and nobility to join the Third in common assembly (a bit late in the day, since the instruction was little more than ratification of what had more or less already occurred). The developments from May through to late June describe an entirely new political constellation. The Third Estate now found itself caught in a two-pronged clash of wills, against both the nobles and the monarchy. The fear of an 'aristocratic plot' remained, but the frontline conflict was now with the king. What began as a contest between the monarchy and the two privileged orders became a struggle between the latter orders and the Third, and finally morphed into a dispute between the Third and the king. In other words, it was a chronology in which, broadly, the original form of the dispute was turned upside down, with the monarch facing a new antagonist. From the point of view of the monarchy, the juridical status of the meeting of the Estates-General was that of a 'consultation' between the king and his subjects, in which the king retained the authority granted to him by divine right. Initially the Third accepted this model, but by late June the stand-off was about an altogether new relation between representation and legitimate power. When in 1787 Lamoignon appeared before the *parlement de Paris* and made the speech in which he categorically stated that 'the King alone must possess the sovereign power in his kingdom', the *parlement* had its own reasons for not warming to this assertion. Had, counterfactually, Lamoignon still been in office in early 1789, it is doubtful that the deputies of the Third Estate would have warmed to it either. Similarly, when, also in 1787, the *duc d'Orléans* protested that the king's insistence that the *parlement de Paris* 'register' his fiscal proposals was 'illegal', Louis replied, first, 'I don't care', and second, 'Yes, it's legal since it is my will.' The new audience for this doctrine was even less likely than the old to find this congenial. It was thus no surprise that the tergiversating monarch simply didn't know whether he was coming or going, nor that the new audience would turn a deaf ear, and finally express itself on the streets of the capital.

The picture of what causally and circumstantially led up to the events of 14 July is above all one in which a number of fault-lines across both the society and the polity became increasingly visible, with ever-growing pressure on all of them. First, there is a set of corporate interests prepared to use any means to resist the fiscal demands of the state. Secondly, there is the plight of the peasants and artisans, burdened by tithes and dues, at the mercy of weather-induced bad harvests, and the victims of the liberalisation of markets. Thirdly, there is a self-created National Assembly, determined but as yet of uncertain status and voice, without the backing of a constitution or formal recognition by the monarchy. Furthermore, having made 'representation' the key issue, it remained unclear what and who exactly were to be represented. As largely a collection of middle-class professionals, along with dissident nobles and clergy, where would it stand vis-à-vis the grievances of the common people? The delayed and turbulent answers to that question would define most of the later course of Revolution in the great *sans-culotte* uprisings and the power struggle between Jacobins and Girondins. Finally, there was a royal administration bereft of coherent ideas, riven by faction and unsure where to place its bets. But it remained instinctively mistrustful of the newly vocal Third Estate, and when the chips were down very likely to side with Privilege. Taming the nobles in order to replenish the royal coffers and strengthen the authority of the state was one thing; siding with the rabble against the nobles was another altogether.

In the public imagination the reputation of Louis nevertheless continued to fluctuate in direct proportion to the fluctuations of his own position. On the one hand, he was the traditional protector, the argument for which had been put by the marquis d'Argenson, according to which monarchy and people were natural allies against the depredations of the barons. A recurrent refrain in the *cahiers de doléance* was the view of, and appeal to, the king as father of the nation. But this conception was now under considerable strain. For example, at the *séance royale* of 23 June Louis had prefaced his remarks by declaring himself 'the common father of all my subjects'. Yet a claim to fair-minded paternity looked increasingly threadbare as he proceeded to reject the demands of the Third, although there is evidence that he was in fact sympathetic to the calls for common assembly and voting by head and had simply capitulated before the pressures of the reactionary party at court. And where the common people were concerned, what mattered even more than politics was the price of bread; if, where the latter was concerned, the king's protection was not assured, then professions of 'love' for his people sounded increasingly hollow when, ducking and weaving as events unfolded, he seemed to have thrown in his lot with the party of Privilege. Stranded between the competing demands of those wanting to hold on to their privileges and those who wished to end them, Louis said one thing and then another; in a moment of private candour, he wrote: 'My greatest fault is a sluggishness of mind which makes all my mental efforts wearisome and painful.' Louis's other brother, the comte de Provence, put it more crisply: 'When you can hold together a number of oiled ivory balls, you may do something with the King.' Louis himself once observed—unhelpfully, one naturally presumes, but, given what he actually said, the presumption is questionable—that his silences mattered more than his words.

It is customary to stress the hesitations of Louis, as if his indecisiveness were causally decisive in determining eventual outcomes. But in fact they reflect more his sheer irrelevance, caught in an array of forces he was powerless to direct. Whatever he did, he was doomed to play a losing hand. Coping with the contradiction of appearing to want some sort of accommodation with the National Assembly and being unable to resile from what, in his understanding, made a king a king, irresoluteness was his only option. Up to a point, the people were prepared to give him the benefit of the doubt, in the form of conditional trust (the condition that was made explicit in 1791: '*Vive le roi, s'il est de bonne foi*'—'Long live the king, assuming his good faith'). But in early July 1789 that trust was stretched to breaking point. It was no longer merely a question of his prevarications but, more ominously, the fear of a double-cross. The outward concessions of June 27 perhaps concealed—as indeed they did—a secret plan for retraction and suppression. The decision to dispatch troops to Paris was the truly bad sign. Why had the king authorised (if, probably, not himself initiated) a pre-emptive military move of this sort? Was it to contain the restive population of the capital? Did he have designs on the newly fledged National Assembly?

By now Paris was a tinderbox. There was no single spark and no single spot for what happened next, across a multiplicity of sites including the Palais Royal, the Hôtel de Ville, the faubourg Saint-Antoine, the Invalides and of course the Bastille. But it is generally agreed that the initial spark was the news of the sacking of Necker on 11 July (one contemporary observer described Necker's sacking as a 'thunderbolt'). Necker after all had been billed as a saviour. Even Robespierre had described him as 'a great man who seems to have been shown to the people merely for them to glimpse the full extent of the happiness they might enjoy, whose elevation was a triumph for genius, virtue and the nation'. What, then, did his dismissal portend—for the National Assembly in Versailles, the price of bread, the safety of Paris and its inhabitants? One of the choicer specimens of Louis's remarkable inability to think straight is to be found in the letter carried by his ministerial flunky, La Luzerne, informing Necker that his services were no longer required: 'It is important to your integrity and reputation that there should be no cause for stir and commotion.' Stir and commotion were precisely what Louis's decision brought about, with huge consequences for the integrity and reputation of others than Necker himself.

These were the questions swirling in an atmosphere of uncertainty and confusion, along with the first intimations of a theme that would dominate the Revolution: fear of plots and treason. As news of Necker's ousting spread by word of mouth across the city on the morning of 12 July, Paris was abuzz with rumour. Rebellion was in the air; speeches were being made. And since the galvanising power of speech, both formal and informal, was one of the major causal instruments of the Revolution, capable of shaping all manner of outcomes (the three great leaders, Mirabeau, Danton and Robespierre, all understood that they were as nothing without speech-making), on the eve of the storming of the Bastille, let us repair in the first instance to that place of talk *par excellence*, the remarkable Palais Royal.

2

A La Bastille!

Imagine a large piece of real estate in the centre of Paris, not only privately owned but—because privately owned—a place where the writ of the policing agencies did not run. There were many such agencies, so many indeed as to produce the complacent boast that in such a well-monitored capital incidents like the Gordon Riots of 1780 in London were inconceivable. However, the potential spanner in the works of this multiform apparatus was that unique late eighteenth-century urban site, the Palais Royal. Originally Richelieu's estate, he bequeathed it to the Crown, Louis XIV in turn ceding it as a private residence to his brother, Philippe, head of the Orléans branch of the Bourbons. When the latter's great-grandson, Louis-Philippe II, inherited it, he sought to demonstrate his 'democratic' credentials (during the Revolution he restyled himself Philippe Egalité) by opening the grounds to the general public. At the same time he redesigned the area as a zone of untroubled leisure and louche transaction, where virtually anything—most notably sex—could be bought and sold. By the time of the Restoration its logic had become entirely commercial (Balzac gives us an unforgettable description in *Illusions perdues*). But in the eighteenth century it also provided a home for the newfound attachment to untrammelled freedom of speech (it was the setting for the outrageously subversive dialogue that forms the bulk of Diderot's remarkable novel *Le Neveu de*

Prise de la Bastille (drawing).
Storming of the Bastille.

Rameau). Here one could say what one wanted to say more or less with impunity, not least because Louis-Philippe, with political ambitions of his own, had an interest in appearing to side with radical causes. With its curious social mixes of strollers, gawkers, men-about-town, pedlars, prostitutes, *philosophes*, journalists, booksellers, rogues, plotters, spies and agents provocateurs, the Palais Royal was one of the most extraordinary gathering places of late eighteenth-century Paris.

When news of Necker's dismissal spread like wildfire on the morning of 12 July, it was naturally here that dissident and seditious opinion was at its most vocal. Danton had already been seen and heard there several times. Jean-Baptiste Poupart, who was to participate in negotiations with the prison governor during the storming of the Bastille, made a speech whose theme was that force must be met by force. But 12 July in the Palais Royal was above all the day of the young man who would die with Danton under the guillotine, the mercurial Camille Desmoulins, in whom a natural excitability turned easily to heady intoxication. Desmoulins, who had stammered since childhood, leapt on to a table in front of the Café de Foy brandishing a sword in one hand and a pistol in the other, and proceeded, with passionate fluency, to speak of a planned 'Saint-Bartholomew of the patriots' (an allusion to the sixteenth-century massacre of the Protestants), and to demand that the people arm themselves against a corresponding threat by the king's troops. From the gardens of the Palais Royal the assembled crowd surged into the streets, growing apace as it made its way along the Boulevard du Temple to the place Vendôme, where, at around 8 p.m., the first important skirmish took place (although there had already been sporadic outbursts of violence elsewhere in the city). A detachment of dragoons tried, but failed, to check the crowd, now numbering in excess of 5,000. The dragoons were rescued by the Royal-Allemand cavalry regiment under the command of the prince de Lambesc, who retreated to the place Louis XV while the crowd forced its way into the Tuileries gardens. Lambesc's men attacked but, under a hail of stones, were compelled to pull back.

The clash in the Tuileries gardens was in reality little more than a botched attempt at crowd control, with a handful of injuries and perhaps a single fatality. It became one of the triggering occasions of what turned into large-scale urban riot by virtue of what it gave rise to, that phenomenon which was to be an integral feature of the whole revolutionary landscape, with tremendous causal powers in its own right: rumour. Talk of a 'massacre' at the Tuileries travelled fast, no doubt exacerbated by the fact that Lambesc's cavalrymen were foreign mercenaries (French troops—the *gardes françaises*—rushed to the scene from their barracks to help the assaulted people). Here was confirmation of Desmoulins' predicted 'Saint-Bartholomew of the patriots', proof of a 'plot', or at least of a concerted plan to use military force to quell the population. Fear thus joined with grievance to convert a disturbance into an insurrection, animated by the slogan 'Arms and bread!' During the night of 12 July the principal action took place at the *barrières*, the toll gates at the city's walled periphery where customs duties were levied on all goods entering Paris (crucially grain and flour for the bakeries). While a reaction to the soaring price of bread, this too belonged in the conspiracy narrative, echoing the ancestral popular belief in a 'famine plot' now suffused with revolutionary anger reflected in the famous (and untranslatable) alliterative jingle: '*Le mur murant Paris rend Paris murmurant*' (haplessly, 'The wall enclosing Paris makes Paris murmur'). There had already been trouble at the *barrières* on 8 July (dealt with by Lambesc), but the violence on the night of the 12th was on a wholly different scale (forty out of fifty-four toll gates were demolished).

Meanwhile, in the city centre, throughout the night and into the next day, there was widespread looting—of the gunsmiths' shops for weapons, of the convent of Saint-Lazare for foodstuffs—along with the liberation of convicts from the

Conciergerie and La Force prisons. From the point of view of the provisional municipality, 'anarchy' threatened, likely in turn to generate a crushing show of force from the royal troops encircling Paris. On the 13th the Paris Electors hastily constituted themselves as a permanent committee, presided over by the floundering and doomed Jacques de Flesselles, and moved immediately to form the *milice bourgeoise*, headed by the marquis de la Salle, that would shortly be named the National Guard. By the middle of the night, 'authority' and insurrection combined to produce one of the most remarkable sights the capital had ever witnessed: a huge crowd assembled on the place de Grève (in front of the Hôtel de Ville) as in a torch-lit phantasmagoria, the defecting *gardes françaises* mingling with the common people and instructing the new civilian militia in the use of firearms. Besenval, meanwhile, had prudently withdrawn the royal troops to the Champ de Mars. But this did little to allay the power of rumour, which continued to circulate reports that the troops were already advancing into the heart of the old city, slaughtering 'patriots' as they went. However impressive the spectacle on the place de Grève, the weaponry in the hands of the insurgents was primitive, vastly more pikes than guns, and thus no match for the king's regiments. Guns, cannon and powder were imperatively required to stave off imminent disaster.

On the morning of the 14th, around 8,000 Parisians, led by Ethis de Corny from the Hôtel de Ville, arrived on the Esplanade des Invalides, with a demand for arms known to be stored there. The governor, Sombreuil, denied their existence (having previously and futilely ordered his small band of infirm pensioner-soldiers to disable the muskets), whereupon Corny's official delegation was swept aside by a mass invasion of people, who proceeded to ransack the stores, seizing twelve cannon and 28,000 guns, but few bullets and—critically—no powder. Corny's plan had been to take the requisitioned arms back to the Hôtel de Ville for orderly distribution to the militia. In the event, he retrieved only a fraction of the muskets, but all of the cannon pieces. Without powder, however, the latter were of no use. Some had already been secured: during the night a barge laden with barrels of gunpowder had been discovered at the Port Saint-Nicolas and taken to one of the bureaux of the Hôtel de Ville, where the indefatigable abbé Lefèvre spent the small hours distributing it, perilously by candlelight, the peril greatly intensified when—the tale is perhaps apocryphal—in wandered an inebriated member of the militia puffing on his pipe. When urged by the abbé to extinguish it, he drunkenly insisted on his citizen's right to smoke, the danger of everyone and everything going up in another kind of smoke defused only when Lefèvre offered to purchase the pipe.

But there was also the very large stock of gunpowder and ammunition that, on Besenval's orders, had been stored in the Bastille for safekeeping. As the events at the Invalides unfolded, a separate crowd from the faubourg Saint-Antoine and adjacent districts converged on the Bastille. This was as much about disarming the prison authorities as about arming themselves. As tension rose in the city, an anxious Launay had for some time been strengthening the Bastille's defences. In early July a detachment of Swiss mercenaries (from the Salis-Salamande regiment) had been added to the ineffectual standing force of eighty-two *invalides*. The embrasures holding the eight-pounder cannons had been widened, visible to all from the streets and—once again the effect of hearsay—interpreted as an indication of Launay's intention to attack the surrounding faubourgs at the earliest signs of trouble. Intentions were in fact mutually opaque to all parties, thus guaranteeing a high degree of contingency and unpredictability (the rest of the day was to be saturated with both). But out of this feverish brew of circumstance, supposition and panic began the process whereby 14 July 1789 was converted into the historic Fourteenth of July. Up went the cry, allegedly uttered for the first time by one Labarthe, a quartermaster to the *gardes françaises*, but in fact without determinate origin, echoing across the whole city, that was subsequently to resonate throughout the annals of the French Revolution: *A la Bastille!*

And so to the Bastille they went, in their thousands. What followed is the sequence of events that has been consistently named, and commemorated, as the 'storming' or the 'taking' of the Bastille (a practice which, out of deference to narrative custom, I myself have followed). Strictly speaking, this is a misnomer; the Bastille was not 'taken'—it surrendered (it had done so on two previous occasions in the fifteenth and seventeenth centuries). Physically impregnable, its inner citadel could not possibly have been 'taken' by a crowd of demonstrators. Built on the orders of Charles V in the fourteenth century to guard the eastern approaches to the capital, it was originally a fortress rather than a prison (the term *bastille* was a common noun signifying 'fortress' or 'fort'). There were many *bastilles* across the land. The Parisian construction acquired both its upper-case designation as '*la Bastille*' and its fearsome reputation when, at the behest of Cardinal Richelieu, it became a state prison where persons could be sent and detained solely at the discretion of the king (on the basis of the infamous *lettres de cachet*). The overwhelming majority of *embastillés* were the victims of '*justice extraordinaire*'. Because the latter practice bypassed all due process (the contents of the *lettre* were not disclosed and the identity of the prisoner was withheld), the Bastille was associated above all with secrecy: who, at any given moment, was there, and for what reasons, were unknown to anyone other than the monarch, his immediate advisers and the prison authorities (the *cause célèbre* being of course the Man in the Iron Mask).

Richelieu's successor, Mazarin, used it extensively to deal with the rebellious and seditious nobles of the so-called Fronde rebellion, while, after Louis XIV's revocation of the Edict of Nantes (which reinstated the civil rights of the Protestant community), it was also where large numbers of recalcitrant

Huguenots were locked up. In addition to its political purposes as a place of detention for those perceived as a threat to royal power, it also housed perpetrators of economic crimes, especially forgers of the currency, as well as providing convenient incarceration for the black sheep of grand families, from the seriously delinquent to the insane (a private application by the family for the issuance of a *lettre de cachet* doing the trick). The aristocratic prisoners were, however, usually well treated, with ample provision of servants, good food, fine wines, furniture, pets, books and other amenities, such that for the privileged the Bastille often resembled more a hotel or a club than a jail (Marmontel congratulated it for the quality of its food, as if granting a star to a restaurant: excellent soup, succulent beef, marinated artichokes, vintage Burgundies and first-class Mocha coffee). The less privileged, on the other hand, were not so lucky, generally confined to the lower dungeons, where conditions were appalling.

During the reigns of Louis XV and Louis XVI, the Bastille continued to receive refractory and transgressing nobles, but there was a marked shift towards using it to punish and suppress the expression of enlightened opinion, especially the authors, publishers and distributors of prohibited and clandestine literature. Its more famous inmates included Voltaire, who had two spells in the Bastille, and the future leader of the Girondin party in the Assembly, Brissot, briefly imprisoned on his return from London for having published anti-government statements in his newspaper. Nevertheless, as a punitive instrument of state censorship, the Bastille, on the whole, exercised a light touch (Morellet even quipped that, for a writer, a sojourn on its premises was a helpful way station to acquiring both a reputation and a fortune), and in any case by the late 1780s it had become something of an expensive white elephant, with much talk of pulling it down.

Relative desuetude was, however, no impediment to incrustation by legend. Bastille literature had become something of a marketable genre, its circulation feeding directly into a collective view of the prison as a symbol of unacceptable power. The two most widely read texts of the 1780s were the memoirs of Linguet and Latude. Linguet, imprisoned for the publication in London of his dissident *Annales politiques* and who appears to have experienced the prison in its more brutally squalid aspect, created a horrifying image of the Bastille as a 'devourer' of human flesh, but where the principal stress was on psychological rather than physical suffering, the prison as a place of existential annihilation and the deprivation of liberty as a radical dispossession of the sense of self; what was lost were not just a person's rights but the precondition of any rights at all, personhood itself. Latude, by contrast, con man and artist of the great escape, in his memoirs regaled the public with the saga of his multiple evasions. His story embodied the spirit of 'liberty' itself, a demonstration that the Bastille (and by implication the state machine it served) was not omnipotent. Along with Linguet's nightmare world of the self utterly at the mercy of secrecy and unaccountability, Latude's narrative contributed to the making of a political argument. The Bastille, it will be recalled, was not just a prison, it was a *prison d'Etat*. Already in the 1760s, the lawyer and jurist Antoine Servan had made the link between the practices of '*justice extraordinaire*' and the doctrine of divine right, thus questioning nothing less than the foundations of the absolutist state (Louis XVI was distinctly unamused by the attack on the Bastille in Beaumarchais' *Le Mariage de Figaro*). Mirabeau, who had spent time in the Vincennes prison (where he met but disliked the Marquis de Sade), joined the argument in 1782 with his *Des lettres de cachet et des prisons d'Etat*. This was the background that enabled Michelet to claim that the siege of the Bastille was essentially a challenge by the Third Estate to arbitrary monarchical power.

This was, however, an exaggeration. On the day itself, the reality encountered by the besiegers when they finally penetrated the prison proved to be very different. The liberation of its prisoners was both accidental and incidental. More an afterthought than an express intention, indeed almost an oversight (initially, the prisoners themselves were completely forgotten when the keys to the cells were taken as a victorious trophy), the actual yield of freed inmates numbered no more than seven, although there was a nice symmetrical irony when, paraded in the Palais Royal later that night, they encountered their jailer for the last time, his severed head on a pike. The seven prisoners included one aristocratic delinquent (the comte de Solages, first imprisoned in 1765 at his father's request for 'infamous and atrocious crimes'), four forgers (La Corrège, Pujade, Bechade la Barthe and Laroche) and two lunatics: Whyte de Malleville from Dublin, first imprisoned at Vincennes in 1782 and transferred to the Bastille two years later, who oscillated between thinking he was God and Julius Caesar; and Tavernier, the illegitimate son of the financier Pâris Duverney, notionally a political prisoner (having been part of the plot to assassinate Louis XV), but who was spectacularly insane. There were in addition the 'fictional' prisoner the comte de Lorges (of whom more in a later chapter), and the infamous 'missing' prisoner the Marquis de Sade. Moved from Vincennes to the Bastille (his accommodation not just *tout confort* but *grand luxe*), the divine Marquis became nevertheless increasingly obstreperous. On his daily walk he took to rousing the passers-by from the faubourg Saint-Antoine with incendiary slogans; and, when his walk was suspended, he began to shout from his cell window that the governor had authorised the strangling of prisoners. An exasperated Launay finally had him removed to the asylum at Charenton in early July, writing to the minister, Villedeuil: 'The whole staff would be obliged if you would accede to their wish to have the Marquis de Sade transferred elsewhere without delay.' On his release from Charenton, Sade restyled himself Citizen Sade, wrote several political pamphlets and became an ardent supporter of Marat.

As the crowd assembled in the course of the morning of 14

July, the image of the Bastille at the forefront of their minds was not that of a 'despot's' prison. Rather it had reverted to its former status as a fortress, its governor a military figure, appointed by the king and in league with Besenval to contain the population. Since it was widely believed that Launay was poised to attack the neighbouring faubourg Saint-Antoine with his cannon, the first demand was that the guns be withdrawn, and—in the name of self-defence—that the prison's store of ammunition and powder be handed over. These were also the principal requests of the first of a series of deputations from the Hôtel de Ville and elsewhere. A small group of lower-ranking officials arrived at around 10 a.m. They were cordially received by Launay and invited to join him for a meal. The governor agreed to the withdrawal of the cannon, but to nothing else (there is little evidence that he was pressed to do so). The repast must have been convivial, since it lasted an hour and a half, during which the crowd grew substantially larger and, when swollen by the large numbers from the Invalides, altogether more restive. At this juncture, the demands escalated: what was now required was the surrender not just of the contents of the Bastille but also of the Bastille itself. The latter was mutating fast into a 'symbol' and the issue becoming one of 'authority'. The increasingly tense atmosphere was also exacerbated by fears that the munching and quaffing delegation had been taken hostage. Some of the demonstrators set off for the nearby district of Saint-Louis de la Culture to report these fears.

The consequence was a second deputation and a major change of tone. It was headed by Thuriot de la Rosière, future deputy in the Convention (the more radical successor to the Legislative Assembly), member of the Committee of Public Safety and, as Robespierre's arch-enemy, instrumental in the latter's downfall. Thuriot's meeting with Launay was nothing like as convivial. Imperiously high-handed and irascible, with a thunderingly loud voice, Thuriot did not attempt so much to negotiate with Launay as to intimidate him. He also upped the ante even further by requiring (not requesting) Launay to place the Bastille in the hands of the civilian militia. Since for Launay that amounted to treason, he naturally refused (Launay was many—largely unpleasant—things, but his loyalty as a servant of the crown was unimpeachable). He did, however, confirm that the cannon had been withdrawn and invited Thuriot to make a tour of inspection. Thuriot appears to have believed Launay's declaration of peaceful intent, but his own domineering attitude succeeded only in worsening the situation, with various unintended outcomes. As he left the Bastille, he disdainfully neglected to inform the crowd of the upshot of his dealings with the governor, a silence that was misread as betokening a sell-out; this was a first indication that the breach between 'authority' and the 'people' was to implicate the people's representatives as well as the king.

Thuriot made his way to the Hôtel de Ville to give an account of his dealings with Launay, from where he was sent back to the Bastille to calm the crowd with the announcement that Launay had agreed not to attack if not himself attacked. He was about to set off when sounds of explosion and gunfire were heard. A dead body is carried in; cries of 'vengeance' come from the place de Grève. Thuriot had bungled his first mission, and his second was destined to fail utterly; when he finally got back to the Bastille, he encountered a scene of such chaos that it proved impossible for him to get inside, let alone take charge. The crowd by now had become a throng, gathered in the outer precincts of the prison (the Cour du Passage) but pressing forward to gain access to the first of two courtyards, the Cour du Gouvernement, which was the site of the governor's lodgings. Access was secured by a moat and two drawbridges, one for pedestrians and the other for carriages. Both drawbridges were raised.

What happened next was one of the two cruxes of the day's events. A couple of young day labourers, Davanne and Denain, climbed onto a shop roof on the north side of the Cour du Passage, and from there, followed by Pannetier, a grocer, Tournay, a carter, and Bonnemère, a soldier, they crossed the ramparts down into the Cour du Gouvernment in search of the guardhouse keys. Unable to find them, they grabbed axes and smashed the pulleys of one of the drawbridges, which, as it crashed down, killed one and wounded several. The crowd poured into the courtyard, shots were fired (who opened fire first was to be endlessly disputed, the eyewitness testimony marked by irresolvable claim and counterclaim); within a few minutes there were nearly 100 dead sprawled out on the ground, mowed down by the defending Swiss Guards.

It was now around 2 p.m. In the space of four hours, the situation had changed dramatically. As things spiralled out of control, there was a third deputation, headed by Delavigne, the president of the Assembly of Electors. Delavigne and his colleagues (most notably the enterprising abbé Fauchet) came with a triple demand: a ceasefire; the surrender of arms and munitions; and—a compromise version of the earlier proposal from the intransigent Thuriot—admission of the militia to work alongside Launay's band of veterans and Swiss Guards in protecting the garrison. Here was a formula for defusing the conflict and imposing some sort of order, in the form of a deal between two sources of 'legality'. The formula did not get even to first base; in the noise and confusion, the delegates were neither heard nor seen. It was all very different from the studiously polite, quasi-ceremonial reception of the first delegation earlier that morning. The firing continued, with further casualties and, from the enraged crowd, a new call—for the 'destruction' of the Bastille itself and 'death' to its governor. In practice this meant entering the inner courtyard, also secured by a raised drawbridge. But this was a task of a different order of magnitude. The inner courtyard was the true citadel of the prison. Launay did not have many troops (and, lacking in foresight, very few provisions), but he had almost unlimited ammunition and of course the cannon on the towers. With the resources at the crowd's disposal, this was an unassailable position. Some carts packed with straw had been brought from Santerre's brewery in the faubourg Saint-Antoine and set alight to provide a smokescreen as cover from hostile fire in the attempt to press forward into the inner courtyard. But even if they had succeeded in lowering the drawbridge, what awaited them would have been nothing short of a massacre (although they did not know it, a cannon had been moved into position just behind the entrance gate from the drawbridge).

Had the situation remained like this, the whole business of 'storming' the Bastille would probably have ended in a stalemate, and the dispersal of an exhausted and ragged throng. It certainly would never have become what it is famed for (a successful siege) without a further crucial development. The abortive third delegation returned to the Hôtel de Ville, where more dead and wounded were being brought in and the able-bodied were calling for arms. The Electors decided to try yet again with a further delegation consisting of Ethis de Corny (now back from the Invalides), Poupart, Boucheron and Piquod (Boucheron was to provide an eyewitness account of this episode), this time accoutred with official regalia, a flag and a drummer. Boucheron and Piquod managed to get into the Cour du Gouvernement, where they persuaded the crowd to stop firing, advanced to the drawbridge and shouted up to the troops stationed in the towers that they had come to negotiate, but on condition that there be not just a ceasefire but a laying down of arms.

For a moment this seemed to be working, the veterans in particular giving every sign that they wanted the situation to end. And then suddenly the attempted negotiation collapsed (according to the insurgents, because Launay refused to cooperate). The first round of cannon was discharged from one of the towers, accompanied by a volley of musket fire. There were more fatal casualties. The delegates, blamed by the crowd for this turn of events, beat a hasty retreat. It was at this juncture that the pivotal transformation occurred, with the intervention of troops from the *gardes françaises*. Up until now the efforts of the municipality to impose its will on both the crowd and the governor (its progressive escalation of demands making it by extension a contest of power with Crown) had been a tissue of failures. With the arrival of the troops, a riot which had turned violent became something more like an organised military assault; it was also the moment when the symbiotic relationship between the Revolution and the Soldier was born.

La prise de la Bastille (oil on canvas), by Jean-Baptiste Lallemand.
The Storming of the Bastille.

The *gardes françaises* were an elite corps, but this meant that their senior officers were even more distant from the common soldiers they commanded than was the case in the foreign regiments. Moreover, since they were garrisoned in Paris, everyday contact with the population affected their sympathies and loyalties; one of their tasks was to police the theatres, in the course of which they picked up many a proto-republican maxim from the plays being performed. Defection was in the air. After the *séance royale* of 23 June, when the crowd had gathered in front of the palace at Versailles to demonstrate in support of representatives of the Third Estate, the *gardes françaises* refused to use force to disperse the demonstration.

Two days later around 3,000 *gardes* swore an oath in the Palais Royal to protect the National Assembly and fellow 'citizens'. On 30 June a group of soldiers was arrested for insubordination and taken to the Abbaye Saint-Germain prison, where they were freed by invading demonstrators, the troop detachments sent to stop them not lifting a finger (Thomas Jefferson, then the United States minister to France, wrote that the troops had been arrested 'on account of their dispositions in favour of the national cause'). During the clash in the Tuileries on 12 July, several troops went to the aid of the people under attack by Lambesc's detachment of German mercenaries, later followed by an exchange of fire between loyalists and deserters in which lives were lost on both sides. The night of 13 July was a time of widespread defections, and when the Hôtel de Ville constituted itself as a permanent committee, the allegiance of deserting *gardes françaises* (many of whom were already active in the districts) was greeted with joy.

Among those imprisoned at the Abbaye were Pierre-Augustin Hulin and Jacques-Job Elie. Both were to play a major part in the rest of the day's events. Hulin, a former non-commissioned officer and currently director of the Queen's Laundry, showed up around 3 p.m. on the place de Grève (he had already been one of the speakers at the Palais Royal on 12 July and on the morning of the 14th was at the Invalides, rallying defectors), where he found two detachments of *gardes françaises*, to whom he delivered a passionate, tear-stained harangue: Launay and his men are murdering 'our fathers, our parents, our wives and children … I swear I will bring you back victorious or you will bring me back dead'. Accompanied by thirty-five gardes, 300 armed militia and four cannon, he made his way to the Bastille, where he was joined by Elie, a second lieutenant in the Queen's Infantry, who had also come from the place de Grève with a contingent of *gardes françaises* originally assembled by Sergeant-Major Wargnier, Sergeant Labarthe and Sergeant Richemont, who invited Elie to take command.

Hulin took charge of firing cannon at the Bastille walls (not very effectively, the walls being too thick). More audaciously, Elie attempted to bring down the drawbridge leading to the inner courtyard. He ordered the removal of the carts of burning straw, which, while useful as a smokescreen, also assisted the garrison forces in blocking access to the second bridge (two of Elie's comrades were killed in the attempt). Two cannon were brought into the Cour du Gouvernement and trained on the raised drawbridge. Faced with these developments, Launay panicked. He wanted a signed capitulation and a written guarantee of safe passage for him and his guards. Without that assurance, he threatened to blow up the whole place with the gunpowder stocks. He tried twice to get to the storeroom, but was prevented by some of the *invalides* (most notably Bequart, who was shortly to be grimly rewarded for his efforts). Having restrained Launay, and knowing the game was up, they cried out 'Surrender!' and flew a white handkerchief. The besiegers appear not to have picked up any of this, although they were aware that the gunfire had ceased. They advanced to the bridge. It was not yet 5 p.m.

And then suddenly it was basically over. Through an aperture in the drawbridge gate negotiations were opened, with a Swiss Guard proposing 'honourable' surrender. This was rejected. The guard then passed through a piece of paper with Launay's terms (guaranteed safety, or he blows the Bastille to smithereens). Planks were thrown across the moat, an unknown assailant tried to retrieve the piece of paper and fell into the moat. At the second attempt, Stanislas Maillard managed to get hold of it and handed it to Elie (not Hulin, as sometimes reported). Elie accepted the truce terms on his 'word as an officer', but the crowd wanted none of it. At that precise moment, however, the bridge was lowered and the gate opened by the *invalides* (they later claimed that had they known what was to happen next, they would not have done so without a written agreement signed by officials from the Hôtel de Ville). First onto the bridge was Grenadier Arné, followed by the others, who surged into the inner courtyard, where most of the garrison troops were stationed, the Swiss Guard on one side, the veterans on the other. But there was still some firing from the towers. The enraged crowd erupted into a frenzy of vandalism.

The principal object of their fury, however, was the 'traitor' Launay. One of the assailants, Claude Cholat, claimed to have been the one to capture the governor, but it was in fact Maillard who, aided by Arné, handed Launay to Elie and Hulin. The latter felt bound by the code of soldier's honour and due process, but the crowd wanted Launay killed on the spot. The *gardes françaises* managed to get him out of the Bastille, although he was already wounded and bleeding profusely. Elie and Maillard left to head a victory cortège to the place de Grève and the Hôtel de Ville, while Hulin remained with the crowd jostling around Launay. Exhausted, Hulin decided to pause for rest and a restorative glass of wine. It was a fatal error. When he rejoined the crowd, he found Launay's head already on a pike.

The governor, it seems, did not take kindly to role reversal and was not a cooperative or docile prisoner. Abusing his captors (*chienne de populace*—'bitch of a people'—apparently the expression he used) was in the circumstances imprudent, although a declaration of undying love for the People would have got him nowhere either (Foulon tried this tack to no avail). As they arrived at the place de Grève, Launay put up a struggle and kicked one Dénot (or Desnot) in his 'republican parts'. This was the cue for instant and gruesome butchery. Bayoneted in the stomach, savagely stabbed over and over again, he was finished off with a bullet to his head. There remained the business of parting the head from the body. The honour fell to Dénot, a cook fired for drunkenness and theft and very much a last-minute revolutionary. Dénot tried to cut off the head with a sword, but, having botched the job, he took a kitchen knife from his pocket and hacked through what remained of Launay's neck. He later described his endeavours as a patriotic act for which he should be given a medal.

Shortly thereafter, on the place de Grève itself, Launay's adjutant, Losme, was slaughtered, while several other Bastille officers were strangled in the rue des Tournelles. Soon it was to be the turn of Flesselles. As *prévôt des marchands*, his basic loyalties were to the *ancien régime*, and it was only under pressure and with great reluctance that he had accepted the formation of a provisional municipal government with Third Estate representation. The crowd that returned to the place de Grève triumphantly bearing Elie was in ugly mood. A message came through from an insurrectional committee based in the Palais Royal that Flesselles, accused—although the record is unclear, it seems with some justification—of having concealed arms that had been promised to the militia, was to be escorted there for an improvised 'trial'. As he came out on to the steps of the Hôtel de Ville, he was shot, his head cut off and stuck on a pike to join that of Launay.

Just over a week later it was the turn of Counsellor of State Foulon and his son-in-law, Berthier de Sauvigny. If Launay's death was frightful, it was nothing compared to what was meted out to Foulon. Appointed as Controller-General of Finances after the dismissal of Necker, he was widely hated, mainly because he was alleged to have said that the food rioters 'were worth no more than his horses; and that if [they] had no bread [they] had only to eat grass'. Having fled the city, he was captured, made to walk barefoot back to Paris, a bundle of hay tied to his back, given vinegar to drink and his sweat wiped off with nettles. Once back at the place de Grève, and despite Lafayette's entreaties, he was dragged across the square and strung up on a lamp post. The rope snapped twice, so they finished him off by severing his head and—now standard practice—impaling it on the end of a pike, with some of the hay stuffed in his mouth. His heart was also ripped out (by none other than Dénot). Heart and head finally ended up in a tavern at the Palais Royal, where they were thrown out of the window. Berthier, meanwhile, was lynched after having been forced to kiss the severed head of Foulon.

Robespierre, it will be recalled, dignified the rough justice of Foulon's murder with the name of the 'people's decree' (Barnave was even more glacial when he asked rhetorically: 'Was their blood so pure?'). But there were also the cases of no justice of any kind. Only the mix of confusion, panic and paranoia could explain the awful fate that befell the heroic Bequart, the veteran who had prevented Launay from blowing up the Bastille. On opening the gate to the inner courtyard, his hand was cut off at the wrist still holding a key and, in the belief that he was one of the prison warders, displayed on the streets as a trophy. A few hours later, mistaken for someone who had fired the cannon at the crowd in the Cour du Gouvernement, he was dragged by the hair to the place de Grève, where he was hanged.

These are the grim footnotes to the day's events. As night falls, the city is gripped by the terrified anticipation of reprisals from Besenval's troops. All Paris is out on the streets, everywhere barricades are being erected and patrols are circulating; everything and anything to hand is being used to improvise arms—pikes, stones, hot ashes (with which to blind enemy troops), boiling oil and water. The Bastille is a continuing scene of looting and vandalism. In essentials, however, the day's 'drama' has played itself out. Indeed the analogy of a drama in several acts is one for which the historian often reaches as a retrospective shaping device. The rush of events can be given a perfectly intelligible design when seen as punctuated by the four deputations and structured by the two critical turning points: the lowering of the first drawbridge and the invasion of the outer courtyard; then the arrival of the *gardes françaises* and Launay's capitulation. But this convenient ordering edits out the sheer scale of fast-flowing mishap, chance and randomness. As one eyewitness put it with masterly understatement, 'It cannot be denied that there was much confusion and disorder.'

First, there were the many misunderstandings and communicative mis-hits, the most consequence-laden being what took place when the chains of the first drawbridge were smashed. Unable to see Davanne, Denain and the others, the crowd mistakenly believed that the drawbridge had been lowered by Launay's men, an error further compounded when, as they poured into the courtyard, the *invalides* yelling from the towers an order to retreat was interpreted as 'enter'—a literally fatal misunderstanding for the many who lost their lives. Then there were the several insurgents who, having swarmed into the towers and appeared in the embrasures, were taken for garrison troops and fired on by their own people. When Launay surrendered, Hulin was taken for the governor and nearly sliced in two by a sabre. Clouet, the senior administrator in charge of the stocks of gunpowder and saltpetre, was also mistaken for Launay and was only saved from certain death by Vielh, at great risk to his own life. Misidentification extended to one Mlle Monsigny, the daughter of the veterans' commanding officer, who, believed to be Launay's daughter, was saved by Bonnemère in the nick of time from being run through by a pike and then burned alive (for this exploit Lafayette personally conferred on him a sword of honour). Misreading and misrecognition could also spin from near tragedy to pure farce: the Swiss Guard were twice taken for Bastille prisoners, once inside the Bastille itself and then later when, to thunderous applause, they were displayed in the Palais Royal.

These were but the accidents of perception and interpretation of a cognitively dishevelled scene. Cognitive mayhem was, however, further intensified by the pervading atmosphere of suspicion and mistrust, and not just where one would naturally expect to find it, between the opposing camps. Launay's alleged 'treachery' made him of course the villain of the piece (when he removed the cannon the crowd thought they were being reloaded), and the carnage in the outer courtyard was held, erroneously, to be the outcome of a dastardly deception, proof that Launay was the agent of a wider 'aristocratic plot'. For his part, Launay was quite capable of reciprocating. The officer of the Swiss Guard, Deflue (who wrote one of the more reliable eyewitness accounts), described Launay as both incompetent and paranoiac ('He was so terrified at night that he mistook the shadows of trees and other objects around him for enemies'); he was especially convinced that the Corny delegation was the setting of a 'trap'. But the most notable instances of potentially life-threatening misconstruction occurred within the camp of those notionally fighting for the same cause, above all in the relations between the besiegers and officials from the Hôtel de Ville. Flesselle's apparent mendacity made him, in the eyes of the besiegers, a sort of mirror image of Launay, and it is thus no surprise that they shared the same fate. But even those who sought to act in good faith fell under a cloud of suspicion: Thuriot's hauteur was misread as betrayal, while the efforts of Corny's deputation to persuade the crowd to pull back were interpreted as connivance with the prison authorities.

Happenstance, paranoia and random violence are thus central elements of the story of 14 July 1789 that the epic myth has tended to elide. Conservative historians, on the other hand, have emphasised them as the essential elements, the stuff of which the story is made. Yet out of the chaos and madness of the day something genuinely revolutionary was achieved. The following day the king accepted Liancourt's advice to go forthwith to the National Assembly to announce the withdrawal of his troops. The announcement was tantamount to a formal recognition of the powers of the new assembly. Two days later he came to Paris, where he was greeted by the new mayor, Bailly, and handed a tricolour cockade. Bailly welcomed him with the following words: 'Sire, I bring Your Majesty the keys of your good city of Paris. They are the very ones that were presented to Henri IV; he had reconquered his people, and here the people have reconquered their king.' This was not intended as a provocation, but it is difficult to imagine that the king could have heard Bailly's words as anything other than an explicit reminder that the grounds of sovereignty had shifted and that the days of absolutism were gone for ever. Mirabeau spoke of the collapse of an 'antique edifice'; it was not merely a building—the Bastille prison—that he had in mind.

By day's end the besiegers were already collectively entering legend as conquering heroes. Four days later, Maillot, a deputy at what by now had been renamed the Constituent Assembly, wrote to Desbroux that they were a group of men virtually without 'shoes and stockings' who in the space of forty-five minutes had seized the most powerful place in the kingdom. But who exactly were they? Some became household names overnight. Hulin and Elie were given entries in the *Petit Dictionnaire des Grands Hommes*, published in 1790. Joseph Arné, the carpenter who had enrolled in the *gardes françaises* and had been instrumental in handing over the captured Launay, acquired instant fame. On 15 July he was driven through Paris in a triumphal chariot. Along with others, he figured in dozens of popular ballads and broadsheets. He was also the principal character of the first play on the storming of the Bastille, staged in September 1789, *La fête du grenadier*. Arné was himself present at the première, and at the end of the performance, in a nice convergence of fiction and reality, he appeared on stage with the actor to standing ovations. The English press, as ever intent on discrediting the Revolution, put it about that he had entered the Bastille only to save a mistress.

Some went on to important roles in the later chapters of the

Revolution. Léonard Bourdon became president of the Jacobin Club and, along with Thuriot, was instrumental in engineering the downfall of Robespierre (he was the leader of the armed group sent to arrest Robespierre). Fréron, the ardent regicide and revolutionary activist, after having enforced the Terror in the provinces with particular brutality, also joined the anti-Robespierre camp. Maillard presided over the 'sort of tribunal' set up at the time of the September Massacres. Santerre made a buccaneeringly roguish career in the National Guard, turned a blind eye to the September Massacres, was central to the 10 August coup and was the militia officer who escorted Louis XVI to the guillotine. Parein Dumesnil became a committed republican and was implicated in the Babeuf conspiracy (though he was acquitted). Joseph Souberbielle, the surgeon, found himself on the jury at the trial of Marie Antoinette. Rossignol became one of Danton's right-hand men. The abbé Fauchet was arrested in 1793 (on 14 July!) as a Girondin, confessed his 'crimes' and was subsequently executed. Poupart de Beaubourg became an agent of the Girondins and of Lafayette, describing Jacobinism as a 'pestilential miasma', and is alleged to have invented a form of invisible ink for the purpose of secret communication.

Yet 14 July 1789 was not the day for those who were about to become or already were major players. Some of the latter showed up later, as tourists. The young deputy Robespierre arrived with other members of the National Assembly on a sightseeing expedition (it is said that he caught the future Madame Tussaud as she slipped on the stones), and conveyed his thoughts in a private letter: 'I could not tear myself away from the place; the sight of it produced such feelings of pleasure and ideas of liberty in all good citizens.' The man of the hour, Mirabeau, arrived in a carriage bedecked with flowers strewn by a mass of supporters lining the streets. Once inside, he demanded the grand tour, especially keen to visit the dungeons. He departed laden with the gift of books and papers mouldering in the cellars. One likes to think they may have included copies of Mably's *Des droits et des devoirs du citoyen*, issued in late 1788 after nearly thirty years gathering dust. Lamoignon, the keeper of the seals, fearful of its 'incendiary' reputation, ordered it seized and had 1,600 copies buried in the dungeons of the Bastille.

As for the individual whose hour had not yet come, during the night of the 16th a certain Captain d'Anton (as he then styled himself) of the Cordeliers district militia turned up with a particular objective in mind. Around 11 p.m. on the 14th, the marquis de la Salle had nominated the elector Prosper Soulès as temporary commander of the Bastille, in a vain attempt to keep some kind of order. Danton had other ideas about keeping order and dragged Soulès off to the Hôtel de Ville to have his papers verified. Lafayette had to intervene to clear the matter up (in Soulès' favour; Soulès provided a written account of this disagreeable experience, but was to undergo the even more disagreeable experience of perishing under the guillotine in 1794). Here was an early example in a minor key of Danton's understanding that the only way to occupy a power vacuum was by the exercise of brute force (the policy which underlay his most famous utterance: 'Dare. Always dare. And again, dare. In this way you will save France.').

These, however, were but walk-on parts, after the event. The overwhelming majority of the besiegers both emerged from and disappeared back into near-total obscurity. Our only source of information about most of them is their appearance in the official catalogue of the *Vainqueurs de la Bastille*. The baptism was not without controversy and much tasteless wrangling. It took the form of a list of names, or rather several lists, the variations reflecting the competitive and sometimes unscrupulous efforts to get on it. The title of *Vainqueur* was a coveted term of official recognition from the point of view of winners' history, a term with which to strike a claim to ownership of a great event. Initially there was some reluctance to be entered, less from modesty than from fear of reprisal on the part of those not yet sure they were on the winning side. But restraint did not last long, especially when it became clear that not just fame and glory but also material recompense were in the offing. Cousin Jacques (the pseudonym of the journalist Beffroy de Reigny) started a list but gave up in disgust when confronted with a number of claimants hugely in excess of the actual participants (in his *Testament* he denounced them as liars and intriguers).

There were three other lists. Maillard, who became secretary of the *Vainqueur* organisation, compiled his own and included 662 names. Dusaulx, the Paris elector, headed a committee of four (the others were de la Grey, Oudart and Bourdon de la Crosnière) charged with devising an official register. Its deliberations were conducted in open session. This created a space for deal-making, in which individuals and groups mutually conspired to attest the presence of one another. To help in processing the depositions, the committee enlisted the help of Bonnemère, Cholat, Elie, Goisset, Hulin, Maillard, d'Osmond, Rousselet, Thuriot and Tournay. The list quickly ran to 871 names, with many false claimants. Exasperated by the scale of dishonesty, the Hôtel de Ville referred the matter to the Constituent Assembly, which raised the tally to 954 (in part by virtue of inadvertently listing various candidates twice).

Yet despite all the wrangling, fraudulence and mutual recriminations, the lists remain a useful, if limited, source of information. This is especially true of Maillard's, which identified 634 persons by trade and address as well as by name, thus enabling at least a rudimentary sociological description of the besieging crowd. Based on these sources, an early twentieth-century study (compromised, however, by its thesis that the storming of the Bastille was basically a Freemasons' plot) discloses a mixture of social classes. There were some students, writers, radical clerics, a handful of middle-class rentiers and assorted foreigners. But by far the largest number consisted of working people: tradesmen, small workshop masters, journeymen artisans, day labourers and unemployed from the working-class faubourgs close to the Bastille. Many, especially carpenters and cabinetmakers, were of course from the faubourg Saint-Antoine. Yet its importance has been exaggerated, contributing to the forging of yet another legend—the so-called 'myth of the faubourg Saint-Antoine'. A leaflet of 21 July, *Les lauriers du faubourg Saint-Antoine*, stated that 'it is undisputed that the fatherland owes its salvation to the citizens of the faubourg Saint-Antoine' (Carlyle was to use the term as shorthand for an ur-version of the *sans-culottes*).

Most of the participants, however, hailed from the neighbouring, and poorer, districts: Petit-Saint-Antoine, Saint-Louis de la Culture, Saint-Paul and Les Enfants-Trouvés. Leaving the professional soldiers on one side (who were initially classified separately as *Volontaires de la Bastille*), they were cobblers, jewellers, gauze-workers, dyers, masons, nail-smiths, hatters, tailors, locksmiths, hairdressers and wigmakers, printers, braziers, upholsterers, potters and stove-makers. They include Etienne Georget, one of the first to use the cannon, and who was shot in the thigh; Toussaint Groslaire, wounded in arm and leg and who, while lying on the ground writhing in agony, is alleged to have declared to his wife that his injuries were 'nothing, my dear, what is my life worth compared to the salvation of 24 million?'; Louis Guignon, the tailor who brought the Bastille register to the Hôtel de Ville on the tip of a bayonet; Mercier, the wine merchant from Saint-Paul, who helped Elie remove the lighted wagons and sustained several wounds in crossing the plank to receive from the Swiss officer the terms of Launay's capitulation; Laurent Pelletier (or Peletier), about whom all that is recorded is that he was stricken with a hernia during the siege; Antoine-Charles Perrin, the journeyman carpenter, also wounded and whom Reigny described as 'a small man, of feeble health, but whose patriotism produced strength and vigour'; and Louis Tournay, the eighty-two-year-old who jumped from the adjoining roof into the Cour du Gouvernement and released the chains of the drawbridge. There was one woman, the laundress Marie Charpentier, who fought like a lion and was one of the twenty-five to get a pension for having been rendered lame from her wounds. Another source speaks of 'une forte jolie femme' trying to restrain her lover from joining the fray, but when he refused she quickly changed into men's clothes and fought alongside him. And how might the bliss in that dawn to be alive have seemed to what appears to have been the youngest of the participants, an eight-year-old boy, Lavallée, the *petit Gavroche* of the storming, who, according to the account he gave later to Guffroy, was one of the first to scale the towers?

Compared with the abundantly documented lives of the Revolution's big hitters, these are but crumbs from the historiographical table, scraps gleaned from a largely empty or depleted archive. Indeed in respect of most of the *Vainqueurs*, what we have is next to nothing. The following entry in the list is typical: 'Baron, *gazier*'—a surname, a trade (gas worker) and then a blank. This is of course both tantalising and frustrating for the historian in search of the past, but there is also something affecting about the archival silence inhabited by these shadow profiles. There is, moreover, a paradox here: in one crucial respect, we learn more from what we don't know about the historical significance of the *Vainqueurs* than from what we do know. For, while it is true that our relative ignorance is a reflection of limited records, it is also the case that the principal story to tell is not of individuals but of a genuinely collective action. It is the first major appearance on the historical stage of the Third Estate as the People.

The latter proved to be a fluid, often dangerously labile term, and was from the outset a subject of controversy. When Mirabeau argued that the elected members of the National Assembly should be designated 'representatives of the French people', it was objected by the lawyers that the word could be taken to mean either the *populus* (the people as a whole) or the *plebs* (the lower orders). This was not just hair-splitting jurists' talk. Not only at the level of ideology and discourse, but at that of deed and action, the Revolution was to a very large extent the (increasingly fraught) negotiation of these two meanings, one ecumenical and 'fraternal', the other more laden with connotations of class antagonism. In the heady atmosphere of 1789 it was by and large the first meaning that prevailed. Even Marat, before casting himself as the spokesman of the plebs, joined the ecumenical party when, in his *Offrande à la patrie* (written in February 1789), the Friend of the People described the People in the inclusive idiom of cross-class allegiances:

> The French Third Estate is composed of the class of servants, mechanics, labourers, craftsmen, shopkeepers, commercial agents, merchants, farmers, untitled landowners and stockholders, schoolmasters, artists, surgeons, physicians, men of letters, scholars, lawyers, magistrates of the lower courts, ministers of the altar, army and navy—a numberless, invincible legion containing within its breast both wisdom and talent, strength and virtue.

To some extent the actors of 14 July embodied this cross-section, but the bit of Marat's description that captures the essential social reality is its first part. This is why we know so little about them; they belong to that form of history 'from below' sometimes called *historia abscondita* (the history that is lost to us as forever veiled). In his account of the storming of the Bastille, Michelet consistently uses the impersonal pronoun *on*. In this context, it does not adequately translate as the English *one*, but is rather the grammatical sign of anonymous collective agency, with a strong connotation of heroically sustained purpose, a trope designed to move and exhort rather than an accurate historical observation designed to inform (the ideological counter-trope was Burke's 'swinish multitude' and the reference in *The Scarlet*

Pimpernel to 'the surging, seething, murmuring crowd ... human only in name'). But in an important sense Michelet got it right. Even when stripped of its intended meaning (the People as Hero), and restored to its evocation of the indeterminate, the pronoun does the requisite analytical work: the true dramatic persona of the historic day remains the *on*, which, however idealised and mythologised, lies in the record for the most part as stubbornly mute. On the other hand, beyond the silence of mass anonymity, there is also the rare and treasured voice of the individual eyewitness.

3

Humbert's Day

'Where were you on the day that JFK was shot? ... the Berlin Wall came down? ... the Twin Towers were hit?' is a popular dinner-table game, or the kind of question with which the inquisitive young invite the knowledgeable old to reminisce. How many times the children and grandchildren of those who stormed the Bastille prison on 14 July 1789, and lived to tell the tale, were so regaled has to be anybody's guess. Many of the insurgents survived into a ripe old age, and it is not at all difficult to imagine them recollecting their adventure at the centre of a hushed and awestruck family circle. This is also how Michelet imagined them. In the chapter on the Bastille episode in his *Histoire de la Révolution française* he attempts to resurrect the past (the moment of the storming itself) as if it were a living present, but also to project a future point of retrospect from which the original besiegers, now old ('vieillards'), speak of and to the meaning of their experience. Yet Michelet does not individualise his ageing *Vainqueurs de la Bastille* (or Heroes of the Bastille, as they came to be known); no one is named or quoted, we hear no personal voices. The imagined voice is once again entirely collective, a rhetorical device designed to carry a particular message: of all the major historical events the old men could have known in the space of their lifetimes, only 14 July 1789 'was the day of the whole people'. This distinction was also to become part of the

Un Vainqueur de la Bastille (colour litho), by Charles Thevenin.
A Conqueror of the Bastille.

ongoing myth of that day's famous events.

Let us make our own first port of call one of these individual voices. It belongs to Jean-Baptiste Humbert, though not as an old man reminiscing to the young, but as the author of a tiny footnote in the vast revolutionary archive, the eyewitness account of the insurrection he wrote sometime in the first half of August 1789, apparently at the request of the newly constituted Paris municipality: *Journée de Jean-Baptiste Humbert, horloger, Qui, le premier, a monté sur les Tours de la Bastille* (The day of Jean-Baptiste Humbert, watchmaker, who was the first to have mounted the Bastille towers). It falls into two parts: a brief prefatory declaration of identity and intention to an assumed readership addressed as 'Frenchmen, my compatriots', followed by the longer narrative account of the 'day' itself. Our knowledge of Humbert derives entirely from this document. In it he tells us that he was a native of Langres in the department of Haute-Marne, and that as of 1787 he was an artisan employed in Paris by the royal watchmaker, Belliard, in the rue du Hurepoix (the street which coincidentally housed the publisher and bookstore Gueffier, which printed the French translation of Thomas Paine's *Common Sense*). He also tells us that he spent some time as a journeyman apprentice in Geneva and was there at the time of the 1782 rebellion demanding equality of political rights and its suppression by the Genevan 'patrician' oligarchy with French military assistance. Beyond these autobiographical facts, we know nothing of his background, especially how and where he would have acquired the relevant literacy skills to compose his account.

Most of the eyewitness reports of 14 July were written by often highly educated journalists and municipal representatives. Humbert was not one of these. His account has a refreshing 'simplicity' in the best sense of the term, unclogged by the kinds of heavy-handed sententiousness that sometimes characterise the more official depositions. As a lens through which to view, in however fragmentary and incomplete a form, the manner in which 14 July 1789 unfolded, Humbert's text is of value for three things. First, it provides a narrative of some of the main events of the day, and crucially the turning point at which the invasion of the prison became a siege properly speaking, the consequence of which was the surrender by the governor, Bernard de Launay; secondly, as an 'insider's' view, it gives some sense of the lived texture of those events, largely as a whirlwind of chance and muddle; thirdly—and perhaps its most interesting feature—in telling us of Humbert's motives, thoughts and feelings as a participant, the document reveals the extent to which it is the reflection of a particular subjectivity caught up in the maelstrom of history.

Humbert's story starts on the streets of Paris, specifically in the district of Saint-André-des-Arts (in the Latin Quarter). It is 12 July 1789. Unbeknownst to everyone and planned by no one, the French Revolution is about to 'begin', with the occurrence two days later of what retrospectively came to be identified as the inaugural event: the storming of the Bastille. What is widely known (presumably by Humbert too) is that insurrection is in the air. Negotiations between the king, Louis XVI, and the newly formed National Assembly over political and fiscal reform have broken down. Louis's finance minister, the popular Necker, has been dismissed. Troops have been dispatched to encircle the city. In part to meet this perceived threat, the Paris authorities have instigated the creation of a citizens' militia to defend the people. This is the context in which Humbert's personal story accedes to the stage of history-in-the-making.

On 12 July he gets news of a clash in the Tuileries gardens between a crowd of demonstrators and a detachment of troops under the command of the prince de Lambesc, the first major indication of imminent uprising. But the lines of conflict have already been blurred. For there is also 'news that the armed populace was attacking the Bourgeois instead of defending them', the term 'Bourgeois' here referring to the hastily constituted civilian militia (it was sometimes called the *milice bourgeoise*). Confusion and contradiction, against a background of mounting fear and violence, thus mark the point of Humbert's entry into the sequence of events that will lead to the storming of the Bastille. He appears to have offered his services to the Saint-André-des-Arts unit of the militia and to have spent most of his time on patrol from Monday 13 July throughout the day and the night into 14 July.

In discharging these civic duties, however, all he and his fellow militia have are 'swords', the 'District having no firearms or only a few'. On the morning of the 14th, 'overcome with weariness and lack of food and sleep', Humbert makes his way, with thousands of others, to the Invalides (the retirement home for aged and disabled veterans), 'where arms for the various Districts were being distributed' (in actual fact less a distribution than a seizure). Humbert arrives at the Invalides at around 2 p.m. All is sheer chaos. On the steps leading down to the cellars, where the weapons are stored, the press of bodies is such that some are crushed, many faint and even more are 'shrieking and gasping for breath'. Humbert is caught twice in the press, falling back down into the cellar, but is 'only shaken and not injured by the fall'. He grabs two muskets, gives one away, and together with a number of other armed citizens manages to impose some sort of crowd control. If, as is indeed the case, a revolution is about to erupt, the ingredients of the revolutionary mix are little short of a mess. The acquired muskets are, however, useless without ammunition and so, in search of powder and shot, Humbert begins stage two of his revolutionary odyssey. This takes him first to the Hôtel de Ville, where he is given 'a quarter pound of powder but no shot, saying they had none' ('they' probably Jacques de Flesselles, the *prévôt des marchands*, in charge of munitions at the city hall, and who was to pay with his life on the night of the 14th for his alleged mendacity over the question of arms). As he leaves the Hôtel de Ville, Humbert learns of another development ('I heard someone say that the Bastille was being besieged'). This is to become his principal destination, but not before a number of Parisian detours hunting for the elusive and desperately needed ammunition. He has a bright idea. Why not buy some nails from an ironmonger ('which I got from the grocer's at the Coin du Roi at the place de Grève') and use these as makeshift shot? On exiting from the grocer's shop, he is 'accosted by a Citizen' who informs him that shot is in fact being handed out at the Hôtel de Ville (a desperate attempt by the municipal authorities to control the circulation of weapons). Humbert retraces his steps, is supplied with 'half a dozen pellets of buckshot' and sets off for the Bastille. En route he passes the Hôtel de la Régie (the excise office), from which several cases of bullets had been raided. Humbert is given enough to fill a coat pocket. Still further detours and adventures await him on his way to the Bastille, one of which we shall return to in another connection.

It is thus quite late by the time Humbert arrives at the prison (around 3.30 p.m.). Much has of course already taken place; there are already many dead and wounded. But his arrival, and hence his story, coincides more or less with the arrival of both professional soldiers (defectors from the contingents of royal troops) and military hardware (cannon), led by Hulin and Elie (both of whom were to become adulated heroes of the siege). It was this development that broke Launay's will and secured a capitulation. Humbert is no mere bystander or observer at this decisive moment. He helps to wheel the cannon into position and on the approach to the drawbridge which leads to the inner citadel he finds himself 'in the front rank'. Stepping over two dead bodies, under a barrage of gunfire, he advances to the drawbridge, while the cannon is trained on the entrance to the inner courtyard. He assists with the laying of a plank across the moat, when a piece of paper with Launay's terms is passed through a gap in the entrance. One man crossing the plank to take the paper is hit by a bullet and, mortally wounded, falls into the moat. Launay's terms are rejected. The cannon is about to fire when the entrance gate is opened. The besiegers pour in, Humbert ahead of the pack, and he climbs—allegedly the first to do so—the steps of one of the prison towers, where he finds and disarms one of the contingent of Swiss Guards assigned to Launay to defend the Bastille (much of the royal army was made up of foreign mercenaries). Still on the tower, Humbert is trying to disable one of the enemy cannon when he receives a bullet in the neck, collapses senseless and is saved only by the ministrations of the Swiss Guard he has taken into custody. This is to produce a further, unexpected and ironically near-disastrous turn of events (to which we shall revert shortly), but in terms of the main drama, Humbert's narrative and the history it reflects—the storming of the Bastille—are effectively over. Humbert has his wounds treated, sets off for home under armed guard (not without further mishap, which results in his taking refuge in the home of an acquaintance), rests up until midnight and then, ever indefatigable, rises from his sickbed to report to the commanding officer of the Saint-André-des-Arts militia for further duties ('under whose orders I remained until the following morning').

For Humbert himself, the main point of his summary was its veracity, the form of that insistence of interest in its own right. But this is scarcely its main point for us. Stripped of its multiple contingencies, Humbert's story can indeed serve as a matrix, encapsulating some of the key reference points which the historian, looking back, uses to shape an intelligible narrative: the atmosphere of collective fear, the self-arming of the citizenry, the formation of the militia, the search for weapons in different parts of the city, the critical moment at which the Bastille fell. But to strip it in this way is to rob the tale of a great deal, above all its immediacy and subjective resonance, the feel it gives us of what it was like on the ground, in all its chaotic unpredictability. The disorder at the Invalides, the uncertainty on 12 July over who is attacking whom, who is friend and who is enemy, are already signs that here is an unfolding situation that, for those experiencing it, is in many ways the obverse of the readily intelligible.

And there is more, much more. Humbert is determined to enrol in the militia, but is unsure which district he belongs to (Saint-André-des-Arts is merely a guess, probably because the militia is in the process of being constituted, such that no one quite knows how it is being organised). Furthermore, on his journey across Paris to the Bastille, like a prototype of the good soldier Schweik, he is caught up in a fast-moving flow of random encounters and bizarre incidents. Perhaps the most startlingly unexpected is what happens at the Hôtel de la Régie. After retrieving the bullets, Humbert hears 'a woman calling for help'. He approaches and is informed that someone is setting fire to the saltpetre store, the motive unknown. In he goes, to find what appears to be a demented wigmaker 'holding a lighted torch in each hand, with which he was in fact setting fire to the place'. Humbert, with no time to enquire why a wigmaker might want to blow up a stock of saltpetre, knocks him over with the butt of his rifle, extinguishes the fire and, before continuing on his way, is asked to deal with another incident: to 'drive out certain ill-intentioned people who had forced their way in and broken into the documents room'.

But the high point of the genre of happenstance and pandemonium is what happens once inside the Bastille and after leaving it. The Swiss Guard who helps Humbert to his feet after he has been shot in the neck is mistaken by the crowd as the perpetrator of Humbert's wound ('seeing me covered in blood, they assumed that the Swiss must have wounded me, and tried to kill him'). Only after words of explanation is the Swiss spared. But there is to be a further twist in this saga of menace based on misapprehension, this time in respect of Humbert himself. On seeing him return home under armed escort after his wound has been treated, the crowd assumes that he has been taken captive and prepares to administer summary revolutionary justice ('we were followed by a crowd of people who mistook me for a malefactor, and twice attempted to put me to death'). Only with the intervention of a bookseller who recognises him and takes him to safety is the danger averted. In fact, cases of mistaken identity and misinterpreted actions were par for the course on 14 July, of a kind that blurs the historical canvas and confounds the historian's characteristic wish for a 'cleanly' delineated narrative.

Finally, there is the question of what impelled Humbert to take part, what he felt, desired, imagined and, relatedly, what it meant for him to write his account a few weeks later. The striking feature is a certain sharpness of political consciousness. All the buzzwords are there: liberty, patriots, citizens, etc. We are in no position to determine independently whether these are load-bearing terms, in the sense of reflecting what actually went through Humbert's mind at the time of joining the insurrection, or alternatively, whether they are afterthoughts expressed in a language instantly and massively put into circulation in the interval between 14 July and the moment of writing in early August. Take, for example, Humbert's reference to his time in Geneva ('where I was working as a journeyman when that Republic lost its liberty'). This already weaves together autobiography and political history. In addition, speaking as someone who has already seen an uprising and has a view on what it meant, Humbert makes a specific allusion to the Genevan episode that has some direct bearing on 14 July and its immediate aftermath:

> I witnessed the dismay of the townspeople, and I heard the curses they uttered against a certain Minister of France, who, they said, had deceived my King; I heard so many sighs, complaints and regrets, that for a long time I bore in my heart something of the same feeling towards that Minister as the unfortunate people of Geneva.

The minister is almost certainly Charles Gravier de Vergennes, in charge of foreign affairs under Louis XVI, who had endorsed

France's support of the American Revolution, not from radical sympathies but because he judged it to be in the national interest, exactly the consideration which governed his support for French involvement in counter-revolutionary measures in Geneva. Humbert's distinction between a deceived king and a manipulative minister raises the question as to whether his were the already formed views of a politically self-conscious individual, such that they go a long way in explaining his motives for participating in the events of 14 July; or were they picked up immediately afterwards as post-facto rationalisations. For, in connection with the events leading up to the fall of the Bastille, the theme of the good king led astray by his ministerial entourage was a commonplace of many of the other eyewitness accounts, and conforms with the political settlement that the leaders wanted, a settlement in the form of a constitutional monarchy, which they believed had been amicably achieved on 15 July, when the king went before the National Assembly, and on 17 July, when he presented himself to the Paris municipality and the National Guard. In other words, was the implied analogy between Geneva 1782 and France 1789 already part of Humbert's world view, inspiring his sense of what, on the day itself, 14 July was fundamentally about? Or did it come to him only later, when, as he sat down to write in the following weeks, the belief in an innocent and well-meaning monarch was already the new orthodoxy, a belief encouraged by those in charge of the propaganda machine and given wide publicity in press and pamphlet? In his account, is he expressing long-held convictions or subsequently acquired ones, even perhaps merely repeating what he knows others would like to hear?

There is no way this question of before or after can be satisfactorily resolved, since we have no further sources of information about Humbert on which to draw. Yet everything about the tone of his report suggests someone whose attitudes and beliefs were formed well before the patriotic slogans were to be found on everybody's lips, and they may well have been forged in his Genevan experience. Here is a man who volunteers spontaneously for the militia, who positively seeks it out while uncertain as to which unit he belongs to. Even more telling is his behaviour throughout the day of 14 July. He is running from pillar to post, and at every single point of his itinerary he responds to calls for or actively offers help. At the Invalides he gives away one of the two guns he has seized. He assists with bringing out the victims of the crush on the cellar steps. On his way to the Bastille he encounters four soldiers of the watch and shares his ammunition with them. At the Hôtel de la Régie he stuffs his pocket with bullets 'to give to anyone who was short'. He answers the woman's call for help in connection with the saltpetre episode. He acts when the 'household staff came to beg me to help them' with the 'ill-intentioned people' who had burst into the documents room. Once inside the Bastille, 'I rushed over to the staircase to help the citizens, whom I assumed to have been driven back'. He helps to save the Swiss Guard from otherwise certain death.

The word 'help' appears on virtually every page, but nowhere is it ostentatiously paraded as illustrating the virtues of the revolutionary Patriot. On each occasion, it is merely noted, as if in passing, as just one detail among others registered as he bumps into whatever and whomever happen to cross his path. The low-key manner makes it tempting to read this as merely expressing the common decencies of the ordinary man. But there is just too much of this sort of thing to sustain that banal interpretation. It's as if a code of civic duty has been fully internalised, as the living demonstration of a consciously assumed ethic of solidarity in the midst of a political crisis; in its understated way, it is tantamount to being the declaration of a creed, close in spirit to what the eighteenth-century political thinkers had defined as the republic of virtue.

There is also the question of what for Humbert were the purpose and meaning of writing down his account. At one level he seems to be in the world evoked by Michelet or the world of where-were-you-on-the-day-that … He tells us how happy he is 'to have given some pleasure to my relatives by the story of my actions'. But he also adds: 'I do not want the town of Langres to give any credence to the information given by my relatives until I have the signatures of all those whom I have mentioned in my statement.' These are the signatures of the 'gentlemen of the Hôtel de Ville'. It amounts to something of an obsession; he wants not just some but all the signatures of those who can attest the truthfulness of his account ('They were witnesses to everything that I have alleged, and so I need the signatures of all these witnesses'). And so it is that the published text carries a postscript signed by some of the other insurgents: Ducastel, Maillard, Richard, Dupin and Georget. There may have been an element of self-interest in this demand, confirmation of Humbert's claim that he was the 'first' to scale the Bastille towers (many other witnesses were to have recourse to the same tactic, often to secure a false claim to fame). But what is clear is that Humbert was offering not just personal reminiscences for a limited family circle ('relatives'), but a record for posterity. He is anxious for private recollections to become, through validation by others, authenticated public testimony. In the later course of the Revolution a quite different politics of testimony was to emerge. With the onset of the Terror, the revolutionary surveillance committees had a standard question for 'suspects', in its general form not entirely dissimilar to the notorious question asked by the Bastille authorities (the euphemistic word for an interrogation often accompanied by torture): *Où étais-tu le 14 juillet?* ('Where were you on 14 July?') In this context, 'memory' was subordinate to ruse, since the answer given could be a matter of life and death, with independent verification often crucial to whether or not the suspect was believed.

Humbert of course could not have had anything like this in mind. The 'days' of the great *sans-culotte* insurrections were some years off. But one thing that his text has in common with that later discourse is lexical: the main term of his title, *Journée de Jean-Baptiste Humbert*. It is almost certain that Humbert intended the word *journée* in the sense in which it is normally understood: a 'day', specifically his day, a day-in-the-life-of, albeit of an unusually charged kind. But it was not long before it came to acquire a new meaning for the revolutionary actors themselves, one that was retrospectively applied to the events of 14 July. While we should therefore beware of anachronism, it is nevertheless hard to resist hearing in Humbert's invocation of his 'day' something of that meaning to come, as one of the framing contexts for understanding the events of July 14 themselves.

4

THE REVOLUTIONARY *JOURNÉE*

The weather, if not always propitious to the French Revolution itself, has often been a godsend to its many romancers and fabulators. On the first anniversary of the taking of the Bastille, the grandly organised spectacle on the Champ de Mars (the *Fête de la Fédération*) was washed out by torrential rain—an incontrovertible sign to those of pessimistic and ironic dispositions that the Revolution was all a terrible mistake. On the second anniversary, however, the weather was glorious, suggesting to those of sunnier temperaments that, despite the political evidence to the contrary, all was for the best in the best of all possible worlds. For the *Fête de l'Etre Suprême* in 1794, the rhyming of Robespierre's famously immaculate sky-blue coat with the cerulean aspect of the heavens seemed like a godsend expressly dispatched by the Supreme Being himself, prompting one of Robespierre's less felicitous equations of benign nature and revolutionary politics: 'Nature, how sublime, how delightful thy power! How the tyrants must turn pale at the thought of this Festival!' (They were more likely to turn pale at the thought of the guillotine, which for the duration of the festival had been discreetly moved from view to—of all places—the site of the now demolished Bastille.)

But by far the most telling alignment of weather and history comes on the day subsequently dedicated by the French state to commemoration in perpetuity, the day of the actual taking of the

Bastille: 14 July 1789. At daybreak, according to Michelet, the sky was 'luminous'. By late morning, as armed crowds swarmed through the streets of the capital, black clouds gathered, threatening a violent summer storm. By late afternoon the city found itself bathed in warm and mellow sunshine; in the course of a few hours, a massive turbulence had been followed by sweetness and light. To the great poet-historians of the Revolution these were irresistible coincidences, as if the physical atmosphere had spontaneously moulded itself to its political counterpart. The equations were, however, flexible, depending on ideological preferences. Carlyle's late-afternoon sunshine has a distinctly bloodshot garishness to it, held to illuminate 'one general wreck of madness', while by 22 July, with all apparently settled and reconciled, 'there is halcyon weather; weather even of preternatural brightness; the hurricane being overblown'.

Days of this world-historical calibre are rare and it is thus unsurprising that writers invest them with all manner of inflated literary currency. The customary historical units for this kind of treatment are the century and the millennium, most notably attracting the convenient shaping fictions of beginning and ending, with a strong emphasis on the latter, the end as the arrival of end-time. But, if these are the standard units, there are others, including the decade, the year and the day (and, on occasion, the night: *Kristallnacht*). The day is something we more typically associate with the rhythms of everyday life, as the measure of humdrum personal time. Days are quite simply, as Philip Larkin's poem has it, 'where we live'. They go largely unnoticed, apart from certain ritual punctuations of the continuum marked by important occasions in the skein of private and family life (birthdays, for example). These are the moments when the routines of the day are interrupted in favour of a Day, a special object of commemoration, celebratory in the matter of birth, doleful in the remembrance of a death.

This translation is not, however, unique to private life. In certain circumstances, the day can become a Day that possesses high public significance. The latter comes in all shapes and sizes. There is the singular day and the cluster of days (the *Ten Days That Shook the World*, *les Trois Glorieuses*). Streets have been named after some of them (the rue du Quatre-Septembre). Some mark customs of national life (the Queen's Birthday). Some are reminders of catastrophic events: Holocaust Day; or 9/11, a number at once singular (a precise date in September 2001) and abstract, its indeterminate reference as pure number nevertheless laden with sorrowful meaning. Some have proved movable (the Ivory Coast became fully independent on 7 August 1960, but Independence Day has since moved to 7 December). Some are simply perverse: Anzac Day in Australia celebrates a military defeat, the irony of which is caught by an Australian acquaintance of mine who every year phones the Turkish Embassy to congratulate them on a victory. And then there is the kind represented by Bastille Day.

To belong to this kind, several conditions need to be satisfied. First, the commemorating Day has to occur on the same date as the commemorated event; fixity appears to be an index of seriousness, whereas mobility seems to grant priority to convenience over solemnity. Secondly, its remembrance must be institutionalised, part of the official fabric of public life, or staging of what the French call a *lieu de mémoire*. Thirdly, it must possess a certain durability, sustained by a consensus of sorts, even when eventually frayed at the edges or subjected to forms of amnesia or indifference. Fourthly—and most importantly—it has to mark a certain kind of event: namely, what is held to be a founding moment, an experience of historical rupture that is perceived as an absolute beginning. Its commanding tropes are 'Dawn', 'Birth' and 'Resurrection'. This condition necessarily excludes days of catastrophe remembrance, conducted as lamentation or in silence, by definition not days of public celebration.

The *journée* was not merely a sum of time. Nor was it just a significant date, of which, in the French Revolution, there are so many as to be almost too numerous to mention. For the year 1789 alone, claimants in this category for the prize of the most significant would include 5 May (the meeting of the Estates-General), 20 June (the Tennis Court Oath), 4 August (the official end to 'feudal' privilege) and 26 August (the Declaration of the Rights of Man and the Citizen). Indeed, if it were simply a matter of dates, the key example would have be the ground-clearing reinvention of dates itself, the Republican calendar promulgated by decree of the National Convention in November 1793 to replace the Gregorian calendar and which, as a political artefact, backdated the new order of time whereby 22 September 1792 notionally became Day 1 of Year 1. In fact, 21 September was the date on which the monarchy officially ended, and—if somewhat squeamishly (the term was smuggled into a revised declaration published the following day)—the Republic came into being on 22 September. If a given point is to serve as foundational, the marker of a new 'beginning', this has to be it. But a calendrical date is not at all the same thing as a revolutionary *journée*. For a day to be classified as a *journée*, it was not enough for it to be deemed historically momentous; it had to involve degrees of unrest, turbulence, menace and, generally if not always, riot and repression; crucially, it had to involve the actions of the common people. The women's march on Versailles in October 1789, the Champ de Mars Massacre of 17 July 1791, the invasions of the Tuileries palace on 20 June and 10 August 1792, the September Massacres of 1792, the siege of the Convention on 2 June 1793, the *sans-culotte* insurgencies of 1–2 April and 20–23 May 1795—these are some of the more memorable *journées* which have taken up permanent residence in the history books.

But, in a field crowded with rivals, it is 14 July 1789 which remains the most memorable of them all, as the only one that has survived in the wider consciousness and the only one to receive the imprimatur of a national festival and a public holiday. If in the Republican calendar 22 September 1792 is the beginning of Year 1 of the Republic, 14 July 1789 is the beginning of what was to be called Year 1 of Liberty. It has, however, acquired this status at the cost of a certain process of 'forgetting' what the day was fundamentally about. For us it is very difficult to access the thoughts, motives and emotions of those who took part in the storming of the Bastille. Even those who in the immediate aftermath committed their own version of events to print are not necessarily reliable guides to what actually went through their minds on the day itself. The storming was not on the whole a collectively focused or cogently led enterprise. But neither was it random 'mob' violence, the anarchic behaviour of the 'swinish multitude', in Edmund Burke's trope subsequently much favoured by right-wing historians. However inarticulate and inchoate, there was a real sense of purpose, albeit reactive rather than proactive.

The call to arms was not to overthrow the state (a ludicrous ambition), but a call to self-defence. It is true that by day's end on the 14th there was already talk of having toppled a symbol of 'despotism' (success breeds its own meanings), but at the beginning of the day the main concerns had less to do with symbolism than with practicality. The crowd that swept across Paris from the place de Grève, the faubourg Saint-Antoine and the Invalides to the Bastille had no plan to destroy a physical structure (the Bastille was, if not impregnable, indestructible), nor was it propelled by a desire to 'liberate' the prison's inmates (such as they were, seven in all, including two madmen and four forgers). It rallied to the cry *à la Bastille!* as a gigantic raiding party intent on seizing an eminently useful commodity: gunpowder (large amounts of which had been removed to the Bastille for safekeeping). For over two weeks the city had been ringed by an estimated 25,000 royal troops. We do not know whether this was on the direct orders of Louis XVI or stipulated by his ministers. Nor do we know what the precise motive was: whether as a policing operation to maintain public order, a gesture of intimidation or a prelude to an actual military repression (most of the evidence suggests the strategy was defensive rather than offensive). Nevertheless, it was seen by the people of Paris as a real threat to both itself and the National Assembly in Versailles. The eruption took place less from anger at unacknowledged grievances and unsatisfied demands than from fear of assault.

It was, however, also a *journée*—this is what makes it authentically revolutionary—in the sense that its violence addressed or precipitated a crisis of authority around the question: who rules France? The question was provisionally resolved the following day. On the 15th the king went in person to the fledgling National Assembly to concede a shift of sovereignty from absolutism to the 'nation', the National Assembly itself converting to a Constituent Assembly charged with the task of designing a constitution binding on all, and in theory based on the promulgation in late August of the Declaration of the Rights of Man and the Citizen. But if 15 July is about the formal delivery of outcomes (the promise of a new constitutional dispensation and a new form of political legitimacy), 14 July has nothing to do with either the constitutional or the legitimate. On the 14th the question 'who rules?' received the answer: on this day no one rules, or the 'people' rules, and it does so not through some representative institution safeguarding and in turn safeguarded by a set of laws, but from the streets. It is a *journée* by virtue of being a day on which legal authority ceased to exist as a practical proposition.

Article 11 of the Declaration included the right of 'resistance to oppression'. The inclusion was intended in part as the retroactive conferral of legal sanction by the Assembly on the uprising of 14 July. But in respect of the 14th itself, the National Assembly was a non-player. It sat in Versailles wringing its hands, debating this and that, sending out deputations and delegations, but was essentially powerless to act (the lines of communication with Paris were broken on the 13th as a consequence of the Sèvres and Saint-Cloud bridges having been placed under military guard). The king of course had the army. Yet, despite some skirmishes, the royal troops encircling the city were not ordered to attack. In fact it can be argued that the real meaning of the fall of the Bastille was not the capitulation of the prison, but that the army was not used to prevent it. In the event, their commander, Besenval, ordered a pullback to the Champ de Mars, probably because he had not received any clear orders, but also perhaps because the evidence of desertion to the side of the insurgents convinced him that, while enjoying overwhelmingly superior numbers, he could not guarantee their loyalty to the Crown. But whatever the reasons, the retreat was effectively to forfeit what some have seen as the very definition of the state: monopoly over the legitimate use of violence.

Finally, there was also the improvised municipal body that was to base itself permanently in the Hôtel de Ville and to take the name of the Paris Commune. Its members—drawn from the Parisian Electors to the Estates-General—understood immediately the importance of force, creating in great haste the civilian militia later baptised as the National Guard under the command of Lafayette. One of its purposes was to organise resistance to the king's troops in the event of an attack. But another—as Humbert's report suggests—was to control the rioters and maintain public order in the face of incipient 'anarchy', a particular source of concern (shared by a large section of the civil population) being the number of vagabonds, convicts (liberated from other prisons) and further uncontrollable 'elements' in circulation on the streets. The bulk of the militia did not see it this way and sided with the 'people'. In the meantime, the Electors tried to assert whatever authority they had assumed by acting as an intermediary body that would negotiate a peaceful solution with Launay, the governor of the Bastille. All their initiatives failed. Indeed, the Hôtel de Ville itself was seriously menaced by the crowd in the immediate aftermath of the fall of the Bastille, on suspicion of harbouring 'traitors' (one of the members of its permanent committee, Jacques de Flesselles, was dragged from the building and shot).

In short, on three fronts—monarchy, assembly, municipality—constituted and self-constituting authority was broken, relinquished or simply non-existent. In this respect 14 July remains the exemplary *journée* by virtue of being the first in a series which laid bare a power vacuum, the attempted occupancy of which defines the 'logic' of the Revolution as a whole. No one grasped this logic more clearly, and more chillingly, than Robespierre. His principal argument concerned the relation between ends and means, based on the view that the Revolution was a transitional zone, a passage from a corrupt political order to the virtuous republic. The transition entailed the separation of 'justice' from law. Since present laws are merely entrenched injustice, the creation of the just society necessarily involves bypassing them. On the overthrow of the monarchy on 10 August 1792 he observed: 'The Revolution is illegal: the fall of the Bastille and of the monarchy were illegal, as illegal as liberty itself.' At the trial of Louis XVI he stated that 'a deposed king in the midst of a revolution as yet unsupported by just laws' cannot enjoy the customary protections of due process, adding that 'a people does not judge as a court of law'. This was a constant of Robespierre's thought, and it can be detected as early as the events surrounding the fall of the Bastille. The lynching of Foulon, the king's minister, in the days following elicited the comment: 'M. Foulon was hanged yesterday by the people's decree.'

Whatever Robespierre's opinions (and our opinion of those opinions), the fact remains that his analysis was unerringly accurate, one moreover shared by figures on the right, although from a very different political perspective (Thomas Carlyle represented Foulon's death as the exercise of 'wild justice'). The French Revolution, especially on its great *journées*, was fundamentally about the suspension of legality, the pressing of a cause by violent means, and the attempted annexation of an 'empty' space of power from which nearly all traditional sources of legitimacy had drained away. For better or for worse, this is what revolutions are. And if, because of his own willingness to go to the limit in the bloodstained chapter of the Terror, we find Robespierre's pitilessly lucid account too inhumanly cold, we can always turn to the more gentlemanly tones of the king's adviser, the duc de Liancourt, whispering into Louis's ear during the night of 14 July: 'No Sire, this is not a rebellion, it is a revolution.' Liancourt was also to state that it is 'very difficult to enter the domain of true liberty through such a door'. Robespierre thought otherwise, and came to grief. In a very different political idiom, Lafayette also thought it was possible, and to do so in such a way that the Revolution could be rendered 'legal'. His own recipe for this reconciled state of affairs came out of the events of 14 July: a monarchy both constrained by a constitution and secured by a monopoly on the use of violence vested in a National Guard commanded by himself. Many of the participants in the storming of the Bastille shared that belief. But in this Lafayette was also to prove hopelessly detached from reality, as the Revolution ran its course in ways he either failed to predict or deeply feared.

Eric Hobsbawm has written in *The Age of Revolution* that 'the capture of the Bastille' has 'rightly made 14 July into the French national day'. Among historians he is part of a large company that, notwithstanding variations of method, style and emphasis, runs from Michelet's *Histoire de la Révolution française* down through the nineteenth century to the present. On the other hand, by no means do all the historians of the French Revolution share this view. Many would take issue with the self-assurance of the adverb 'rightly', from a set of historiographical and political alignments closer in spirit to the conservative tradition opened by Burke's *Reflections on the Revolution in France* (among the French historians of today, Pierre Chaunu is the most vitriolic partisan of this school of thought, for whom even the revolutionary abolition of the Church tithe was an abomination). The question has always been what 14 July 1789 is to be remembered for, and the answers given have always reflected different interests, preferences and agendas. 'Memory', in this context, has always been less about remembering a past than about interpreting its 'legacy'. To some extent this reflects sheer manipulation, and to some extent the benefits of hindsight history, the knowledge of eventual outcomes unavailable to the actors themselves. What is certainly clear is that on the day itself, whatever objectives and aspirations were invested in the storming of France's most notorious prison, few, if any, had the faintest idea exactly what was happening and what, consequentially, was about to unfold. It became a great day only in retrospect, albeit immediate retrospect: namely, as from 15 July, when the king went to the self-declared National Assembly to formally acknowledge its authority. From there the day proceeded to become a self-conscious Day, starting in the quick of revolutionary events themselves, with the first *Fête de la Fédération* on 14 July 1790, and culminating in the creation in 1880 of Bastille Day.

The hallowed place 14 July was to acquire in the annals of national memory was intended to be a place beyond controversy. Its theme was to be the unity of the People and the Republic, one and indivisible. But unlike 4 July, which, while subject to varying interpretations, has not been as such deeply controversial among Americans (few would see it as anything other than positive), the official versions of 14 July have masked profound disunities built into the remembering process itself, along with fierce disputes over not just its meaning but also its *value*. To take but two very well-known examples from the field of nineteenth-century historiography: for Michelet it was a glorious moment in the emancipation of the People, while for Taine it was but a spectacle of wanton destruction by the rabble (an 'excited and wild animal') and its subsequent remembrance a 'festival of murder'. Behind the public mask, division has always been there, from the beginning through to the Bicentennial, as faction and party, ideology and politics have scrambled to take 'ownership' of memory and adapt it to a present set of priorities.

There are many reasons why this is as it should be, not least that it exemplifies one of the things 14 July is supposed to stand for: a certain 'democratic' liveliness of debate, along with a rich array of registers—epic, tragic, ironic—for its depiction. Yet it has also proved to be something of an embarrassment for the official mythology. From this point of view, 14 July is supposed to stand, not for difference and division, but for national unanimity around the shared ideals of liberty, equality and fraternity. This has required the manufacture and projection of a consensus built in large part on the elision of what has made 14 July controversial: namely, the fact that it was a revolutionary *journée*. What on the historical ground was a massive disturbance of the peace must not be allowed to enter disruptively into the agreeably peaceful space of commemoration (not least for the reason that, if this were permitted, it might encourage further real disturbances of the peace). It thus becomes a matter of remembering the Revolution by forgetting what made it a revolution, burying the question Robespierre put with devastating clarity: 'Citizens, do you want a revolution without a revolution?' Whence the paradox of 14 July 1789 being consistently billed as a world-historical event while the very thing that made it, or its consequences, world-historical is equally consistently repressed.

To some extent, this is understandable. Presumably only a Robespierrist or the modern political equivalent could affectionately commend 14 July in terms of its being the day the 'people's decree' prevailed in the form of lynchings and decapitations. Certainly no sane person would want to follow through with Robespierre's logic to celebrating the Law of Suspects (forerunner of the show trial) and the reign of the guillotine. If there is any dignified form for representing this, it would have to be the idiom of tragedy, not epic (and perhaps only a Shakespeare could manage the Jacobin Terror). Nevertheless, Robespierre's characterisation of 14 July coincides very much with what 14 July was. One may or may not like this, but frankly neither affection nor hostility has much to do with it. It is not or should not be the task of the historian either to sentimentalise or to moralise history, and, whatever one's politics, it is a matter of plain historical record that violence was at the centre of the events of 14 July; it is what made the day a *journée*. If memory is to be not just another legitimation (or delegitimation) narrative, it has to be true to what is being remembered, however variously interpreted. Collective memory is not much good at this; it tends to turn its face away from what it would rather not see. In other words, collective memory can be many things, including a contradiction in terms.

On the other hand, as a cultural force it has done its work with considerable success. But alongside the operations of that commemorative machine, there has also been another force in play from the moment Bastille Day was declared a public holiday. This is the form in which, for the wider population, the festival has on the whole survived. In modern times the celebration of 14 July as a popular uprising has been largely confined, and even there but sporadically, to the politically militant districts of working-class Paris and other cities. Otherwise, *le quatorze* today retains little felt connection with 14 July 1789. In its official guises it is pure display—a military defile, a presidential broadcast followed by a garden party in the grounds of the Elysée palace. Meanwhile, the general public to which the president's speech is notionally pitched, takes a break. The village streets of France are bedecked with tricolour flags and pennants, but it is extremely unlikely that the exploits of the *Vainqueurs de la Bastille* are uppermost in anyone's mind.

At this level, the contemporary social reality of 14 July is close in spirit and practice to 4 July, both now simply a day of leisure for the majority of the working population. This has in no way damaged the remarkable elasticity of the political claims that can be made on either. President Bush, scrabbling around for bits and pieces to justify a democracy-exporting foreign policy, identified 4 July as 'the birth of democracy'. President Chirac, in his doomed attempt to persuade the French people to vote for the European Constitution, claimed the latter to be in direct descent from 1789. It is, however, doubtful that either ploy resonated deeply in the public imagination. In reality 4 July for Americans and 14 July for the French have become essentially a day off work, much prized if it happens to facilitate a long weekend. The politics of memory have migrated elsewhere: when Zhou Enlai said of the impact of the French Revolution that it was too early to tell what it has been, he was absolutely right, but he might well have been dumbfounded to see the truth of his observation verified in his own backyard. Who would have predicted the citing of 14 July 1789 by the protesting students on Tiananmen Square?

These domestic etiolations, the loss of original meanings even as origins are celebrated, are dispiriting but probably inevitable. Of the original day, Thomas Carlyle wrote that 'to describe this Siege of the Bastille (thought to be one of the most important in History) perhaps transcends the talent of mortals'. Happily, Carlyle did not inflict on himself the self-defeating position of taking literally his own words on the unavailability of words. The closest his fiery prose came to extinction was in the famous episode of the first draft of *The French Revolution* being consumed in the flames of John Stuart Mill's domestic hearth as the consequence of Mill's maidservant mistaking the manuscript for waste paper. Unfazed—he had no backup copy—Carlyle sat down and wrote it again from memory. Carlyle was far closer to the events he wrote about, and, whatever one makes of his often hysterical politics, endowed with incomparable literary gifts.

As a storyteller, only Dickens, in *The Tale of Two Cities*, could hope to emulate him. Nevertheless, the place of 14 July 1789 in the historical record remains unique, and uniquely challenging to the powers of the historian (other than those who have had a vested interest in anaesthetising its significance). By contrast the Day, as something repeated from 1880 over a period of 125 years, no longer possesses anything like the same degree of glamour. Initially a spontaneously joyous as well as a politically engineered collective occasion, Bastille Day has, over time, come to look an altogether shoddier affair, progressively mummified into formal ritual orchestrated by assorted dignitaries, its culmination that extended piece of media kitsch, the Bicentennial. Event and memory, ideally supposed to blend in a harmonious story, in fact have gone their separate ways.

On the other hand, it would be an error merely to lament the divorce, not just because of the unstoppably eroding effect of the work of time, but also because of the paradoxical relation between revolutionary event and the category of memory. It its purest ideological form, the Revolution wanted to sweep the past away and start anew from ground zero (Michelet thought that the only proper space of memorial for the Revolution was the Champ de Mars, not because it had been the site of festive occasion, but because it was in his own time, an 'empty space'). Memorial was not logically the Revolution's natural ally, but the temptations proved too great and those involved fairly quickly sought to make it their friend. Shortly before his death, the radical Jacobin Saint-Just (Robespierre's right-hand man during the Terror) wrote a sort of testament in which he spoke of leaving a 'legacy to memory'. Where Saint-Just himself is concerned, memory has not, on the whole, chosen to respect his wishes (he has been comprehensively written out of the commemorative script). But, even discounting the particular case of Saint-Just, the wish itself, in its general form, sits oddly with the ideological and affective investments of the revolutionary actors themselves in the erasing power of the new. And however one handles that intractable paradox, there remains the brute force of erosion, the ineluctable disenchantment that time brings to original enchantments. The nineteenth-century historian and thinker Edgar Quinet, commenting on Saint-Just's testament, observed, sadly but wisely, that modern human beings have limited resources for sustaining the 'contract' between event and memory:

> To give credit to the ideal Being, the Fatherland, to go so far as to accept the ideal recognition of future generations as payment for our services, who would want such a contract today? ... This idea and all others of this kind have been extirpated from the human soul ... They have become so alien and hostile that it is difficult to render them in a persuasive manner. Our present language refuses to express them. Yes, these ideas are dead.

There have been many attempts to rewrite the contract, many 'languages' of remembrance, some of them reputable attempts at fidelity to the original 'pledge' 14 July was held to embody, most of them, alas, travesties, reflecting for the most part the tawdry designs of politicians on increasingly inert national symbolic property. Nevertheless, remembering and commemorating have proven to be an abiding and apparently indestructible aspect of July 14, written into the story from the beginning with the first *Fête de la Fédération*.

5

The *Fête de la Fédération*

In a pamphlet of 1788, Camille Desmoulins, sensing what lay just round the corner, exhorted his small band of readers (the pamphlet was circulated in handwritten form): 'Patriotism spreads day by day, with the devouring rapidity of a great conflagration. The young take fire; old men cease, for the first time, to regret the past. Now they blush for it.' After July 14 the blushing time was over. In the minds of most, the *ancien régime* was strictly *ancien*, finished. The past that mattered was not last year but yesterday, and it was indissolubly linked to what might and should lie ahead: the Revolution triumphant. Hot on the heels of the literal 'yesterday', Antoine-Louis Gorsas, the editor of *Le Courrier de Versailles à Paris*, wrote: 'Yesterday will be forever remembered in the records of our history: it opens the way to the greatest and perhaps the most fortunate revolution.' In similar spirit, the ubiquitous contemporary commentator, Louis-Sébastien Mercier, composed a 'Farewell to the Year 1789', whose peroration brought memory, or more accurately the prospects for memory, centre-stage (Mercier's text has been neatly described as an exercise in 'pre-emptive nostalgia': 'Great year! You will be the regenerating year, and you will be known by that name. History will extol your great deeds.'

This was relatively quick off the mark, so fast indeed as to evoke a paradox in being concerned more with the future of

La fête de l'Unité et de la Réunion, sur la place de la Révolution (oil on canvas),
by Pierre-Antoine Demachy.

memory than with its object in the past. Proleptic talk of this sort about how 14 July would be remembered was common in the immediate aftermath of the Bastille episode, and it points to one of the more intriguing difficulties faced by the historian of the French Revolution in distinguishing between 'events' and their commemoration. The latter process started immediately, inside events themselves, and may be said to have contributed in some measure to the subsequent development of the Revolution as it moved into new stages. Strung out across memory and desire, prospect and retrospect, the already accomplished and things yet to be accomplished, the capture of the Bastille came to occupy an unusual temporal grammar in which past, present and future tenses jostled alongside one another. Much later, in the twentieth century, Charles Péguy collapsed the temporal distinctions entirely, arguing that the storming of the Bastille was its own instant commemoration, its 'zero anniversary': 'The fall of the Bastille, history tells us, was strictly speaking a festival, it was the first celebration, the first commemoration and, so to speak, the first anniversary of the fall of the Bastille. Or, in a word, its zero anniversary.'

The dominant medium for this instant commemorative flurry was, of course, that of print, above all the sudden explosion of journalistic ventures, as reportage simultaneously straining for the monumental. In one of the best known of these, *Révolutions de Paris*, Loustalot reached as early as 17 July (it was the newspaper's first issue) for the language of memorialising hyperbole: 'this glorious day ... the triumph of justice and liberty'. And so it went on, in similar rhetorical vein, across the whole terrain of a feverishly improvised print world. Hyperbole is close to the making of fictions, and the one strayed into the other at the hands of the remarkable Jean-Louis Carra. Carra was one of those ferociously energetic oddballs that the Revolution regularly threw up, as if at random. In pre-revolutionary times, he was, like Marat, a scientist of sorts (particularly interested in the physics of electricity). Also like Marat, at the outbreak of the Revolution he became a journalist and with Mercier founded in October 1789 the *Annales patriotiques et littéraires*, probably the most successful and widely read of all the revolutionary journals (it was especially popular in the provincial Jacobin Clubs). Himself a fervent Jacobin, Carra was subsequently elected as a deputy to the Convention, although these radical affiliations did not seem to inhibit his wilder ideas, such as the proposal that the French monarchy be handed over for safekeeping to the Duke of York.

In his guise as journalist, the inventive Carra immediately cottoned on to the marketability, both financial and political, of Bastille tales, and, in association with his inaptly named *Mémoires historiques et authentiques sur la Bastille*, he published a short book called *Le Comte de Lorges* (the non-existent but legendary prisoner said to have been liberated from the Bastille on the 14th). The 'authentic' was at a premium in this business (Latude was to title his own memoirs *Mémoires authentiques*), but few could rival Carra for sheer chutzpah: as a measure of the veracity of his story, Carra claimed to have met with and questioned the Count on his release (and prior to the all too convenient disappearance after which he was never to be 'seen' again); nothing could be more 'eyewitness' than that, and thus at a stroke a purely fictitious personage was spirited into the realm of attested historical memory. Brought to life as a figure of testimonial, the Count was given an exhortatory speech in which memory, wish and prophecy converged on the theme of festival: 'I want to celebrate for ever, yes, I desire that the Fourteenth of July be a day of festivity in eternity.'

The *Comte de Lorges* also found a place in a medium that was in some ways even more important than print, if only for the reason that it was accessible to the illiterate. The future Madame Tussaud, Marie Grosholz, officially the niece but probably the daughter of the Swiss impresario Philippe Curtius, who ran a waxworks establishment in the boulevard du Temple in

Paris, made a model of de Lorges. Curtius effectively invented the recipe that was to be the staple of waxworks exhibitions (the combination of the famous and the villainous). His most renowned show was mounted—where else?—in the Palais Royal in the 1770s, featuring such Enlightenment luminaries as Voltaire, Rousseau, Necker and Benjamin Franklin. He was also employed to make wax funeral effigies in the classical style. For Voltaire's cortège organised by Jacques-Louis David, he produced a model to accompany the corpse swathed in vermilion robes. Naturally, it rained, and the vermilion dye stained the effigy, thus inadvertently plastering an early form of modern kitsch on the attempted revival of an ancient funerary tradition.

The effigy was to have a more macabre role in the economy of both action and representation before and during the Revolution, variously paraded, mock-executed or burned. Indeed to this day on the far left it retains something of its revolutionary force; on the night of Nicolas Sarkozy's election as President, protesters who had gathered at of course the place de la Bastille, burned an effigy of the successful candidate. Straw replicas of Brienne and Lamoignon were consumed by fire in front of the statue of Henri IV on the Pont-Neuf, as were the straw-doll copies of Réveillon and Hanriot during the April riots. Wax, however, was a more durable (and a more potent) medium, and for a time Curtius's shows became a mix of running commentary on events (what much later, in the nineteenth century, in connection with the Paris waxworks, was to be called a 'plastic newspaper') and a form of propaganda, a means of inciting the populace to patriotic thoughts and deeds. This was to take a grimly recursive turn, circling from wax to human, back to wax. On 12 July 1789, inflamed by Desmoulins' speech in the Palais Royal, the crowd demanded from Curtius the wax busts of their heroes, Necker and the duc d'Orléans, to carry around the streets as a gesture in support of reform. Two days later it was the turn of the victims, the decapitated Launay and Flesselles. Within hours of their removal from the pikes, the heads were rushed to Marie; in her memoirs she records taking the impressions while seated with the bloody heads on her knees. Naturally, when the guillotine went into overdrive, there were heads galore, supplied by both the enemies of the revolution and the Enemies of the Revolution. The most popular collection featured wax busts of Louis XVI, Marie Antoinette, Carrier, Fouquier-Tinville, Robespierre and Hébert, with, in the foreground, Marat in his bathtub (later Madame Tussaud claimed that David used her work as a model for his *Marat assassiné*).

But all these efforts pale into insignificance when compared with the entrepreneurial tenacity of that one-man memorial machine, Citizen Palloy. After the capture of the Bastille, Palloy, a master builder by trade who had done very well out of the Paris construction boom of the previous two decades, was immediately commissioned to supervise the demolition of the hated prison. This was not quite the symbolic act of bidding farewell to the *ancien régime* it seemingly resembled. Demolition had been on the cards for some years, the expense of its upkeep held to outweigh the prison's usefulness. Several argued that it was better to retain it as a reminder of despotism, while the actual reason for ordering its destruction was the practical, if unfounded, fear that, by means of a series of hidden tunnels, it might be reoccupied by the king's troops. On 15 July Palloy arrived on site with a large contingent of building labourers to dismantle the edifice, stone by stone (the task was more or less completed by the following November).

Palloy was, however, an ardent patriot as well as an enterprising building contractor (he was officially listed as one of the *Vainqueurs* on the basis of a somewhat dubious claim) and conceived the idea of using the materials of the prison for commemorative purposes. The idea was to develop over the years into a veritable culture industry, mixing sentimentality and fetishism on a grand scale: inscribed slabs and plaques made from the Bastille stones, memorial medals, miniature models of the prison, paperweights, dominoes (made from the marble that had adorned the governor's windowsills), replicas of Latude's rope ladder, a stone bearing a chiselled portrait of Mirabeau and another inscribed with the Declaration of the Rights of Man and the Citizen. The project was of course partly designed as a money-spinner, but Palloy's primary motive was less mercenary than political (his obsession was to ruin him financially), dedicated to disseminating memorabilia across the whole of France as a way of binding together the national-patriotic community: 'It did not suffice for me to have participated in the destruction of the walls of this fortress. I had the desire to immortalise the memory of its terrors.'

Most of Palloy's efforts had as their backdrop the revolutionary festival, both unofficial (often initiated by himself) and official, starting with the first *Fête de la Fédération* on 14 July 1790. As early as 18 July 1789, Voltaire's protégé Charles Villette (originally a marquis, he burned his letters of nobility) had called for a publicly institutionalised celebration of the fall of the Bastille. Spontaneous festivity had already broken out in the course of 1789, especially in the provincial towns and cities. The most noteworthy event in Paris was a procession in mid-September from the faubourg Saint-Antoine to the church of Sainte-Geneviève, led by a contingent of the National Guard carrying a miniature Bastille made from cardboard, along with papier-mâché images of the wounded and the dead. Towards the end of the year, the thought that there might and should be a national festival on an annual basis, to take place on 14 July itself, began to gather pace. In December 1789, Clément Gochon, a worker from the faubourg Saint-Antoine, submitted a proposal to the Commune, *Projet d'une fête nationale pour être exécuté le 14 juillet 1790*, and, with Palloy at his side, suggested that its centrepiece be a huge balloon, each of its four sides to be painted with a representation of the great events, from the invasion of the Invalides through the storming of the Bastille to the king's journey to Paris on 17 July. Bailly approved, stating: 'We suggest that this meeting ... be sworn on the next 14 July, which we shall all see as the time of liberty: this day shall be spent swearing to uphold and defend it.' The institution of a national festival was, however, properly the remit of the Constituent Assembly, not least because it was anxious to retain control of popular demonstrations, no matter how joyous. The last thing it wanted was a repeat of the revolutionary *journée* itself, although Mercier was to write that the truly great festivals were the *journées* themselves, 'barbaric festivals' bathed, as in ancient Rome, with the stench of carnage. The Assembly began the process of sedulously eliminating all allusion to raw violence. In June 1790 it approved the demand forwarded from the Commune (with Talleyrand as intermediary) for a 'general Federation' to take place on 14 July. It was to be called a festival of federation in order to include all the municipalities of France and the regionally federated branches of the militia (as head of the militia, Lafayette, with an eye to the starring role, insisted on a strong military colouring to the proposed event).

The further decision to hold the festival on the Champ de Mars (at the time outside the city limits) created a problem that was in turn to become something of an occasion, in its own way the actual heart of the construction, both literal and metaphorical, of communal memory. The plans were not finalised by the Constituent Assembly until 21 June. With just over three weeks in which to make preparations, the Champ de Mars was subjected to a renovation blitz. The field, already a quagmire from the heavy June rains, had to be levelled, terraces to seat 400,000 had to be built, along with a triumphal arch, an Altar to the Fatherland, and a grand pavilion in which to seat the king and his party. Despite employing 15,000 workers, it became clear that the work could not be completed on time. And so was organised that gently fraternal version of the *journée*, the so-called *Journée des Brouettes* (the Day of the Wheelbarrows). We do not know who made the suggestion, but, as of one mind, the people of Paris, from duchesses to dustmen, priests and soldiers, rich and poor, along with thousands of delegates from the provinces, repaired to the Champ de Mars to dig, shovel and shift. It was backbreaking work; indeed the field had to be not only levelled but also lowered by several feet in order to ensure the visual prominence of the Altar to the Fatherland at its centre. But the work, it seems, was conducted in a spirit of genuine cooperation and good humour. In terms of egalitarian goodwill, the high point of the festival was attained before the festival itself properly speaking began. 'It was there', wrote Mercier, 'that I saw one hundred and fifty thousand citizens of all classes, ages and sexes making the most superb picture of concord, labour, movement and joy that has ever been witnessed.' This of course was Mercier in characteristic overdrive, but his picture was not a mere travesty of the facts.

The first *Fête de la Fédération* was conceived as a 're-enactment', not of the actual events of 14 July 1789, but of their 'meaning', understood as the founding moment at which the social 'contract' that sealed the Nation as a unified entity was drawn up and proclaimed. Hegel famously remarked that history repeats itself, the first time as tragedy, the second time as farce. If that is so, it is a law that applies *a fortiori* when the second time round is history as re-enactment. The Russian anarchist Kropotkin (who wrote a history of the French Revolution) described it as 'one of the most beautiful popular festivals ever recorded in history'. But to a large extent he must have consulted the records with his eyes half shut. Impressive it might have been as a choreographed event, but the one thing the authorities could not predetermine was the weather. It poured, in buckets, nearly all day long. Around 8 a.m., the assembled National Guard, along with the provincial delegates, the Commune deputies and regulars from the army and the navy, proceeded from the boulevard du Temple (presumably past Curtius's wax-works and of course past the site of the Bastille) to the place Louis XV, where they were met by the representatives of the Constituent Assembly as well as an assortment of foreign dignitaries ('Swedes, Spaniards, Polacks, Turks, Chaldeans, Greeks', as one source has it); there was also, authorised by the Assembly, a delegation from the United States which included Tom Paine. Crowds lined the streets in their thousands, singing the revolutionary 'Ça ira', in some sort of counterpoint to military drumbeat and salvo. Militia, Army, Assembly, People were as if fused in a collective celebratory affirmation; Paris had never seen anything like this before.

They were also soaked to the skin. Numbering well in excess of 100,000, the bedraggled but still enthusiastic procession reached the Champ de Mars, by now a sea of mud, several hours later, entering the field through the strategically placed Arc de Triomphe, to a correspondingly triumphal shout of welcome from the waiting spectators (an estimated 260,000 Parisians). It took another hour or so for the procession to file in, and around the middle of the afternoon formal business began in unrelentingly atrocious conditions. The ceremonial focal point was the Altar to the Fatherland, suitably adorned with patriotic image and text. First came the 'Mass' (which has to go into inverted commas, not least because it was officiated by that parody of a churchman, the Bishop of Autun, who specialised in never showing his face in Autun, Charles Maurice de Talleyrand-Périgord). Talleyrand didn't believe a word of what he uttered; one story has him begging Lafayette at the altar not to make him laugh, and after it was all over he repaired to more agreeable precincts, the private gaming table of a high-society viscountess, where he proceeded to take all the players to the cleaners. Apart from the difficulty of keeping a straight face, there were also the impediments of rain and wind, his robes sodden, incense that wouldn't burn, his voice more or less inaudible, but at least they had the merit of stripping away some of the layers of charlatanism.

Yet somehow he got away with it, delivering in pseudo-religious garb the essential revolutionary-federative message of the New Dawn ('on this day France has been made anew'). Indeed it is a remarkable feature of both this and other revolutionary festivals that they drew extensively, if eclectically, on bits and pieces of religious paraphernalia. Palloy, for instance, called his Bastille stones 'patriotic relics' and his miniature Bastilles 'votive sculptures'. Even more bizarrely, according to one contemporary newspaper account, the National Guard in one of the Parisian districts presented the local church with 'consecrated bread of considerable size in the shape of the fortress of the Bastille'. Mercier was later to fulminate: 'No idols, no idolatry in our Republic.' But revolutionary iconoclasm, along with the more general aversion to external signs of 'difference', had a hard time extirpating deeply rooted attachments to religious symbolism. Robespierre expressly resisted much of the later 'de-Christianising' phase of the Revolution and was personally responsible for that strange revolutionary invention, the Festival of the Supreme Being.

The Mass was, however, but a prelude to the Oath, with this time Lafayette as the star performer. Where Talleyrand just about managed it, Lafayette provided fabulous theatre. Battling the elements, he rode his trademark white charger from the altar to the pavilion where the king and his family were placed, humbly asking His Majesty's permission to swear the oath of 'federation'. Having both obtained permission and appropriated majesty, he rode back to the altar, itself adorned with various images and slogans, the most important bit of text trinitarian in character: 'The Nation, the Law, the King'. Having taken the precaution of distributing a very large number of surrogates around the field to declaim in unison with him (the inaudibility problem), he drew his sword, advanced to the altar and declared:

> We swear to be forever faithful to the Nation, to the Law and to the King, to uphold with all our might the

> Constitution as decided by the National Assembly and accepted by the King, and to protect according to the laws the safety of people and properties, transit of grains and food within the kingdom, the public contributions under whatever forms they might exist, and to stay united with all the French through the indissoluble bonds of fraternity.

The oath was then successively repeated by members of the National Assembly and the gathered multitude. As for the king, Louis had arrived late, and remained in his pavilion, conspicuously aloof from the whole proceedings. He did, however, swear his own oath, to use 'all his powers' to defend and uphold the (as yet unwritten) constitution. Sceptics parsed this as ambiguous, in the sense of Louis intentionally implying that his powers in this regard might prove strictly limited. On the other hand, whatever he meant by the oath, he was obliged to declare it as 'King of the French' (not 'King of France'). The change spoke volumes, signifying an end to the mystical bond of monarchy and territory underpinned by the doctrine of divine right; it was not long before he would be simply referred to as Louis Capet. Marie Antoinette then rose to her feet, holding the young dauphin aloft and declaring (presumably between gritted teeth): 'This is my son, who, like myself, echoes the same sentiments.'

Despite the weather-induced debacle, the festival was carefully planned and monitored. Of all the proposals submitted to the organisers, only three were approved: the procession of the militia, the mass and the oath, all three related components of a consciously orchestrated ceremony. The most resonant was the oath, its general importance as a secular-political ritual captured by the art of David in the unfinished sketch of the Tennis Court Oath, but above all in that earlier and prescient masterpiece of oath-taking, the *Horatii*, with its tensed arms converging on a single point in pictorial space. *The Fête de la Fédération* reproduced that pattern on a mass scale, the right arms of all present raised and directed towards the centre occupied by the altar, the physical expression of a common allegiance. In principle the oath engaged the whole 'nation'; in reality, as well as ceremonially, it was the affair of the *fédérés* of the National Guard, an early form of the new cult of the citizen-soldier and the militarised *patrie*. When not playing at churchman, Talleyrand got it right when he observed: 'It is France armed that is going to gather together, not France as a deliberating body.' Notionally, the festival was about the militia and the people, bonded as on the day of the storming of the Bastille. From the point of view of those controlling the festival, however, it was to be primarily about the militia *rather than* the people. Behind the façade of a theoretically all-inclusive consensus, the structure and meaning of the *fête* were to be defined and organised by a hierarchical system of subordinations and exclusions.

The officially excluded category was of course the Aristocrat, minus the large number of enlightened nobles, such as Lafayette, who had cast their lot with the Third Estate. Symbolically, the Aristocrat fulfilled the role of the ritual scapegoat. But the exclusionary logic also extended to the People (as the potential troublemaker). The People figured as an abstraction, but not the people as such. They were present as spectators rather than as participants, kept at the edge and on their best behaviour within a rigorously calibrated pecking order. Keeping the People out or at the margins was one of the concerns implicit in the extensive 'topographical discussions' on how to arrange bodies relative to the Altar of the Fatherland. The official visual symbol (along with the federative flag) was a triangular design representing Nation, Law and King. But in the placings of the audience around this symbol of egalitarian concord, some were clearly more equal than others. The disposition of persons was shaped as a set of concentric circles: the inner circle for the soldiers and the militia, the next for assorted political notables and the outer circle for the assembled multitude. This was the true image of France reborn.

After the 1790 festival, Mirabeau rationalised these arrangements and their meanings in a programmatic treatise on the subject, in which he made it quite clear that civic obligation was to come before popular exuberance, and that since carnival was associated with riot, appropriate methods of containment and control were to be the order of the day. This was intended to detach festival from festivity. The popular *fête*, when it took place at all, occurred elsewhere, especially in the provinces, and, when left to its own devices, was altogether more genuinely spontaneous. In Paris there was a three-day feast, but mainly for the benefit of the National Guard. Palloy organised a post-14-July street party for ordinary Parisians. This was an improvised affair, and the beginning of a cultural breach between the official and the unofficial, a parting of the ways between ceremony and holiday that was to come to define the social reality of the 14th for the vast majority of the population. The midday banquet and the evening *bal musette* could, and did, merge as a shared embrace of revolutionary civic virtues, in this regard often drawing on older religious traditions (for example, the meal as a secular equivalent of the Eucharistic feast). But they were just as much about entertainment, a time in which, released from daily labours, the people could let their hair down.

From the point of view of those in charge of the new political order, the *Fête de la Fédération* was stage-managed, not just to contain the common people, but also to consolidate a particular version of the Revolution; as throughout the whole history of the revolutionary festival, 'memory' was to be at the disposal of one agenda or another, and the past subordinated to the perceived requirements of the present. Behind the public display of concord, the festival was designed to outflank a political adversary (already the theme of the Enemy lurking behind the veil of Fraternity) in a barely concealed contest for power over not just what the Revolution meant, but to whom it belonged. Thus the Oath, as outwardly the spectacularised confirmation of the national Pact, gathering and transcending all interests, was in fact subtended by the politics of faction and party, namely Lafayette's. Above all, 14 July 1790 was Lafayette's day, and *fayettiste* was soon to emerge as an adjective for the political settlement the festival had ratified (a constitutional monarchy). One of the first places (along with the site of the Bastille) visited by the federates arriving from the provinces was the Tuileries, as a kind of holy site at which one might catch a glimpse of the king. The purpose of the festival itself was to protect, not disturb, the peace, to 'complete' the Revolution through an act that, in commemorating a beginning (14 July 1789), also marked an end. The abbé de Patry summed it up when he claimed that the festival 'puts the final seal on the most memorable of revolutions'.

There were of course dissenters, notably among the radical journalists. Desmoulins mocked the festival, with in particular a coruscating snapshot of Lafayette in strutting mode, as ego run amok, and Louis as a pathetic, humiliated wretch (on this point at least Edmund Burke agreed with Desmoulins, though naturally without sharing the latter's glee at royalty's abjection). Loustalot described the 'ensemble' of the festival as a 'beautiful' display of unanimity before, however, switching to its 'details': 'a crowd of idolators dazzled by M. Lafayette', the *Vainqueurs* ignored, not a word in memoriam for those who perished on 14 July 1789, self-prostituting leaders of the Constituent Assembly, the 'insolence' of marshals and generals putting themselves before their troops, a 'thousand ruses' to rob the citizen of all capacity to 'reflect', a moment 'poisoning' the well of memory and dedicated more to 'forgetting' than remembering. This was strong stuff (and in many respects also devastatingly right). But it was the acme of restraint alongside Marat's characteristically venomous broadsides of 16 and 18 July. In his first report, Marat described the proceedings as a brazenly 'shameful' charade mounted by a collection of fat cats bent on optimising the political conditions for lining their own purses, while betraying the true interests of the common people, broken by unemployment and hunger. The festival promoted a 'false image of public happiness' to 'distract the citizen from public affairs' (by which more concretely he meant preventing the Parisian 'sections' from preparing for the forthcoming elections).

The image both masked and accentuated the reality of a 'divided' nation. But Marat's denunciation went one stage further, beyond the exposure of a gimcrack fabrication to the charge of 'conspiracy'. With his unique mix of the hysterical and the lucid, he went for the political jugular by attacking the centrepiece of the occasion, the Oath. This was not just a confidence trick practised on the vulnerable, but the crucial element of a 'plot' engineered by royalists and Lafayettists to secure collective support for the 'constitution before it has been ratified'. It was a recipe not for establishing rights but for sacrificing them, not for democracy but for 'tyranny': 'Sustained by your support, if you refuse to underwrite oppression and tyranny, they will remind you of the oath you swore, and force you into becoming the oppressors of your comrades, from fear of perjuring yourselves.' As the voice of the *sans-culottes*, Marat had every reason for writing: 'Why this unbridled joy? Why these evidences of foolish liveliness? The Revolution, as yet, has been merely a sorrowful dream for the people!' Part of the point of the *Fête de la Fédération* was to declare the Revolution 'over'; for Marat it had yet to begin. From the purely predictive point of view, Marat won the argument, although this was something of a self-fulfilling prophecy given that he himself was partly instrumental in bringing about what he foresaw.

This brash mix of the splendid and the tawdry, genuine enthusiasm and cynical opportunism, was an unrepeatable one-off. In the rich pageant of festive revolutionary stagings to come (literally thousands of them), there were competitor festivals (perhaps the grandest and the strangest the Festival of the Supreme Being). But where 14 July is concerned, none of the successors came anywhere near matching the bravura of the first. The only muffled or discordant note, drowned out by the collective clamour of *Je jure*, was the semi-detached attitude of the king. By the following year he was fully, and permanently, detached, the oath he had uttered deemed worthless. But he was not the only historical actor to renege on a pledge solemnly given. The problem with oaths is that, however solemn and publicly ritualised, they can be betrayed, or at least their meaning varyingly interpreted. By 1791 the political landscape had changed substantially and the 1790 compact was in the process of unravelling. Whatever the construction the king had put on the constitution he swore to uphold, he had no intention of relinquishing the veto powers traditionally vested in the doctrine of divine right. In the meantime, he and the rest of the royal family had absconded, his image as Father of the People irreparably damaged by the flight to Varennes in June 1791, from where he could—though whether he intended to remains uncertain—summon the émigrés and foreign armies just across the border threatening to put an end to the still-nascent Revolution. The festival of 1790 which had promised 'closure' now stood as a hollow promise, and the 14 July celebrations were never to be the same again. If there was a large quotient of sheer fakery in the 1790 *fête*, there is still something to Kropotkin's view that it was 'one of the most beautiful popular festivals ever recorded in history'. (Wordsworth, who found himself in Chalon, on a boat with a contingent of *fédérés* returning from Paris, remarked on the atmosphere of 'benevolence and blessedness spread like a fragrance'.)

Certainly 14 July 1791 was a beautiful day, but, along with the sun in the sky, there was also insurrection in the air and the festival itself, if this time spared the torrential downpours of the original, was nevertheless something of a washout. The real crowd-pulling event had taken place but a few days previously: Voltaire's funeral (more accurately his secular canonisation, namely the transfer of his remains to the Panthéon, a former church recently converted into a resting place for the 'great men' of the nation). This was an extraordinary public consecration, the purpose of which was to appropriate the reputation of the great man for the Revolution (all very different from the time of his actual death in 1778, when newspaper obituaries were prohibited and the French Academy barred from holding the customary memorial service for deceased members). To make the point, the coffin was deposited at the ruins of the Bastille the night before the procession (the ghost of Enlightenment thus marking the spot of the fall of Despotism). The procession itself did not get to the Panthéon until around midnight the following day, the sarcophagus accompanied by members of the Constituent Assembly and the Paris Commune, and the casket inscribed with the words: 'Poet, philosopher, historian, he made a great step forward in the human spirit. He prepared us to become free.'

In a sense, therefore, the Bastille celebration had already taken place (the Bastille connection strengthened by one of Palloy's miniatures, made from the prison stones, being one of the main embellishments of the cortège). But there remained a score to settle. The king was not only personally absent from the second *Fête de la Fédération*; the ignominy of Varennes meant that all trace of his consecrated place in the national compact was expunged. The original triangular dedication on the Altar to the Fatherland had been emended: 'the Nation, the Law, the [ ]'. Lafayette once again hogged the limelight, but this was not to be a re-run of Lafayette's day. Suspicion and disappointment had replaced jubilation. Marat's talk of 'plots' now seemed all too plausible and his hyperbolic description of Louis ('crowned brigand, perjuror, traitor, conspirator') far more likely to find a sympathetic audience; Lafayette was doubtless much disconcerted on hearing cries of 'Down with the king' as he pranced on his white charger. The Constituent Assembly moreover sent a mere token representation and declined to suspend its sitting, one of its tasks for the day the hearing of a petition from the radical

Cordeliers Club (Danton's base) calling for a referendum on the future of the king. Moderates in the Assembly managed to defuse the situation, initially 'suspending' and then reinstating Louis within the terms of the still-unratified constitution. On 16 July, however, a further petition—this time demanding the deposition of the king—was drafted, read out, from the four corners of the Altar to the Fatherland, to a large crowd gathered at the Champ de Mars, and by early evening signed by over 6,000.

The following day Lafayette and Bailly, determined to put an end to these stirrings of 'popular democracy', came to the Champ de Mars with a contingent of National Guard to enforce martial law (decreed the previous evening). The crowd refused to disperse and the militia opened fire (estimates of fatalities ranging from thirteen to fifty). This—what came to be called the 'Massacre of the Champ de Mars'—was the bloodiest incident since the taking of the Bastille, this time, however, with a capital difference: the people's militia had attacked the people. The petition was subsequently lost in the fire that devoured the Hôtel de Ville in 1871 during the Communard uprising, but is known to have included the names of many of the *Vainqueurs de la Bastille*. It seems that Danton, who read out the petition at the Champ de Mars, did not actually sign it (perhaps from considerations of prudence). As for Robespierre, while he argued in the Assembly for the immediate trial of the king, and wept copiously at the Jacobin Club for the victims of the 'massacre', he kept both the petition and the petitioners at arm's length. Yet nothing was to be the same again. The hallowed locale of collective revolutionary memory, and in particular the Altar of the Fatherland (on the steps of which many had lost their lives), were now stained with blood, and as a consequence, commemorative festival was about to acquire a distinctively 'republican' aura.

The next *Fête de la Fédération* was something of an antclimax, the day itself mattering less than the speeches and manoeuvres around it. The happily inclusive slogan 'Nation, Law and King' must by now have seemed a distant memory. Despite Varennes, Louis persisted with his claim that the royal veto was consistent with the letter and the spirit of the new constitution (finally promulgated in September 1791). In this he succeeded only in making himself even more unpopular, while, for his part, Lafayette, when not detested for his role in the Champ de Mars repression, was widely perceived as a figure of fun. The royalist cause, however tempered by liberal-constitutional nicety, was rapidly becoming a lost cause. On 20 June a demonstration was planned to protest against the king's veto powers (the date consciously chosen as the third anniversary of the Tennis Court Oath). This was to comprise a further petition (to be presented to the Assembly) and the planting of a Liberty Tree in the Tuileries garden. Once again the National Guard was summoned to disperse the crowd and once again the prospect of a further 'massacre' loomed. Although the crowd did not get to plant the tree in the garden, they did succeed in invading it. This time the militia did not fire, chiefly because their orders failed to come through, but also because the National Guard was now torn asunder, many siding with the demonstrators. The crisis was defused, but it was a foretaste of what was to happen two months later, the outcomes of which were to transform the face of festive Paris.

The domestic political temperature was further raised by the fact that France was now at war with Austria and Prussia. In early July the Assembly had issued the proclamation of *la patrie en danger*. 'Danger' was indeed now the watchword, and it presided over arrangements for 14 July. In the spring the new Legislative Assembly had delegated to the Committee of Public Instruction the task of drafting a bill for the regulation of public festivals. Shortly before, Robespierre made a speech to the Jacobin Club for a new kind of *Fête de la Fédération*. Elected detachments of the militia would gather in Paris from all over France, to swear fealty to a martial slogan: 'Liberty or Death' (the original version of the Revolution's most famous rallying cry being 'Liberté, égalité, fraternité ou la mort'). Death was now the proud, and exclusive, partner of Liberty, as Robespierre moved to his peroration: 'Come, on the tombs of our brothers let us mingle our tears and weapons, remind ourselves of the pleasures of the celestial virtues, and die tomorrow, if need be, from the blows of our common enemies.' This was a formula for a more Spartan festival, in which moreover the entire Legislative Assembly would take part (Robespierre coupled this demand with a proposal for the construction of a new Assembly building on the site of the demolished Bastille, big enough to allow the common people to observe, and monitor, the actions of their legislators). The idea was to break once and for all with the corruptions of pomp and circumstance, in favour of an austere if overwhelming spectacle of militarised civic virtue. The speech was intended as a mobilisation against the enemy both without and within. But, in its linking of sacrifice and death to ancestor-worship (not just those who had fallen at the front or, the previous year, before the Altar of the Fatherland, but all who had martyred themselves in the cause of the Revolution), Robespierre's address also hit a truly ominous note: invoking and appeasing the spirits of the nation's dead was to become a central feature of the blood-and-soil nationalism of the far Right (although its partisans would never have dreamed of seeing Robespierre as one of their own ancestors).

It has been said that on 14 July 1792 the Champ de Mars was more like a 'military encampment' than the site of a festival. For the there was a circle of eighty-three tents (representing the eighty three departments of France), in the centre a huge marquee for king and Assembly, a memorial for the war dead (Robespierre's idea) and a Tree of Feudalism adorned with various symbolic baubles representing Privilege, which the king was supposed to set on fire. The royal family sat through the whole thing in tears, with the king as ever abstracted and the crowd hostile. After reviewing the procession, he had to push his way through the crowd to swear the oath at the altar; though under military protection, there were fears for his person in the crush. He went through the motions of swearing the oath, but balked at being required to burn the tree. His authority in tatters, he was escorted at his own request to the Ecole Militaire: it was his last public appearance of this kind. In 1791 the king's name had been effaced; in 1792 it was the turn of the institution itself. Danton placed a motion before the Jacobin Club that the National Guard from the provincial departments should remain in Paris until 'liberty' had been established (now equated with the Republic and the end of the Monarchy). Late in July the militia contingent from Marseilles arrived belatedly, singing Rouget de Lisle's song, henceforth, by association with the singers, to be baptised and immortalised as the 'Marseillaise'. Less than two weeks later, on 10 August, came the coup d'état, many of the National Guard that had remained in the city marching on the Tuileries. The Monarchy had come to an end, the Republic was shortly to be declared, and 14 July now had a rival, 10 August.

If 1792 was the year of the 'Marseillaise', it was also, from the point of view of the federative festival, the moment of its dreary swansong, inaugurating a trajectory of decline followed in turn by a long slumber (from which it was to be aroused only in 1880). Officially both 14 July and 10 August were to be celebrated; in his curious XVI Patriotic Commandments, Palloy urged the case for both: 'Always preserve the memory of the days of 14 July 1789 and 10 August 1792 and pass it on to your progeny.' This, however, was a difficult mix to sustain and in practice 10 August was now to be the date that mattered. In May 1793 the Convention passed a motion to establish a 'Republican Federation of the French People'. The term 'federation' had originally been coined to evoke the principle of unanimity (Desmoulins had called it a 'sublime idea'), but in fact no one had really known what it was supposed to mean. It was a fourteenth-century word, and not to be found in any of the late seventeenth-century or eighteenth-century dictionaries, although the adjective *fédératif* occasionally appeared in discussions of the Dutch Republic. Yet, even with its new republican inflection, 'federalist' in the context of revolutionary politics resonated in problematical ways. It was associated with the resistance of the Gironde to the Jacobin stress on the centralised state, and by June 1793 the Girondin party in the Convention had been routed, although the federalist revolts continued in the provinces (some of them brutally put down).

As for the 10 August festival, it was decided literally to superimpose it on the memorial place of 14 July. The theme was to be 'regeneration', and a Fountain of Regeneration, a female statue in the form of the Egyptian goddess Isis, was erected on the site of the Bastille. It was supposed to look as if made from stone, but was in fact a plaster fabrication; it collapsed in 1799, as, politically speaking, did so much else. In any case, the public mood showed little sign of the regenerated. The festival was regulated, seemly, and dead. There were a few improvised events beyond the control of the Convention, often held in secret, with occasional bouts of revelry, and here and there a touch of the parodic, scoffing at authority. What large-scale animation there was proved to be essentially vengeful, as when on 10 August a sizeable crowd descended on the Basilica of Saint-Denis, intent on dispersing the bones of the dead kings of France. A mere footnote, 14 July was marked by a small ceremony within the precincts of the Assembly. It was, moreover, squeezed on both sides by the death of Marat, assassinated by Charlotte Corday on the evening of the 13th and followed on the 15th and 16th by the mass viewing of his decomposing corpse in the Cordeliers church.

The years 1794–5 were, broadly, the time of the Revolution as graveyard and the graveyard of the Revolution, through the height of the Terror to 9 Thermidor (the arrest and death of Robespierre). The conditions for commemorative festival, on July

14 or any other date, had never looked bleaker. Furthermore, as the reference to 9 Thermidor indicates, there was a further complication. It was not just that 14 July now had a competitor, either coexisting with it or officially ousting it (10 August). Strictly speaking, '14 July' no longer existed as a date at all, as a consequence of the promulgation of the new republican calendar the previous October (rescinded twelve years later by Napoleon). The calendar additionally proposed a host of new days of revolutionary festivity and remembrance, most notably the five *sans-culottides*, tacked on in order to get the numbers right and respectively named Talent Day, Labour Day, Virtue Day (*fête des actions*), Rewards Day and Opinion Day. For leap years there was to be a sixth *sans-culottide*, invested with special prestige and called Day of the Revolution.

Yet, if it no longer had a calendrical existence, public consciousness of 14 July as indelibly memorable remained strong, though, in the fraught circumstances of 1794, somewhat bruised. From this point of view, the old and new calendars in practice lived side by side. However, with the guillotine operating daily, this was hardly a time for commemorative jubilation. Executions were in fact suspended for the day, but this made little difference. Paris was tense and frightened; there were sporadic banquets, but the general atmosphere was apathetic at best. Robespierre disapproved of the banquets: France cannot 'celebrate' while there are still Enemies to destroy and the true work of the revolution to complete (in reality Robespierre was probably more concerned about seditious and conspiratorial talk around the banquet table). This was all a far cry from Lafayette's calculation in 1790 that the *fête* would signal an end to a fully accomplished revolutionary project.

With the fall of Robespierre later that July, the whole festival apparatus begins to wind down, with 14 July in particular poised to leave the stage, not so much with a bang as with a whimper. In 1795 a decree was issued on 10 Thermidor (the day after the anniversary of Robespierre's overthrow) stipulating that both 14 July and 10 August were to be commemorated. In respect of the former, this meant a festival for the following year, but by then the post-revolutionary regime known as the Directory had been installed, and with it came an explosion of frivolity and blasé indifference to public life. The people had lost interest in civic virtue and wanted not so much to commemorate as to party. The Directory abandoned all pretence at coherence and voted to celebrate *pêle-mêle* 14 July, 10 August and 9 Thermidor, a ragbag of contradictions sometimes politely referred to as a compromise-formation.

The underlying desire, however, was to forget rather than remember. The deputy Grelier made a speech that caught the prevailing temper:

> In evoking 14 July and 10 August, our aim is not to celebrate bloodshed and the punishment of the guilty. On the contrary, we are trying to remove them from our memory in order not to poison the pure joy that the triumph of Liberty inspires in us.

With the advent of the Consulate (the successor to the Directory), it was then but a step from extinguishing memory of the unpleasant to the extinction of memory *tout court*. As one of the three consuls, Sieyès made a couple of dutiful speeches on the importance of 14 July and 10 August. But Napoleon Bonaparte had other ideas, all geared to burying revolutionary memory. For a few years 14 July was continued, but essentially as a means of glorifying military victories abroad. By the time he became emperor, Napoleon decided to abolish the festival altogether, the significant date now to be 15 August (the date of his birth). The final blow was delivered by the plan to erect a giant elephant on the site of the Bastille, also known as the Elephant of Revolutionary Oblivion. This may have had something to do with one of Napoleon's many self-images (the identification with

Hannibal), but no one really knew what it was supposed to mean. In *Les Misérables*, Victor Hugo put it thus:

> One knew not what it meant. It was a sort of symbol of sorts of the force of the people. It was gloomy, enigmatic and immense. It was a mysterious and mighty phantom, visibly standing by the side of the invisible spectre of the Bastille.

It was another cheapjack plaster construction and, after the fall of Napoleon, it became the home of the city's vermin and quietly rotted away. But with it the work of oblivion had been more or less accomplished. Erased, suppressed or driven into underground clandestinity, the Fourteenth of July ceased to exist until resurrected by the Third Republic in 1880.

6

Bastille Day

In 1880 the government of the Third Republic decided that it was in the interests of both the Republic and itself to awaken the 14 July festival from its long nineteenth-century sleep. It was henceforth to be an annual event in perpetuity, legally sanctioned as both an official commemoration and a public holiday for the general population. This was the moment of the invention of Bastille Day. The campaign to restore the festival in some form or other had been under way for the best part of a decade, notably sponsored by the radical politician Léon Gambetta and, in a series of addresses to the Institut de France, by the scholar Henri Baudrillart. As early as 1872, Gambetta had written in his newspaper, *La République française*, of the 'need' a 'free nation has of festivals', and in one of his best-known public speeches, also in 1872, called specifically for a Fourteenth of July event, on the teleological argument that all the 'decisive *journées*' of the Revolution, including 10 August and 22 September, were 'contained' in the inaugurating *journée* of 14 July. The right-wing government, recovering from the trauma of the Paris Commune uprising, did not agree. It sought to impose a nationwide interdiction on the 14 July popular banquet, though in both Paris and the Midi the ban was often ignored. That government fell in 1877.

La République sur la barque du Progrès (engraving), by Albert Bellenger.

On 21 May 1880 deputy Benjamin Raspail proposed a motion, signed by sixty-four fellow deputies, that 'the Republic adopt 14 July as the day of an annual national festival'; it became law on July 6. But if the formulation of the law was simple, the politics behind its framing were complex. The idea of a 'national' festival was explicitly billed as a 'festival of the Republic'. Yet the meaning of the term 'republic' and its relation to the legacy of the French Revolution were politically delicate issues. Just how delicate is clear from the debates, both within and outside the Assembly, that accompanied Raspail's motion. Some deputies argued that the appropriate date to be remembered was 4 August 1789 (the date of the official abolition of 'feudal' privilege), while a smaller number favoured 5 May 1789 (when the Estates-General convened at Versailles). Others maintained that 9 Thermidor (27 July 1794), the moment of Robespierre's fall, was more suitable (in order to ensure public dissociation of the 'republic' from the memory of the Terror). The lone voice of the feverishly intransigent Henri Rochefort (*L'Intransigeant* was the name of the newspaper he created) held out for 21 January 1793, the date of Louis XVI's execution and naturally went entirely unheard. What no one proposed was the actual date of the founding of the First Republic (22 September 1792), indelibly linked to the coup of August 10 and the September Massacres. That would have been altogether too uncomfortable, a reminder among other things of the invasion of the Tuileries, the insurrections of 1848 and, closer to home, the violent insurrection of the Paris Commune in 1871 (which had razed the Tuileries).

The agreed solution (14 July) was, however, also problematic, not on the logical grounds that the political demands it embodied had little, if anything, to do with 'republicanism' (for the Republican parliamentarians of 1880 it sufficed that July 14 could be posited as the historic challenge of 'modernity' to feudalism, clericalism and monarchy), but because it too was, if on a much lesser scale, stained with blood. Here was a prime case of publicly ratified 'collective memory' being brought face to face with the recalcitrance of history: the deputies wanted memory to be shaped to the needs of the fully legal republic, but 14 July 1789, however you cooked the historical books, had been unambiguously illegal. The solution was to finesse the matter with the argument that the reference of '14 July' was a double one: simultaneously to the date of the storming of the Bastille (a time of strife) and to the date of the first *Fête de la Fédération* the following year (a time of reconciliation and concord). Thus emerged the prima facie odd proposal for a festival that was to celebrate not so much an event as another festival, though it could be maintained that event and symbol, action and theatre, were so closely intertwined during the Revolution itself that the borderline between the two categories was blurred. The rationale of this ingenious superimposition of the two dates was supplied in a speech by the politician-historian Henri Martin in the Senate:

> But let us not forget that behind this 14 July, when the victory of the new era over the old regime was secured by armed struggle, let us not forget that after the day of 14 July 1789 there was the day of 14 July 1790. One cannot charge the latter with having spilled a single drop of blood, of having produced the slightest degree of division in the country. It was the consecration of the unity of France. Yes, it consecrated what had been prepared by the ancient institutions of the monarchy. The latter had, so to speak, created the body of France, and we have not forgotten this; the Revolution, on that day, 14 July 1790, formed, I will not say the soul of France—only God made the soul of France—but the Revolution made France conscious of herself; it revealed to France her soul. Let us thus recall that on this day, the most beautiful and the purest of our history, from one end of the country to the other, from the Pyrenees to the Alps and to the Rhine, all Frenchmen joined hands.

Politically speaking, Martin's effort was a tour de force, aversion of the past designed to satisfy nearly all mainstream parties: music to the ears of 'moderate' Republicans, a generous titbit for restive monarchists (many of whom had opposed the whole idea) and a firm repudiation of any claim on the revolutionary past by the revolutionary Left (there was an attempt to co-opt remaining dissidents by granting amnesty to former Communards on 11 July 1880). The speech provided an account of the meaning of the new national festival perfectly tailored to the requirements of a legitimation-narrative for the Third Republic that would be uncontaminated by contact with everything that was unsettling and controversial about the original Republic. In short, it represented yet another proposal to remember by forgetting. On 14 July 1790 France may still have been more than two years away from becoming a republic, but never mind, it provided not so much a precise political analogue as a vocabulary. The new *fête* was to be a resurrection of the tropes of Resurrection. ('What we celebrate today', wrote a contemporary journalist, 'is the resurrection of France.')

Ironically, telling the truth in the minimal sense of sticking closer to the facts fell to the royalist right (in a series of pamphlets). They opposed the idealised fairy tale (stressing, for example, the derisory yield of liberated prisoners in the storming of the Bastille), but of course not from a disinterested commitment to truthful chronicle. They had agendas of their own, and if 'fact' was mobilised to subvert fiction, it was in order to discredit the whole revolutionary enterprise. When General Ambert referred to the festival as 'la fête de la désertion' (of the *gardes françaises*), he highlighted a historical truth, but missed the essential point, primarily because he wanted to identify desertion not with patriotism but with treason. Moreover, the (selective) stress on fact over fiction was no impediment to producing lurid fictions of their own: 14 July as 'madness', the 'festival of assassination' and the 'first act of the Terror', along with the storming of the Bastille as 'satanic', a scene of 'carnage and cannibalism'. The purveyors of this agitated idiom were doubtless inspired by Taine's *Origines de la France contemporaine*, the volume dealing with 1789 having been published in 1878. The upshot was that the faithful were asked to stay at home and fast, as a mark of contempt for the republican banquet. Some placed religious symbols on their balconies, in counterpoint to the republican flags which adorned the city.

The programme for the first Bastille Day comprised several elements: alms-giving to the poor, public concerts, firework displays, illuminations. The two main ceremonies were to be the presentation of colours to the troops at Longchamp, with President Jules Grévy in attendance, and the inauguration of a monument at the place de la République under the auspices of the Paris municipality. Both involved the introduction of new ritual and symbolic motifs, most importantly the flag and the statue. The military theme that had always been at the forefront of the 14 July celebrations was now unambiguously what the state wished to emphasise most (as a way of healing the wounds inflicted by defeat in the Franco-Prussian War). The dominant conception was 'nationalist' rather than 'republican', and its rallying point the union of army and nation under the flag. The tricolour became a public revolutionary emblem in 1789 when, on 17 July, Bailly, the mayor of Paris, presented a submissive Louis with the red, white and blue cockade. The colour scheme—which may have been Lafayette's idea—combined the red and blue of the city's coat of arms with the traditional white of the French monarchy. Those wedded to new conceptions of sovereignty were inclined to see the placing of the white band between the red and the blue as a conscious statement of the king's subordination to the will of the people; those of less polemical dispositions saw it rather in terms of an ecumenical embrace carrying the promise of a well-ordered constitutional monarchy.

In 1794 the Convention adopted this design when it decreed

the *drapeau tricolore* as the national flag to replace the two royal standards, the oriflamme and the fleur-de-lys. The oriflamme (its colour flaming red and its name from Latin *aurea flamma* ('flame of gold') was originally a religious banner belonging to the Basilica of Saint-Denis (as the burial site of monarchs, it was France's equivalent to Westminster Abbey) and, from Carolingian times, was used only in battle (its bearer a military post of considerable honour and prestige). The white flag embroidered with a fleur-de-lys (a symbol of purity) as the royal coat of arms, was alleged to have been first adopted by the Frankish king Clovis on his conversion to Christianity towards the end of the fifth century, but it was especially associated with the Bourbon dynasty and the doctrine of divine right. It made a brief reappearance after the fall of Napoleon during the Bourbon restoration and, in altogether more provocative mode, during the Vichy regime under Nazi occupation.

The politics of the flag were thus highly charged. The symbiosis of soldier and citizen was a crucial component of the revolutionary legacy, including the history of its commemoration from the first *Fête de la Fédération* onwards. The first Bastille Day took this a stage further. The flag was not confined to the official military parade at Longchamp, but was displayed across the whole city, festooning streets and buildings (an echo of the 'pastoral' festival two years previously which Monet painted as an impressionistic sea and swirl of colour). The idea was to saturate civilian life with reminders of the civic meanings of the military ethos. The running context for this was the bitter conflict between laity and Church, the principal battleground of which was in the sphere of education. The decade 1880–90 was the time when 14 July was vigorously and successfully used to prosecute the campaign of anticlerical secularism that was the hallmark of the Third Republic's version of 'republicanism' (the final separation of Church and State occurred in 1905).

The school was seen as a place of civic instruction and as

a breeding ground for the production of the good citizen. The inculcation of lay-patriotic values in schoolchildren, concluded the Paris *conseil municipal*, should be one of the primary purposes of the festival ('one cannot associate them too soon with national and republican festivals'). In 1882 schoolboy battalions were included in the 14 July military procession (precedent was furnished by the children's battalion in the 1790 *Fête de la Fédération*); as miniature soldiers, to whose hands the security of the fatherland would eventually be confided, the schoolboys constituted a preparatory sketch in which past (glory), present (celebration) and future (safety) could be combined. This implicated not just the social but also the biological reproduction of the good citizen. The Municipal Council further stressed the importance of associating girls—the future mothers of the nation—as well as boys with the festival: it is 'only republican women who can make good republicans of our children'. Naturally, the Church disagreed; its 1909 index of prohibited works included a number of school history books, especially those devoted to the French Revolution and specifically the events of 14 July 1789.

The second major innovation was in the choice of a public representation to embody the spirit of the Republic. This was the figure of Marianne. Its origins as a political icon are obscure. Some have maintained, a trifle implausibly, that the name is a deformation of Juan de Mariana, the sixteenth-century Jesuit who wrote a defence of tyrannicide. Other exotic sources include an off-the-cuff improvisation by Paul Barras during the government of the Directory (he was one of the five executive Directors): at a dinner party he allegedly asked the name of his hostess, the wife of his political colleague Jean Reubell; on learning that it was Marianne, Barras is claimed to have remarked that it was a name 'which befits the Republic just as much as it does yourself, Madame'. Serious research, however, has uncovered a more authentically revolutionary origin in a Provençal folk song by the poet Guillaume Lavabre, routinely sung during 1792 in the area around Toulouse, and in which Marianne represents the Republic. In September the same year the Convention decreed that the new seal of state should be marked with a woman holding a pikestaff and sporting a Phrygian cap, though she was not explicitly named as Marianne. She was, however, to lead an extremely active radical afterlife, from her appearance in Delacroix's famous picture of 1830 (*Liberty Leading the People*), a pictorial image that was to become ubiquitous, on the back of official authorisation by the Ministry of Interior, during the short-lived Second Republic. During the Second Empire depictions of Marianne were driven underground, where they served as a clandestine symbol of opposition to the imperial regime.

The retrieval of Marianne by the Third Republic was nevertheless not uncontroversial. The Church deplored Marianne replacing Marie (on 14 July 1880 the devout placed busts of the Virgin on their balconies), while the royalist Right referred to her contemptuously as 'Marie-Anne' (allegedly her original peasant name). But these were largely disgruntled noises off-stage. It was within the republican camp itself that the significant division of opinion was to be found. For, if there were to be busts and statues of Marianne publicly displayed in the town squares of republican France, what was she to wear? In particular, what was her headgear to be? Revolutionary tradition had consecrated the Phrygian cap (in ancient Rome worn by emancipated slaves to mark their freedom), and the Paris municipality followed tradition when in 1879 it commissioned the statue that was to be situated at the place de la République and ceremonially unveiled on 14 July 1883. But this was not the face of the Republic that a queasy government wished to endorse (too redolent of insurrectionary *sans-culottes*, Communards and striking workers), and it asserted its preference for the alternative to the *bonnet rouge*, the more bucolic and peaceable wheatsheaf crown (the president and his government ministers stayed away from the unveiling). One barometer of tensions between 'moderate' and 'radical' republicans throughout the Third Republic is the extent to which the crowned and the bonneted, the placid and the fiery images of Marianne vied with one another. One thing that was universally agreed, however, was the adoption of the 'Marseillaise' as a national anthem.

As deputies, ministers and mayors debated meanings and bickered over symbols, what did the first Bastille Day look like from the point of view of the common people? The most widely read daily newspaper in Paris, *Le Temps*, reported that the 'whole population of all classes and all nuances took an active and joyous part'. This obviously has to be journalistic hype, but all the evidence suggests that the politically manufactured chimed with the popular mood. Other than in the Vendée region (still scarred by memories of what was claimed to have been 'genocide'—the revolutionary suppression of the royalist uprising in western France), the whole of France appears to have greeted and joined the festival with unforced alacrity. What precisely was being celebrated of course varied considerably. In Paris allusions to the storming of the Bastille were conspicuously absent. Some street vendors sold small replicas, but this was more a knick-knack trade, equivalent to the later buying of a replica Eiffel Tower from a street hawker. In the provinces, and especially in the south, the political tone was sharper. In Saumur a descendant of Aubin Bonnemère, the *Vainqueur* who had presented one of the Bastille stones to his native town—it had since been buried somewhere in the cellars of the Hôtel de Ville—campaigned successfully for it to be taken out and dusted down.

But the key to the generally amiable sociability of the 1880 festival is the fact that it was also, for the first time, a public holiday. If the 'people' was to participate fully in 'its' national festival, it had to be given a day off work, and thus republican 'memory' was joined with and expressed through a collective form of the modern leisure culture. Over time the two were to diverge so far as to leave very little felt connection between them, but in 1880 the general euphoria was such as to mask the early stirrings of that eventual rupture. Entertainments, both planned and improvised, included bonfires, fireworks, races, cockfights, boules and, above all, feasting and dancing (the republican banquet at midday and in the evening the popular *bal*). Some of the primmer advocates of republican civic programming saw the dancing as training for the body, a useful preparation for military service. But this was a truly fatuous rationale, with no purchase at all on the ordinary working people, for whom the *bal* combined ancient festive practices and sheer pleasure (in Paris the dance halls were also pick-up places, the more louche transactions of popular festival in the capital caught by some of the Impressionist painters; no surprise, then, that the conservatives described festive Paris as 'a cheap dance hall' and 'an immense orgy').

Where the political capture of the popular imagination was more successful lay not in imposing a disciplinarian blueprint on mundane pleasures, but in creating pleasures that, by their very nature, could serve the cause of social tranquillity even as a revolutionary past was being marked. This seems to have been one of the intentions behind the use of the new technologies of illumination. Illuminated Paris on 14 July 1880 was typically described in the contemporary accounts as 'féerique', the momentary conversion of the urban landscape into a kind of fairyland, offering not only a brief respite from the grindingly ugly world of daily work, but also an escape from memory itself, in which a potentially uncontrollable revolutionary heritage was replaced by an agreeable mirage. For, along with the festive affirmation of the legitimacy of the republic against its enemies on the Right, there was also a real fear of trouble from the Left (the fall of the Bastille was to be celebrated as 'a definitive victory, not as a battle to be recommenced', as one provincial newspaper put it on 18 July 1880). Especially sensitive to recollections of, and continuing attachment to, the 1871 uprising, the government prohibited 14 July gatherings at Père-Lachaise, where so many

Communards had fallen in a bloodbath. There was considerable anxiety over what might erupt at local republican banquets, with fighting talk fuelled by alcohol. There was also the worry, at a time when republic and capital were now on exceedingly fraternal terms, that an outburst of radical sentiments might have an adverse effect on the stock market (the Bourse in fact rose the day after the festival). Illuminated dreamlands were one way of seeking to secure the appropriate political slumber, amusement as less a training of the body than a seduction of the mind.

The 1880 festival created a template that, with some modifications and a few wartime exceptions, has been continuous. The detail of that annual self-reproduction, as basically a saga of repetition, need not concern us here; there are, after all, few changes one can ring to a fixed repertoire. By far the more compelling story lies in the attempt to capture, by way of a series of snapshots, something of the changing circumstances and fluctuating allegiances of Bastille Day at and around certain key historical moments, typically—and understandably—moments of stress, convulsion and recovered solidarity in the life of the nation. Six such spring automatically to mind: 1889, 1899, 1919, 1935–6, 1940–42 and 1945, six dates related successively to the Second International and the new forms of worker militancy nourished by Marxism and Socialism; the climax of the Dreyfus Affair; the Armistice of the First World War; the formation of the Popular Front; the Vichy regime under the Occupation; and the Liberation of 1945. In their different ways, these are the moments when the ideological fix, of which the *fête* was a major ingredient, gluing together the terms republic, nation, revolution and people, came unstuck from the pressure of internal conflicts, only to be reapplied when France faced and emerged from the external threats of two world wars. In short, the history of Bastille Day from the late nineteenth century to the end of the Second World War can be seen as a kind of prism through which to view critical moments in the social and political history of modern

France.

If 14 July 1889 was the date of the centennial (a subject for the next chapter), it was also, and not by coincidence, the date of the First Congress of the Second International. From the point of view of the emergent worker and socialist movements, 14 July carried a distinctly 'red' meaning. During the 1848 insurrections the red flag was often flown, while workers in the more militant faubourgs defied prohibition and organised their own 14 July banquets. With the founding in 1879 of France's first socialist party, the Federation of the Socialist Workers of France (initially, the *Parti ouvrier socialiste révolutionnaire*), the class-based struggle over the revolutionary heritage of 1789 became more visible. The issue here for the Third Republic was not the dispute between laity and Church, or the parliamentary conflict between republicans and royalists (the latter, however vociferous, were clearly on the losing side of history), but the antagonism between labour and capital. In this mighty confrontation, a simple but stark question was posed by the radical Left: what, or rather who, were the Republic and its symbols for? The revolutionary socialist, Guesde, who with Marx's son-in-law, Lafargue, had founded the breakaway *Parti ouvrier français* in 1882, was in no doubt. The memory of the Bastille had been hijacked for the construction of a new citadel of incarceration: 'a Bastille of the capitalist class'. Two of the terms of the Revolution's great slogan, 'liberty' and 'equality', were in some vital respects now enemies rather than friends (the third, 'fraternity', remained variously interpretable on a spectrum from just being nice to one another to the need for organised solidarity).

Where the state-sponsored festival itself was concerned, there were two options for the Left, reappropriation or boycott. The socialist leader Jean Jaurès supported the first option, repudiating the official association of 14 July with the theme of class concord and—while remaining careful not to advocate revolutionary violence—staking a claim to the true 'meaning' of 14 July in terms of popular rebellion (specifically the beginnings of the *sans-culotte* role in the making of the republic). For Jaurès and his followers the festival was not just the formal property of the modern republican state, now stamped RF, but belonged naturally to the People in a more radical and class-conscious sense of the term. Others, however, identified this as a trap and called for outright abstention (or alternatively showing up with a black flag). There was now, moreover, a rival to 14 July: the Second International, acting on a motion proposed by Raymond Lavigne, declared 1 May as International Labour Day (in commemoration of the victims of the 1886 Haymarket riot in Chicago). Although not invoked by Lavigne, there was a sort of revolutionary precedent for this: when in October 1793 Fabre d'Eglantine presented to the Convention his plan for a new republican calendar, it included the recommendation of a labour day to fall annually on (in the old calendar) 19 September. Assuming anyone recalled it at all, Fabre's innovation was not invoked, one imagines, because it was more a proposal to celebrate work than the granting of a day's release from it.

In 1892 the unions at Saint-Nazaire voted to 'abstain' from 14 July celebrations and 'henceforth recognise only 1 May' as a festival date. This failed to attract widespread support, most probably less from strong worker identification with the official festival and more because the latter was a public holiday. The State of course refused to establish 1 May as a national holiday until well into the twentieth century. It accordingly became more an occasion of protest and riot than a festive gathering. In the United States, as a reaction to the 1894 riots in Cleveland, Labor Day was moved to September (thus at a prudent distance from memories of the original May troubles in Chicago). In France hostility to the 14 July ceremony on the syndicalist left became increasingly vocal. Spouting the mantras of 1789 was but a political narcotic administered to the masses, the republic's version of the 'opium of the people'. In the early years of the twentieth century, with Clemenceau's authoritarian premiership and his (merited) reputation as a strike-breaker through the use of armed force (though he had previously been a committed Dreyfusard and supporter of Zola), union resistance to 14 July found an echo in the caricatures of the anarchist Aristide Delannoy (the heir of Daumier, he was sentenced to a year's imprisonment because of his work). In one of these a debauched Marianne is figured as receiving a bunch of flowers from the bloodstained hands of Clemenceau. In another, the words 'liberty', 'equality' and 'fraternity' are illustrated in the background by three representatives of a grasping and repressive ruling class (a banker, a magistrate and an officer), the caption a homophonic play which can't be carried over in translation: '*Des mots … des maux.*' ('Words … evils.') There were renewed calls for 1 May to replace 14 July, and to the extent that the latter was to be observed at all, it had undergone an important mutation: for the militant workers it was more a time for manifestation than a time for *fête*.

The new fractiousness signalled by the First Congress in 1889 acquired another context a decade later, when in June 1899, and in the light of hitherto suppressed evidence, the Dreyfus case was reopened (only to be promptly closed again in September). This was the affair that split France in two, around the trial of the Jewish army captain Alfred Dreyfus on trumped-up charges of spying for Germany. Prior to the eruption of the Dreyfus Affair, several of the secularists of the Third Republic had stressed the superior 'civic' values of the Jewish (and Protestant) communities in denouncing the retrograde attitudes of the Catholic Church. It was possible to mobilise 14 July on the side of this campaign, most notably by recalling the impeccable pedigree of the abbé Grégoire. Few remembered that Grégoire had presided over the marathon sixty-hour Assembly session in Versailles that ran concurrently with the taking of the Bastille. Many, however, would have recalled his efforts to promote equal rights for Protestants and Jews, although today we will find both the title and some of the actual arguments of his *Essai sur la régénération physique et morale des Juifs* not a little unnerving. This, however, would be a mere antiquarian quibble alongside the virulent anti-Semitism of the Dreyfus Affair, which crucially infected the military. While the army remained loyal to the state, much of its officer class was averse to republican values; Dreyfus was in part the scapegoat for that aversion.

In short, 14 July 1899 was something of a minefield. How could the festival sustain the fiction of a unified national family based on a sacred bond between army and people when it was the army itself that was centrally implicated in the affair? (Many commentators on the right, most famously the writer Maurice Barrès, touched rock bottom by arguing that national unity required that, even if innocent, Dreyfus should be found guilty.) On the day itself both Right and Left assembled to affirm the army, but for diametrically opposed reasons: the Right (especially the Ligue des Patriotes) to defend the 'honour' of the army at all costs (including the dishonourable); the Left (especially the Ligue des droits de l'Homme) to 'save' the army from those who sought to abuse and pervert the 'republican' ideals it was there to defend. Jaurès moved boldly, and controversially, to occupy the high ground of 1792; the army, he claimed, belonged to the people under 'the flag of the First Republic'.

Nationalism and republicanism, which since the Revolution had been the two sides of the same coin, were now locked in mortal combat. It took a victimised Jew to open an ideological fault line that had been more or less successfully concealed for over a century. In several places things turned nasty. In Rennes a group of young nationalists went on the rampage, shouting 'Down with the Jews', and smashed the windows of Victor Basch, a prominent member of the Ligue des droits de l'Homme and a well-known Dreyfusard. The fault line, moreover, widened to reveal an even deeper fissure. If the principal bone of contention between Left and Right turned on the question where, to what and to whom the army belonged, its proper relation to the state and the rule of law, there was also a more radical anti-militarist strand of opinion, arguing that the affair was not just about a few rotten apples in an otherwise healthy institution, but implicating the whole spirit of militarism and revanchism in a way that constituted a genuine threat to democracy itself. Unlike Jaurès, who sought to reclaim ground stolen by his political adversaries, the anti-militarists, like the syndicalists (they were often the same people), sought to transform the festival into a site of contestation. This was to happen again in the run-up to the formation of the Popular Front in 1935 (in which Victor Basch was to have a prominent role).

If the aggravated relation between Bastille Day and the Dreyfus Affair replayed some of the tensions of the 1889 festival, it was also fundamentally about something else: France and its 'others'. Anti-Semitism was the bridge joining nationalism and ethnicity, the army, the nation and the flag linked as the meeting ground for what, in right-wing circles, was increasingly called 'the good Frenchman'. This had little to do with republican 'patriotism' in the older sense, but rested more on the invocation of 'stock', blood and soil that characterised the language of Action française (itself born of the Ligue des Patriotes). This group detested the Revolution and all its works, arguing not so much for an adaptation of revolutionary memory as for its liquidation, and for the replacement of Marianne by Joan of Arc. They felt that 8 May (the date of the liberation of Orléans by Joan's army in 1429) should usurp 14 July in the commemorative calendar. The original *prise de la Bastille* had been a disaster for the nation, a conspiracy of foreign Freemasons, mainly from Germany, and the source of that 'collective tyranny' otherwise known as democracy. The modern, and true, Bastille was the 'Bastille of the Republic', run by a mongrel collection of democrats, Freemasons and Jews.

In this scheme of things the unwanted ethnic 'other' was a

parasite on the body of the nation. If this was to have a place at all in the festive proceedings, it was as an exotic exhibit. The 1889 World Exhibition, timed to coincide with the centennial of 1789, had as one of its displays a 'Negro Village' in which around 400 natives were put on show in a kind of ethnological zoo. As if to make amends, in the 1950s de Gaulle invited a group of African leaders as guests at the 14 July celebrations to mark the policy of decolonisation and the creation of something called a new French Community (a kind of Commonwealth). But making amends was not so easily done. To grasp the wider history—of slavery, colonialism and racism—to which the Dreyfus episode belongs in connection with Bastille Day, it needs to be framed by both a flashback and a fast-forward. First, back to Toussaint L'Ouverture, the Haitian leader of the slave rebellion who in the late eighteenth century threw the Declaration of the Rights of Man and the Citizen back in the faces of the colonial masters. The revolutionary leaders (and later enemies), Brissotin and Robespierre, had both voted in support of anti-slavery motions, but it was only after Toussaint led the slave uprising into a military alliance with Spain and Britain in the war with France that the Convention voted for full emancipation. Toussaint figured nowhere in the 14 July celebrations (until he was, belatedly and somewhat disingenuously, wheeled on to the stage of the great 'multicultural' jamboree that was to define the bicentennial). If we then fast-forward to 14 July 1953 and the time of the Algerian War, immigrants from North Africa assembled on the place de la Nation to stage their own counter-event. It resulted in a violent confrontation with the police, with seven dead and over 100 injured.

For all the tensions and conflicts surrounding it, Bastille Day nevertheless went on to reproduce itself more or less placidly throughout what remained of the belle-époque. The imminence and then the outbreak of war brought a rude awakening. The agreeable times were gone; mobilisation, of both men and mood, was the order of the day. On 14 July 1913 there was a huge rally at Longchamp. Anti-militarism was a dead letter, disreputably eccentric when not flagrantly treasonable. The following year, with the nation actually at war, the Bastille found a new metaphorical incarnation: Germany, its prisoners Alsace and Lorraine. The year 1915 witnessed the attempted bracketing of the festive in the festival.

The divergence of ritual and holiday into separate realms had been under way for over three decades, but the disconnect was now an embarrassment to this new incarnation of the *patrie en danger*, for which ceremony and revel could not that easily coexist. The government decreed that 14 July was to be 'exclusively patriotic and commemorative'. Street festivities were banned, partly because of blackout requirements, but also because it was felt that wartime was not party time.

The Armistice saw the return of the festive atmosphere, in one of the most extravagant 14 July *fêtes* ever. But it was primarily festivity in the service of a military achievement. In addition, 1919 saw the release of Abel Gance's film *J'accuse* (an echo of Zola's famous intervention), but this was not a time propitious to recalling the Dreyfus Affair. The army had distinguished itself, saved the Republic, and the first Bastille Day since the end of the war was to be a Victory Day. Its official themes were Victory, Right and Law, with much talk of the ancient Germanic foe, going back to the fifth-century Teutonic invasions of Gaul and the institution of feudalism. In early nineteenth-century historiography a link had been established, notably in the writings of Augustin Thierry, between an oppressed medieval Gaul and the Third Estate of 1789, generating an analogy between the Germanic warrior-barons of the early Middle Ages and the exploitation of the common people by the 'feudalism' of the *ancien régime*. Its transfer to the defeat of Germany was of course blatantly opportunistic, mere dressing for what had been a contest of nation-states, and revenge for defeat in the Franco-

Prussian War. And to the extent that the French Revolution was evoked, the emphasis fell only on the first term of the expression, as something distinctively 'French' rather than revolutionary.

The nation and its borders were what mattered. The autochthonous blood-and-soil ideology of the far Right had a field day, its inspiration more the more nationalist theses of the historian Fustel de Coulanges than the liberal historiography of Thierry. There was not a trace of the Third Estate, or the insurrectionary *sans-culottes*, in any of the official discourses. All was swamped by a semi-delirious greeting of the returning soldiers, in a procession led by Marshals Joffre, Foch and Pétain. Two hundred painters were employed to produce gigantic pictures to accompany the victory parade along the stretch from the place de la Concorde to the Arc de Triomphe. Fragments of destroyed German artillery capped with the effigy of a triumphant *coq gaulois* were held aloft. There was no music, the silence finally broken by a thunderous ovation for the saviours of France. This is doubtless why Barrès recorded that on that day he was in seventh heaven.

Throughout the 1920s and the first half of the 1930s there is little of note to report on the fortunes of the 14 July festival. Peace had restored the more peaceable forms of collective remembrance, with also a pull away from the collective to the personal, the public to the private. In 1933 René Clair's film *Quatorze juillet* struck the relevant note, as the affectingly poignant love story of a taxi driver and a flower seller against the background of the *bal musette*. Then, in 1935, a new page was turned in the modern history of the festival, a page written largely by the constellation of forces on the Left from which was to emerge, the following year, the Popular Front government headed by Léon Blum. Its text was informed by two urgently pressing questions. First, what was the point of victory in the First World War if, with the rise of fascism, Europe was hurtling towards the second? In addition, with the onset of the Stalinist purges and show trials just round the corner, what of that post-1917 phenomenon: the narrative crafted mainly by historians and intellectuals in or close to the French Communist Party (founded in 1920) which furnished both a telos to the French Revolution and a pedigree for the Russian Revolution, such that the latter could be seen as the political relative of the former and the storming of the Bastille the natural predecessor of the Potemkin mutiny (the more sceptical, however, might have reached for the Kronstadt uprising)?

The great rally organised by the Rassemblement populaire for 14 July 1935 was an attempted answer to these questions, loud and clear in connection with the first, more muted and blurred in connection with the second. There were two Bastille Days. With one significant variation, the official ceremony was business as usual, a military procession down the Champs-Elysées received by assorted politicians and functionaries. The variation was the permission to allow Dreyfus's funeral cortège (he had died two days previously) to pass the place de la Concorde through the assembled ranks of troops, with much of the officer class presumably poker-faced; it was not until 1995 that the army officially acknowledged Dreyfus's innocence. The real event of the day, however, was the march orchestrated by the Rassemblement populaire from the place de la Bastille to the place de la Nation. It was a massive display of working-class strength and Left solidarity. Its committee president, Victor Basch, spoke on the theme of the anti-fascist cause. The communist and non-communist Left buried the hatchet. Jacques Duclos, a leading figure in the French Communist Party (and in many ways a hard-core Stalinist), made a speech interpreting 'fraternité' as fraternising under two flags (albeit reserving his own as the flag of the future): 'Our enemies want to see the red flag in conflict with the tricolour, the "Marseillaise" with the "Internationale". In vain. We see in the tricolour flag a symbol of past struggles and in our red flag the symbol of future struggles and victories.' The separation of the Revolution and the Republic, much desired by the founders of the Third Republic, was now to be overcome, through the recapture of 'the great revolutionary tradition which made of 14 July a day of hope'. There was also a reprise of the public oath that had been the centrepiece of the *Fête de la Fédération* in 1790, now sworn to defend democracy against the threat of fascism, as well as to ensure peace and economic justice.

The following year, with the Popular Front government installed, 14 July was more a time of celebration. Once again there were two processions, but now not as rivals. The numbers were so great that two separate itineraries to the place de la Nation had to be devised. But if on 14 July 1936 the pleasures of simple festivity were recovered, it remained a *fête du peuple* in an almost lost revolutionary sense of the term 'people'. It was a day of speeches, and where there were entertainments, these were primarily directed to enhancing consciousness of a political heritage. They were reminders of a revolutionary past and its continuing obligations, the latter understood as loyalty to the Blum government, but also as the carrier of the yet unrealised promise of the Revolution. It was in many ways the exact opposite of the original Bastille Day in 1880 and the Third Republic's view of itself as the deliverer of promised outcomes in the form of its version of republican 'modernity'.

To be sure, the stress fell on fulfilling the promise by non-violent and constitutional means, thus, like all its predecessors, writing out everything about 14 July 1789 that had been violent and unconstitutional. The radical journalist Albert Bayet wrote in his paper that on 14 July 1936 the 'soul of the people' had 'relived the spirit of 89', but was quick to add—enthusiastically but falsely—that the latter had been not only both 'formidable' and 'peaceable', but all the more formidable because peaceable. Yet the sense that something was indeed being 'relived' was palpably real, not so much a commemoration of the past as its re-enactment. Romain Rolland's play *Le Quatorze juillet* (written in

1902) was staged to full houses, its form precisely that of a living re-enactment, as if on the evening of 14 July 1936 the storming of the Bastille were taking place all over again.

In 1939 (the year of the sesquicentennial), the Popular Front was a thing of the past. As the nation moved closer to war, via the Munich settlement, Prime Minister Daladier tried to reinvoke the 'federative' example of 1790, calling the anniversary festival 'the festival of national unity', while President Lebrun spoke of 'federation' and 'defence of the fatherland'. But there were not many listening (or in attendance). By far the larger event was the procession from the place de la Bastille to the place de la Nation sponsored by the French Communist Party, its participants billed as 'the sons of the *sans-culottes* who faced the army of Coblenz' (the Hitler–Stalin pact not yet signed). Over 50,000 joined in, although—a sign that the solidarities of 1935–6 had evaporated—the Socialist Party dissociated itself from the occasion. Meanwhile, the far Right reverted to form, reminding its supporters that the appropriate image of 14 July 1789 was that of a 'pool of blood as indelible as the drops on Macbeth's [*sic*] hands'. Once again political conflict was exercising acute disintegrative pressure on the festival and its meanings. Georges Lefebvre published his great book on 1789 (*Quatre-vingt-neuf*), the citizen offered as sustenance for dark days ahead; Vichy banned the book.

The long history of *le quatorze* from 1790 to 1940 had more than its fair share of the evasive, the manipulative and the dishonest. But its one and only truly ignoble moment is to be found in that travesty of 'liberty' known as the *zone libre*, the gesture of the occupying power in 1940 towards a parodic remnant of national sovereignty. The Nazi way with 14 July was not without its own, distastefully bizarre contradictions. On 14 July 1941 the *Pariser Zeitung* published an editorial proclaiming the date as a 'significant European date' in opening a revolutionary tradition that culminated in the great twentieth-century revolution, the

National Socialist one. There was also the grim coincidence that the decree of the *Gleichschaltung* banning political parties came into effect (a project that the comte d'Artois could only have dreamed of when the Estates-General convened in May 1789). The converse, and by far more influential, view was that robustly taken by Goebbels: '14 July shall be erased from history'. In the occupied zone the erasure machine went to work immediately, with a special emphasis on banning any display of the tricolour. With limited scope for resistance, ordinary Parisians fought back with resourceful cunning. Jean Guéhenno recorded in his *Journal des années noires* seeing women in Belleville wearing handmade dresses and headscarves, the resemblance of their colour scheme to the tricolour—'of course, officer'—a mere 'coincidence'. For the more soberly dressed menfolk this was a hard act to follow; obliged to be more circumspect, they adopted the artifice of a box of matches decorated with a small illustration of the *cocarde* that protruded, at once discreetly and defiantly, from the jacket pocket.

For the Vichy regime, divesting itself of the title 'French Republic' (rebaptised the 'French State') and the motto 'Liberté, égalité, fraternité' (replaced by 'Travail, famille, patrie'), 14 July was an encumbrance. Pétain's far-Right supporters were unhappy with the whole business on any set of terms. They wanted to bury 14 July and Marianne for ever, and came up with the novel suggestion that, if there had to be commemoration, it was better dedicated to Marat's assassin, Charlotte Corday; one wonders whether any of them were familiar with Cruickshank's engraving in which Corday is depicted as Joan of Arc, the true heroine of the Right. An alternative suggestion was for celebrating the Crusades. Pétain, however, had marched with Joffre and Foch in the grand victory festival of 1919. Simply eliminating it would be a step too far. Instead of a burial ceremony, there would be the next best thing: in the words of Pétain's minister of the interior, 'a ceremony for the dead', especially dead soldiers. This was not to be a festival in the celebratory sense, but a day of mourning. Pétain himself made a speech the following year in which he defined 14 July as a time to reflect and meditate on those who had fallen in the defence of French soil. This was close in spirit to the forms of nationalist ancestor-worship favoured by the extreme right-wing movement, Action française. And, as a pointed farewell to the secularist Third Republic, the regime also brought the Catholic Church back into the proceedings, Pétain's first stop on the day being mass at the church with the archetypal crusader name, Saint-Louis de Vichy. One concession to Third Republic precedent, however, was retaining the day as a public holiday. Out of residual deference to this mockery of the 'holiday spirit' (all public festivity was strictly forbidden), the *grande rafle du Vél d'Hiv* (the biggest round-up of the Jews) was postponed until 16 July.

As at once cause and consequence of this humiliating insult delivered to republican tradition, 14 July in its more recognisable guises was claimed by the Resistance. In 1940 a brochure by de Gaulle was secretly circulated in which, predictably, the new 'Bastille' was the prison of Occupation and 14 July not a day of mourning but of recollected and renewed promise; the Resistance was the true heir of the Revolution. In his 1941 broadcast from London he declared: 'Your 14 July is not dead', and to signal that it was still alive, he requested all concerned to wear the cockade. With Laval's return to the Vichy government as 'prime minister' and the end of the *zone libre* in 1942, de Gaulle issued a call to more active resistance: it was now a 'national duty' to 'demonstrate' on 14 July, wearing the tricolour and singing the 'Marseillaise'. In parts of the former free zone there was a massive turnout, along with acts of sabotage, arrests, confrontations between demonstrators and the future collaborator *Milice*: in Marseille the forces of order opened fire with machine guns, leaving several dead and wounded. Laval, as the most pro-German of the Vichy politicians (it was under his premiership that Vichy would later deport Dreyfus's granddaughter to the Nazi extermination camps), was a particular focus of hatred; for every cry of 'Vive de Gaulle', there was a 'Hang Laval'. On the morning of 14 July 1942 Pétain and Laval attended a perfunctory ceremony in Vichy; afterwards over 500 people gathered and stood in silence in the town centre.

The opposite of an impotent yet resolute silence was the explosion of joy that accompanied the first 14 July after Liberation. Collective exuberance could not, however, paper over the fact that here was a nation not only exhausted but also split. First, there was the reckoning with Collaboration, and secondly, the tussle over political ownership of the Resistance. Here was the start of the scramble for domination of the post-war political landscape. The Left was already muttering that Gaullist ambitions signalled the beginnings of the 'monarchical republic', with a strong whiff of Bonapartism. The Communist Party campaigned for a sovereign constituent assembly, and to that end had organised a gathering of Resistance fighters in Paris, provocatively named the Estates-General of the Resistance. Nevertheless, 14 July 1945 was not a day for airing differences and dissensions. A huge procession of liberating troops marched from Vincennes to the place de la Bastille, where they were reviewed by de Gaulle as the new head of state. This was followed by a motorised parade from the place de la Bastille to the Arc de Triomphe. Later in the day came the celebration of the Resistance, the route now reversed, from the place de la Concorde to the place de la Bastille (thus nearly all the sacred urban spaces of 14 July commemoration were honoured). We can call this stage-managed, an attempt to rebuild the solidarities of national festival after the cracks of the 1930s and the disintegrations of the 1940s, a politically crafted recovery of the discourse and rituals of 'unanimity' that had informed the first *Fête de la Fédération*. But this account, while true at some level, also reflects the condescension of hindsight history, and completely overlooks how it was felt at the time. Where now the Marats and Loustalots who had spoken so contemptuously of the 1790 celebrations as an empty farce? Nowhere in sight.

Above all, 14 July 1945 is remembered as an ecstatic three-day street party, untrammelled release on a mass scale after the years of humiliation and deprivation. It has often been compared with the Armistice *quatorze* of 1919, for the obvious reason that both took place at war's end. But this is misleading. The latter was essentially a victory parade celebrating a feat of arms, whereas 1945 was more about deliverance, not just from the scourge of war but also from the nightmare of occupation. The restoration of 'liberty' rather than the affirmation of military prowess was its guiding theme. This is the main reason why the comparison with 1919 does not work. In the stress on liberation from an oppressor rather than victory in an external war, 1945 had a more natural affinity with 1789 than did 1919. 'Liberty', gained or regained, was the watchword (one of the largest local gatherings in Paris took place in the 19th arrondissement where an old revolutionary practice was recovered, the planting of a Liberty Tree). Liberty doubtless meant, in both 1789 and 1945, as many different things to different people as it does to the cast of characters who, in the ensemble set piece of Mozart's *Don Giovanni*, sing 'Libertà' in unison. But on the streets of Paris the unison was as much a reality as a convention or a fiction, at least in the shared affirmation of a word, if not common agreement on what it meant.

Of all the 14 July *fêtes*, there are five which stand out: 1790, 1880, 1919, 1936 and 1945. Of these, arguably the greatest was 1945, when the French people were at last freed from the long night of the worst 'Bastille' ever imposed. It is virtually impossible for historians to feel their way into the complex arc of emotions aroused and nourished by that three-day street festival—relief, sorrow, exhilaration, rapture, solemnity. It was a time when the founding trope of the founding moment—'birth'—must have resonated in a peculiarly deep way. It was also a time when formal ceremony and festive sociability fully came together. If 1968 invented the politics of pleasure as a slogan, 1945 was a moment when the political and the pleasurable were really as one. By virtue of the presence of allied forces and diplomats, it also had an international dimension, embodying the 'universalist' thrust of Victor Hugo's line in his novel *Ninety-Three*: 'The overthrow of Bastilles is the deliverance of mankind'. There had been nothing quite like it before, and there has certainly been nothing at all like it since. If Vichy represents the nadir of the Fourteenth of July, then 1945 is its zenith, after which it follows the trajectory of a prolonged, generally quiet and increasingly pale sunset, until arising, phoenix-like, from the ashes in that multicoloured confection, the centennial.

7

The Centennial and the Bicentennial

By 1889 there had been eight Bastille Days, all of which had unfolded more or less in the intended manner, if against the background of the intensifying stand-off between labour and capital. The Third Republic appeared to have settled confidently into the ritual presentation of its own self-image as the republic of all, with no inkling of what lay on the horizon, the eruption five years later of the Dreyfus Affair. The ninth Bastille Day, however, fell into a special category, as the moment when the Day was folded into the embrace of that weightier historical unit, the Century. Yet, as it turned out, in the elaborate preparations for the centennial, 14 July did not figure as the jewel in the festive crown (in the calendar of memorable events, 14 July 1889, expressly chosen as the date of its First Congress, belongs rather to the Second International). There was a proposal from the Paris municipality to host a grand 14 July banquet, to which—in a conscious echo of the 'federation' of 1790—all the mayors of France would be invited. While the government showed no real enthusiasm, it took place, albeit adjourned to 18 August. As for memories of the Bastille, their sole major representation was a cardboard replica built in 1888 on the avenue de Suffren.

The reasons for this partial eclipse of the 14th were not ideological, but stemmed from purely practical considerations regarding schedules. It had been decided that the centennial would be a year-long affair (celebrating 1789 as a whole), to run from late July 1888 to June 1889. In fact it did not really get under way until the spring of 1889, and moreover ran beyond the prescribed cut-off point, with the last event taking place on 21 September, the day before the legislative elections. The key date of the whole sequence was 5 May, designed to precede the real event of the centennial, the opening the next day of the Exposition Universelle. The question of which dates to mark, and which to highlight, was nevertheless a source of controversy. The indefatigable journalist and amateur scholar Charles-Louis Chassin (his name crops up everywhere in debates about the centennial) favoured a programme that would embrace 5 May, 20 June, 14 July and 4 August 1789, plus 21 September 1792. For its part, the government chose to emphasise the 'peaceable' dates, 5 May (the meeting of the Estates-General) and 4 August (the end of 'feudal' privileges). The former was declared the 'official' occasion, and included a pilgrimage to Versailles. On 20 June the Tennis Court Oath was also commemorated by a small event in Versailles, organised by the municipality, with but three ministers in attendance. Then 4 August saw the transfer to the Panthéon of the remains of Lazare Carnot, grandfather to the then President of the Third Republic, Sadi Carnot. Naturally all reference to Lazare's role on the Committee of Public Safety as the technocrat-politician who, although not centrally involved in its implementation, did not oppose the Terror, was kept under wraps; in the year of the Exposition Universelle, his reputation as a mathematician, scientist and engineer probably mattered more than his standing as a player during the high period of radical Jacobinism.

The importance granted to scientific enquiry and accomplishment by the modern secular republic underwrote the two distinctive, and lasting, aspects of the centennial celebration: the archival and the monumental. In the first place, memory itself was to be given a duly scientific pedigree through the constitution of a documentary corpus that would enable a properly 'factual' understanding of the revolutionary past. This did not of course detract from the irreducibly political character of publicly sanctioned memory, but it gave the latter a new context: the battle of the scholars, as, methodologically and institutionally, the study of the French Revolution became more and more the province of the academic profession and the specialist review. The ideological cleavage was the familiar one. In 1889 Emile Faguet—enthusiastic supporter of the Ligue des Patriotes—published his *Dix-huitième siècle*, a book that followed Taine's reactionary line in rubbishing the Enlightenment and its misbegotten offspring, 1789. This was part of a wider campaign by the Right, reflected in a stream of brochures and pamphlets, the most erudite of which was *La Revue de la Révolution*, albeit that erudition was generally geared to the aims of propaganda.

The counter-attack was mobilised around the commanding figure of Alphonse Aulard, the first holder of the newly created chair in the history of the French Revolution at the Sorbonne, and himself centrally involved in the planning of the centennial. Intellectually, Aulard's principal adversary was Taine, his reckoning with the latter (*Taine, historien de la Révolution française*) published in 1908 as a thorough, if also polemical, critique of Taine's historical 'method', although it was not long before Aulard also had to look to his left flank, when confronted with the even more radical 'Jacobinist' historian Mathiez. Aulard's own work, mainly in the field of political history (and evincing a strongly pro-Danton bias), attracted the loyalties of a group of scholars, both within and outside the university. Its principal organ was the journal *La Révolution française* edited by Aulard under the auspices of the Société de la Révolution française, around which was spawned, especially in the provinces, a cluster of centennial societies and committees. Supported by government funding, they produced a centennial *Histoire de la Révolution française* (also issued as a cheap 'popular' edition in instalments). The primary goal was the production of a 'scientific' historiography, but one that was also the bearer of a legitimation story, as evidenced by the stupendous non sequitur that Charles-Louis Chassin put before the municipal commission: the 'facts established by positive method' are such as to 'prove' the 'legitimacy of the demands of our forebears'. Positivist history, in short, constructed an equation binding 'science', education, citizenship, republic and nation. The extent to which the equation could raise the temperature to boiling point is illustrated by the extraordinary incident in which someone tried to shoot Aulard after one of his lectures in the august precincts of the Sorbonne.

The constitution of the archive was thus the foundation stone of an ideological canopy designed to cover the whole nation as it prepared for the centennial celebrations. The canopy was to be further embellished by a new emphasis on the monumental. Refurbished buildings were to be political statements, most notably the Hôtel de Ville (though the huge sums devoted to cleaning it up after it had been gutted by the Communards proved controversial). But the major commemorative raids on public space took the form of what has been called 'statuomania'. Statues sprang up everywhere. The most famous was the statue of Danton, commissioned for the centennial, its inauguration, however, delayed by uncertainties over where to place it. It was finally unveiled in the Latin Quarter in 1891, but, to mark the original inspiration, the pedestal was inscribed: 'A Danton/ la Ville de Paris/1889'. This was not to be interpreted as an endorsement of the violent events of 1792–3. The intended image was of Danton the 'moderate', the eventual victim of the Terror rather than one of its initiators. The more general objective, however, was simply to saturate space. Emile Bin, at once a painter and mayor of the 18th arrondissement, took this to heart with a sequence of twenty gigantic paintings depicting various revolutionary episodes and figures, which he staged as an outdoor exhibition in the Buttes-Chaumont district. The exhibition was instructively called *Musée historique du Centenaire de la Révolution française*, the 'museological' term an index of the attempt to bring the archival and the monumental together as partners in the Third Republic's centennial vision.

The distinctive monument was not, however, a statue or a painting, but a prodigious feat of engineering, the Eiffel Tower, itself the landmark exhibit of the Exposition Universelle. The link between the latter and the centennial anniversary was umbilical. Bureaucratically, the commissariat in charge of the Exposition was also responsible for organising the centennial programme. Symbolically, the connection of one to the other was reflected both in the schedule which arranged the opening of the exhibition for the day following the 5 May commemorative event and in the spectacular blitz which accompanied the festivities of 4 August. Carnot's inaugural speech stressed the link:

> Today France glorifies the dawn of a great century which has opened a new era in the history of mankind. Today we contemplate, in its brilliancy and in its splendour, the work born of this century of labour and of progress. … She [France] has the right to be proud of herself and to celebrate with head erect the economic centenary, as also the political centenary, of 1889.

The governing idea was the republic as the natural home of a technological avant-garde, the grand Machinery Hall and the Eiffel Tower as the embodiment of a modernising rationality, in contrast to the Bastille, now defined as 'medieval'. The retrospective view was cast entirely on a prospective grid. The commission turned down the proposal for an actual Museum of the Revolution as too backwards-looking. It was similarly unenthusiastic about the attempted resurrection of the *Fédération* festival (the proposal for a mayors' banquet). The buzzword was 'progress', the principal set piece a Fountain of Progress, designed by Jules Coutan and placed on an axis linking the Central Dome and the Eiffel Tower. It is doubtful that anyone heard an echo of the Jacobin 'Fountain of Regeneration'. This was less about the purifying power of water than about the transforming power of electricity, a technically accomplished trumpeting of Technique and its material benefits. The electric lights, illuminating the entire 228 acres of the Exposition, converted the entire site into a fairground image of Paris as the *ville lumière*. The Eiffel Tower was dotted with enamel panels coloured red, white and blue, lit up at night as the tricolour writ large. If the illuminations of 1880 had for a brief moment made over the city into fairyland, by 1889 this had become an explicit iconographic motif: the most popular print produced for the occasion was Jules Chéret's poster 'The Land of the Fairies—The Enchanted Garden'.

Placing the centennial under the aegis of the Exposition Universelle thus meant that it was less about the claims of the past than about the priorities of the present and the possibilities of the future. It also consequentially meant that what was being commemorated and what was being fêted were distinct objects. The centennial was, as one commentator has aptly observed, less an anniversary of 1789 than a paean to the nineteenth century, of which 1889 was both a culmination and a spearhead of the future. It was in fact the first time that the notions of 'commemoration' and 'celebration' started to diverge, the latter more the Third Republic acting as cheerleader to itself. Naturally the Republic called on its citizens to salute 1789, as the historic launch pad for the process that had yielded the power and prosperity of the last decades of the nineteenth century and beyond. But this was to respect the past while insisting that it stay put. The Modern had arrived as if by natural selection. Darwin's theory indeed figured as one of the exhibits in the science section of the fair. It was not difficult to catch the hint of a political analogue: successfully managed adaptive change had secured the survival of the fittest in the sense not only of the scientifically and technologically advanced, but also of the regime most fit to rule. If the Revolution had been midwife to the child, the child was now a fully mature adult who had long since flown the nest. Enough was enough.

Enchanting the collective gaze with spectacularised representations of industrial modernity was in part a way of disenchanting, or at least discouraging, revolutionary thoughts. Revolutionary icons were expressly banned from the fairgrounds of the Exposition, and few, including possibly members of the government, would have counted the 1,792 steps of the Eiffel Tower (the illuminated tricolour by now essentially non-controversial). For, while basking in the glow of the image it had forged both of and for itself, the Third Republic was also looking anxiously over its shoulder. The cause for concern was not so much the agitations around the Second International (much of which had declared itself to be 'moderate' and 'parliamentarian'), or even the anarchist groups (in 1889 Emile Pouget started his anarchist paper *Père Peinard*, which was explicitly modelled on Hébert's incendiary revolutionary paper *Père Duchesne*). Perhaps a spectre was still haunting Europe, but it was almost twenty years since the Paris Commune, and there was little that could not be handled by a robust policing operation.

The real worry was over the possibility of insurrection and coup d'état under the auspices of the right-wing populist movement known as Boulangism. Hero to the army, expert in manipulating the revanchist mood (he was nicknamed 'General Revanche'), supporter of the Ligue des Patriotes, opportunistic player on the political chequerboard as simultaneously or successively conservative republican, neo-royalist and ultra-Bonapartist, General Boulanger had become a force in the land. For a moment early in 1889, he looked like being able to mobilise the resentments of the disaffected 'little man' behind a coup. By April the plot—if that is what it was—had fallen apart; Boulanger fled to Belgium, where two years later he blew his brains out over the grave of his mistress.

Several historians have suggested that one reason the plan failed was because the public mood was already entranced by the imminent opening of the Enchanted Garden. The magic worked, not only by virtue of its seductive power over the imagination, but also for the more practical economic reason that the commercial payoff in terms of tourism, exports and increased employment was considerable. It worked, moreover, not just in defusing the Boulangist threat, but also in the longer run. There were still to be revolutionary movements and conspirators plotting coups. But these were essentially splinter formations, fractions of the body politic. There were to be no more revolutions in France. The centennial said thank you to 1789, but it also said goodbye to all that.

In certain respects the shadow of the centennial fell over its younger sister. 1889 had brought commemoration into contact with commerce not merely by linking it to, but by subsuming it under, the Exposition Universelle. For the bicentennial, President Mitterrand wanted a repeat, and in this he was strongly supported by business leaders with an eye to the establishment of the single European market. There was also the small matter of the G7 economic summit, cleverly timed to open on 15 July, thus securing the presence of world leaders, several of whom (crucially Margaret Thatcher) were not notably fans of 1789. What better showcase for the view that France was now more about making money than about making revolutions? These, however, were recessionary times and the prospect of longer-term profits was outweighed by the immediate burden of cost. Jacques Chirac, mayor of Paris, prime minister during the period of 'co-habitation', and in 1988 failed contender for the presidential crown, effectively vetoed the proposal, albeit on grounds as much political as economic.

In the process Chirac made his own substantial contribution to overdosing collective memory with the charlatanesque. While as prime minister he refused, allegedly for budgetary reasons, funding for an Exposition Universelle, the would-be and future president of the French Republic, in a bid for the conservative vote, had already floated the impressively quixotic idea of a counter-festival to celebrate in 1987 the thousandth anniversary of the French monarchy (987 the beginning of the Capetian dynasty). Money, in its symbolic form, was to be part of this enterprise (the government authorised the issue of a ten-franc piece stamped with the fleur-de-lys). The best Mitterrand could manage in terms of his European aspirations was the secular canonisation of Jean Monnet, the founder of the EEC, whose remains were transferred by presidential order to the Panthéon. But, if there was to be no new Exposition, there was always the legacy of the old, especially the Eiffel Tower. The bicentennial of the Revolution and the centennial of the tower were notionally married in a music and fireworks spectacular (lasting of course exactly eighty-nine minutes), although Mayor Chirac—the tower being municipal property and its festival therefore the domain of the Hôtel de Ville—went out of his way to ensure their divorce. And to match further the monumentalising energies of the Third Republic, there was the inauguration of that ultra-modern building, the Arche de la Défense, on a stunning visual axis running west from the place de la Concorde and the Arc de Triomphe; the new business quarter (uncharitably, but not unreasonably, described as a 'business slum' and as the most anti-Paris place in Paris) was now tied into the commemorative fabric of the city.

This was not simply wilful vulgarisation and exploitation, but a token of shrinking options. For what in the late twentieth century did France now have to say to itself about its revolutionary past? What did it want to remember? How to reinvent, on an appropriately grandiose scale, an occasion that for nearly half a century had progressively ossified, the life drained from it? The last truly great 14 July festival had taken place in 1945. Throughout the Fourth and Fifth Republics, despite the ongoing conflicts between Gaullists and Communists, the *fête* had become little more than a cardboard cutout, the only new addition the display of missiles to signal France's accession to the nuclear club. By the 1960s it was essentially moribund. Not even the riots of 1968, with parts of the capital barricaded, disturbed much. Largely unruffled, 14 July proceeded in its stately way, but on gammy legs and tired feet. Take the case of 1974, on the presidential watch of Valéry Giscard d'Estaing, when 'feet' became an explicit topos under the aegis of practical reason. Giscard declared it was time for the festival to be 'reborn'. As an inclusive gesture designed to flatter what was left of the Left, it was decided that the military parade should proceed from the place de la Bastille to the place de la République. It would, however, have been a mistake to see in this an invitation to scale the heights of revolutionary memory. In a newspaper interview outlining his 'vision', Giscard contrived what was, so to speak, a remarkably flat-footed recommendation. If the festival was dying on its feet, the way to bring it back to life was by putting a newly invigorated step into the feet themselves. He thus determined that, since the storming of the Bastille had taken place on foot ('*à pied*'), the military review would take place likewise (no cars, no tanks), adding to this view of historical symmetry the eminently practical thought that 'the savings in petrol would be far from negligible' (it was the time of the oil crisis). This may have been a politically astute way of making a point to the modern 'consumer', but hardly counts as inspired. Even the French Communist Party seemed to have given up the ghost. In connection with the festival for the following year, the best its newspaper, *L'Humanité*, could muster was a limp proposition that could have come from virtually any source in the centre ground of French politics, on both the left and the right: 'the festival is a way of celebrating liberty'. By 1983 the only illustration the conservative paper *Le Figaro* could come up with to mark the festival was an image of Launay's head on a pike, accompanied by an article suggesting that 14 July 1789 had been a minor, as well as an unpleasant, event, quite unworthy of the historical myth it had been required to sustain.

These were the symptoms of a heritage grown arthritic, not to say threatened with terminal senility. It certainly meant that by the time of the bicentennial the cultural materials and political atmosphere to hand were somewhat threadbare. This, however, was no impediment to inflated expectation. They do these things differently in France of course, but perhaps only Jack Lang, Minister of Culture (also nominated, for the duration, Minister of the Bicentennial), could have pulled off this hyperbolic flight of fancy as the core of his mission statement:

> In Paris, on this symbolic night of 14 July, a night of fervour and of joy, at the foot of the timeless obelisk, in this place de la Concorde that has never been worthier of the name ... a great and immense voice ... will cast to the four winds of history the song expressing the ideals of the 500 *Marseillais* of 1792.

One thing left unsaid in this uplifting dithyramb was the fact that the 'Marseillaise' originated as a war song (also known as 'Chant de guerre de l'armée du Rhin'), composed by the army engineer Rouget de Lisle while posted in Strasbourg, to send off the army to fight the foreign enemy on the eastern front. What was also left unsaid was that the 500 from Marseilles who had arrived too late for 14 July 1792 were instrumental in overthrowing the monarchy. At first sight Lang seemed to be implying a bold commemorative move: the important date was not 14 July 1789 but the date of the coup, 10 August 1792. Not since 1793–4 had such a suggestion been floated; August 10 was strictly taboo. Was Lang lifting a nearly 200-year blanket of silence to propose that France celebrate the act which preceded and made possible the formal declaration of the republic in September 1792? It is highly doubtful that this was the intention, but, even if it was, it was a message strangled at birth. Nowhere in his hymn of praise to the 'Marseillaise' and the marching *Marseillais* was August 10 mentioned. This indeed was unsurprising given the view enunciated by Prime Minister Michel Rocard of the 'meaning' of the bicentennial: 'it convinced a lot of people that revolution is dangerous and that if one can do without it, so much the better'—all too true, but not quite the point of a commemorative event focused on what after all was a revolution.

The lead spot for the rendition of the 'Marseillaise' was not given to anyone from Marseilles, but to Jessye Norman, who naturally converted a robustly menacing anthem into a lovely aria, delivered with professionally exquisite precision; it led one disenchanted wit to suggest that the ideal venue for the *soirée* was the place de l'Opéra, presumably overlooking the irony that on 12 July 1789 the crowd forced the closure of the Opéra. But the point of enlisting Norman's services was not just her status as an internationally renowned singer. It was also because she was an African-American, a descendant of slaves and a focal point for a commemorative arch stretching across the Atlantic to the United States. To a large extent this was President Mitterrand's doing. The Fox played a long game, trimming his sails to shifts in the prevailing winds as the preparations unfolded. But on one fundamental point he was admirably consistent and forthright: there was a commemorative object and it was, warts and all, the French Revolution. Perhaps his finest moment was when he appeared before a gathering of historians at loggerheads and told them bluntly that commemoration meant taking the Revolution 'en bloc', the rough with the smooth (although he later adjusted this bold position to a less controversial one by saying that what he actually meant was taking the *legacy* of the Revolution *en bloc* rather than the thing itself). Certainly when push came to shove, the basic message he wanted sent out was the one all could rally round (apart from those for whom the Revolution was, under any description, an irredeemable abomination): the Revolution as cradle of human rights.

Jessye Norman singing the Marseillaise on the Place de la Concorde.

The truly important date, therefore, was 26 August 1789, a date that so far had not found a place in the official commemorative calendar: namely, the moment of the Declaration. But this, it will be recalled (it wasn't much recalled during the bicentennial), was a declaration of the rights not just of 'man', but also of the 'citizen'. Three years before the formal promulgation of the Republic there was here already the whiff of a republican conception, although what a republic of citizens was to mean became one of the most violently contested issues of the Revolution itself. While Mitterrand made it clear that the foregrounding of human rights was intended to echo the Declaration, the expression 'of the Citizen' was nevertheless on the whole left quietly to one side. The implicit idea seems to have been to align the legacy of the Revolution with the juridical basis of European and transatlantic conceptions of rights. The choice of Jessye Norman to sing the 'Marseillaise' evoked a link with the American Bill of Rights and also the abolition of slavery (although the Bill of Rights itself had evaded the slavery question). But the distinctive feature of the French Revolution which sought to tie the law-based rights of individuals to the political rights of the citizen was either buried or blurred.

Once again, memory was tailored to the needs of the present. It was thus no accident that, in the protracted and intense discussions of whether it was right to mark the two hundredth anniversary of the Revolution by selectively picking out the 'good' bits and discarding the 'bad', and, if so, which bits qualified as good and bad, the recurrent figures of speech were those of the supermarket and the butcher's shop, in which the consumer hunts for the best bargains and the choicest cuts. The *Nouvel Observateur* described the theme of human rights as prime sirloin; the stakes seemed to have become indistinguishable from their homophonous partner, presumably accompanied by a portion of *frites* and washed down with a bottle of *rouge* (Marcel Amont's popular song of 1972, 'Bleu, blanc, rouge et des frites', was dusted down for the occasion). The steaks might be served with a touch of radical garnish, but were to be dextrously trimmed of excess republican fat before being popped on the grill.

In so far as the notion of citizenship survived, it was as the cosmopolitan idea of the citizen of the world, and hence the legacy of 1789 as the universal reach of (a liberal version of) human rights in the age of multiculturalism and globalisation. This was how Jean-Noël Jeanneney, appointed president of the bicentennial commission, interpreted Mitterrand's brief. Jeanneney found himself in a tight spot, caught between the pressure of schedules and the manoeuvres of politics. His predecessor in the post, that expert prowler of the corridors of power, Edgar Faure, died in 1988 and bequeathed what by any standards was a somewhat exiguous dossier. His own signal contribution was the counterfactual thought that there were two individuals who could have prevented the Revolution from taking place at all, Turgot (about whom Faure had written a book) and himself, the thought further deepened by the observation that, alas, Turgot had died too early and he, Faure, had been born too late. Jeanneney adopted what looked like a crisper approach, characterised in some quarters as evincing a muscular 'Jacobinism', with much talk of 'civic virtue' and the like, although it would be profoundly mistaken to construe the patrician Jeanneney as a closet Robespierrist. To his credit, he tried to rescue the bicentennial from a soporific consensualism based on the heart-warming incantation of '*droidlomisme*' (the rap version of, and comment on, *droits de l'homme*). Yet the universal and cosmopolitan framework of human rights was exactly what was needed in respect of another self-denying ordinance: 'Let us guard against all forms of Gallocentrism.' This was all very well if intended as a warning against tub-thumping nationalism, but it immediately raised a dual question: what could it mean for France to commemorate a revolution and what could it mean for France to commemorate Revolution?

What Jeanneney came up with was, minimally, weird and, maximally, disingenuous. The commemoration would highlight four 'representative' figures: Condorcet, Grégoire, Monge and Toussaint L'Ouverture. The choice of Monge, the renowned mathematician who had helped with the calculations involved in devising the new republican calendar, was non-controversial (an echo of the foregrounding of Carnot by the centennial as the embodiment of scientific enlightenment). The abbé Grégoire was selected as standing for 'equality', notwithstanding the fact that his conception of citizenship emphasised republican sameness rather than multicultural difference (an emphasis translated into practice through his concerted effort to stamp out regional patois and dialects in favour of a uniformly imposed common language). Nothing was made of his speech to the Convention on 21 September 1792 in which he famously argued that 'kings are in the moral order what monsters are in the natural'.

As for the token inclusion of the leader of the Haitian slave rebellion, Toussaint, perhaps the least said the better. No amount of African-American operatic cosmetics could disguise the fact that Jeanneney was being a trifle economical with the *actualité*. The uprising of 22 August 1791 galvanised the Assembly into rescinding the rights of free blacks and mulattos (the slaves themselves not figuring anywhere on the political radar screen), the consequence of which was the burning of plantations and the murder of white masters. And, in addition to editing an intractable past, there was also an awkward present. A group of poor nations (including Haiti) organised a meeting in Paris to coincide with and protest against the rich man's club represented by the G7 meeting. More generally, the notionally global template of the whole affair did not in practice prove to be open house. Later the president's wife, Danielle Mitterrand, confessed to her fury at the exclusion of certain—unnamed but readily identifiable—Latin American nations on the grounds that this would have been displeasing to the United States (pulling no punches, she described it as 'shameful').

The figure in the quartet who carried the greatest weight, however, was Condorcet, the 'good' Girondin, spokesman for the 'rationality' of the market and champion of human rights (he was an admirer of the American Constitution and Bill of Rights). As the jewel in the crown, Condorcet was to be given his rightful place in the Panthéon (in the form of a plaque, his remains having disappeared without trace at the time of his death while imprisoned during the Terror). But then what of those ultimately responsible for his imprisonment and death, Robespierre and Saint-Just? Their role in the Terror and the infamous Law of Suspects was hardly an advertisement for a liberal conception of human rights. But it was Robespierre who, in his last speech to the Convention, as his support crumbled around him, said: 'The French Revolution is the first to have been founded on the rights of humanity and the principles of justice.' For his part, Saint-Just, on the day of his execution, saw hanging in the hall of the Conciergerie prison the tables of the Rights of Man and allegedly proclaimed: 'After all it was I who did that.'

This may have been—to put it mildly—a claim misplaced, but, however unpalatable, the complex relation of belief and practice to the discourse of human rights that characterises Robespierre and Saint-Just would have to be part of any commemorative picture that, as Jeanneney put it in one of his braver moments, would respect the 'virulence' of the Revolution and avoid a false unanimity based on taking the 'lowest common denominator'. These brave words would be merely warm words if they did not extend to the inclusion of the Revolution's most controversial figures. But in the end this was simply too divisive. Since the Jacobin leaders were bad news, they were to be no news at all, written out of the scenario for what was to remain a comfort zone untroubled by 'virulence'. Robespierre appears to have figured but once in the history of the 14 July festival, on a poster at the great rally of the Popular Front in 1936.

Jeanneney's mission was basically a hopeless one. While demanding a certain autonomy, he had to remain sensitive to the sinuous moves of his political masters, cope with inter-ministerial rivalries, not to mention the obstructions of the arch-rival ensconced in the Hôtel de Ville, Mayor Jacques Chirac. At the same time he had to plan and deliver a range of actual events. In one of his interviews he spoke of his determination to give the festival 'a clear civic meaning'. Yet, for all his intelligence and dynamism, clarity was the very last thing he produced. In the end, and despite his own warnings against tendentious cherry-picking, he capitulated: 'Let everyone take from it what they want.' This laissez-faire, anything-goes attitude was probably born of desperation before the dwindling chances of salvaging a moderately coherent programme. But it was just as much a reflection of the fact that none of this really *mattered*. For the real objective was to produce a variant of the Greatest Show on Earth, a multicultural image-fest MTV style.

In one fundamental respect the bicentennial outstripped the centennial. It did not merely juxtapose commemoration and commerce, it succeeded in commercialising commemoration itself, through the figure of the advertising whiz kid Jean-Paul Goude, whose first reaction to being asked if a bicentennial commission might interest him was the quintessential expression of postmodern cool: 'Why not?' Goude was a gifted maker of commercials with—crucially important—an instinctive understanding of the mass appeal of television (more ominously, he was an admirer of Leni Riefenstahl's filming of the Nuremberg Rally). Goude was more Lang's man than Jeanneney's, in some respects a pawn in the low-level power struggle between the two.

Nevertheless, Jeanneney, a specialist in 'media history', appears to have found collaboration easy ('We worked closely and harmoniously with Goude and his people') and made his intention clear: the 14 July festival was to be a 'media-performance in top gear' that would 'respond to the aspirations of a contemporary sensibility' in a manner linking 'the syncretic message' of contemporary 'world music' to 'the near-universal adherence today to the message of 1789'. The nature of the link was far from clear, in particular what relation it bore to all the well-meaning talk of 'civic virtue' and revolutionary aspiration. The formula now was to be that what works is what sells. Farewell to the carmagnole and hello to the pulsating Afro-rhythms favoured by the Goude style, notwithstanding Goude's murkily exploitative relation to 'blackness' (blackness and 'animality' was one of his favourite tropes).

Goude was a truly inspired choice for the times. He candidly acknowledged that 'in the terms of show biz' (i.e. his terms), the 'Revolution … is something that is very hard to represent'. Indeed it was, a difficulty aggravated by the fact that Goude knew next to nothing about, and showed very little interest in, the history of the Revolution. The best he could manage was the official mantra: 'For me, it's first and foremost human rights. The rest is just memory.' For the purposes of commemoration, memory had oddly ceased to count for much. What counted was what could be counted, with the foot: 'I wanted the whole of France to tap with its foot, as if in a club,' Goude proclaimed. He didn't have the Jacobin or Cordelier Clubs in mind. There was of course that last refuge of antiseptic indifference to the past, postmodern irony (Warhol was Goude's role model). 'Parody' was a term that crossed Goude's lips often as he spoke of his conception, but, since this was unlikely to recommend itself to his masters, what emerged, with a few visual jokes thrown in, was the governing theme of 'fraternity' on a planetary scale and 'revolution' defined as 'the birth of a global sound', the hybrid mixtures of world music.

The show, named for form's sake 'The Marseillaise', is virtually indescribable: that is to say, indescribably awful, a procession of floats, tableaux and images for the age of the *société du spectacle*. Only a Flaubert in unusually caustic mood could have done justice to it—a vast extravaganza of cultural and musical clichés tossed into a high-temperature melting pot, in which the melt succeeded in reducing to ashes anything intelligibly resembling commemoration of the French Revolution. Its notional openness to multiple cultures (*fraternité sans frontières*) was belied by the predominating representation of the five countries with a history of revolution (France, Britain, Russia, China and the United States) that happened also to be the five permanent members of the UN Security Council. Black Africa and little chunks of Islam were thrown into the pot, but tricolourised by projector light, which led some to wonder, with good reason, exactly what message was being projected. Toussaint of course was nowhere in sight, perhaps from sensitivity to the extraordinary advice Goude, in an interview, claimed he had received from Jacques Attali: '"Some blacks, by all means, but not too many." He was right.'

The media swooned, somewhere over the moon (perhaps

inspired by the Michael Jackson 'moonwalk' routine that had been the centrepiece of the finale provided by the contingent from Florida). Hardcore voices from the left mellowed overnight, rushing to sign up for membership of the Goude fan club. Those who remained obdurately sceptical were chided by Jeanneney, who, now abandoning his earlier insistence on at least an element of intellectual seriousness, reminded all and sundry that the commercial was a legitimate art form in its own right and that the hostility of the intelligentsia to the advertising world was an 'old refrain' to which no one in their right mind would pay any attention. The sole reservation President Mitterrand allowed himself was the remark that it had perhaps 'dragged on' a bit (presumably mindful that the taxing demands of the G7 summit called for early nights). And that was that, the *jour de gloire* as animated fresco of 'clips' vanishing in a puff of smoke and leaving behind no trace apart from the bills to be settled (Goude remaining steadfastly coy about the size of his own fee). Jacques-Louis David had acted as pageant master to the later revolutionary festivals, including the most fraudulently meretricious among them. But, as an artist, he had also transformed and revitalised the pictorial vocabulary of European history painting. By contrast, the centennial got Jules Chéret and the bicentennial got Jean-Paul Goude.

So, what did this glitzy show really amount to? Was there any point to it at all? Was anything being 'remembered'? Had the tocsin of 1789 given way to its death knell? At a far remove from the world of show business, but with a canny eye to the value of media exposure, came a devastating reply. Enter stage right the with-us-or-against-us, winner-takes-all guru of 'revisionism', hailed by some as 'the king of the bicentennial', the distinguished historian François Furet. The intellectual and professional complexities of the historiographical disputes preceding and surrounding the anniversary far exceed the brief of this short book. Furet's contribution bears mentioning because of its effort to occupy not only the citadel of the historians but also the wider public sphere, as a ruthless, even pitiless, campaign to sabotage the celebratory aspect of the commemoration in terms far more sophisticated than those of the traditional counter-revolutionary Right. One of the thousands of publications timed to coincide with the bicentennial was the *Dictionnaire de la Révolution française* compiled by Furet and his colleague Mona Ozouf. This was the culmination of what previously, down from the historians' version of Mount Sinai and reaching for the regal performative, Furet had proclaimed the Revolution to be: 'over'. What primarily he meant by this was certain ways of thinking and talking about the Revolution and its legacy, first and foremost the domination of memory and historical scholarship by the Jacobin tradition which, in various guises, had run from Aulard through Mathiez to Lefebvre and Soboul, inflected en route by the experience of the Russian Revolution and the prestige of Marxism on the French Left (a great deal of Furet's take was comprehensible only as a settling of scores with his own past as a member of the French Communist Party).

More radically, however, it was 'over' in that there was no longer any place for affectively charged memory and interpretation of the Revolution in a nation that had finally learned the difference between the 'democratic idea' and the 'revolutionary idea', critically the lesson that the former had little to do with the latter's experiment in 'popular sovereignty'; although when the going got tough Furet was prepared to concede that 1789 could be said to have provided a historical impetus for the birth of democracy, albeit in a manner pre-programmed to devour its own offspring. Pacified and normalised, the modern French republic – the 'republic of the centre' – required an end to the interminable rehashing of the 'meaning' of the Revolution. The time had come to call time on the 'debate' itself. In 1868 the polymathic roving ambassador of French intellectual life, Edgar Quinet, remarked of the main actors of the French Revolution:

'However dead they may be for us, they are still in the fray. They go on fighting and hating.' Quinet meant of course the battles fought on their behalf in the nineteenth-century aftermath. He found this puzzling. Furet, himself a great admirer of Quinet, considered it pointless. Also baptised the 'pope of revolutionary studies', he issued the equivalent of a papal bull instructing the sectarians to stop squabbling over what by now was a non-issue.

Furet's was in many ways an odd demand for an end to the 'civil war' (as he put it) of interpretations on the matter of the Revolution. It was essentially an appeal backed by an act of intellectual *force majeure*, stipulating armistice on Furet's terms. The irony, not lost on several commentators, was that, in seeking to clear the decks and shut up shop, the militant anti-Communist came to resemble nothing so much as his Stalinist adversary in effectively aiming at a 'purge'. There were to be simultaneously both no more words and a last word (Furet's own), suitably refined by the band of disciples, acolytes and collaborators that came to be known as the 'galaxy', but itself fundamentally immune to historical reflexiveness over its own status as a product of the final spasm of the Cold War (November 1989 saw the fall of the Berlin Wall). From the point of view of a pluralist culture of 'debate', this looked more like an ominous restoration of (historiographical) divine right than a further expansion of the democratic 'marketplace of ideas'. After all, and however one orchestrated the story, kings, including a 'king of the bicentennial', were not supposed to be part of it. In the immediately ambient surroundings—the world of historians, writers, intellectuals, journalists—the imperious call, though influential, happily went unheeded, and everyone carried on quarrelling. In respect of the bicentennial programme itself, Furet at least acted consistently, if a trifle churlishly. King François, while gladly accepting his crown ('I won!' he triumphantly declared to the Spanish newspaper *El Pais*), did what by his lights was the decent thing, relating to the bicentennial jamboree as a committed refusenik: 'Let's not play with words: at this point the bicentennial of 1789 seems to us the shroud of tradition.'

Quite phenomenal amounts of high-grade intellectual energy went into these disputes. Yet, when seen in the broader national perspective, the jousting amounted to little more than shadow-boxing, so much sound and fury signifying nothing. As he looked down from his position of Olympian hauteur, the self-absenting monarch could not have been entirely displeased by the ideological tone of the bicentennial. Despite his (grotesque) fulminations against the governing socialists as the heirs to the Jacobin heresy, it was broadly, if unavowedly, on Furet's terms that the wider commemoration took place—the market, individual rights, liberty as the play of private interests—in short, the panoply of liberalism. While one revolution with which the French variant had long been associated was receiving its burial rites—namely, the Bolshevik one—another from a faraway place had come, tacitly but ubiquitously, to take up abode in the commemorative consciousness: the American one (although, towed along by the undercurrents of the revisionist wave, the English revolution also got a good billing; the nationalist gesture of Maggie Thatcher, who tried to handbag the proceedings by invoking Magna Carta, was of course a huffing and puffing sideshow). But the date that really mattered now was not 14 July 1789, and still less October 1917, but 4 July 1776. Tocqueville had prevailed over Marx, with Lafayette rising from the grave to applaud the new ideological arrangements as a reprise of the 1790 *Fête de la Fédération*, minus the military bravura and the oath-swearing ceremony at the Altar of the Fatherland. Furet may have pretended not to be listening, or have continued, perversely, to insist that Mitterrand's men were singing from a different song sheet, but this must have been music to his ears.

Yet in an important sense, diagnostically if not prescriptively, Furet was right, though in ways that he himself did not quite have in mind. The historians could continue quarrelling forever, but where 'memory' in its more collective and diffuse forms was concerned, the game was up, 'over' in the more dismal sense of general indifference to the debate, to any debate, whatever its terms. Even Michel Vovelle, the historian tasked by the Ministry of Research with breathing new life into the scholarly dimension of the bicentennial, had his doubts. Notwithstanding his own strong political convictions (as an active member of the French Communist Party), Vovelle made every effort to sustain a sane dialogue between the warring parties. He grasped that what was 'good' about the 'legacy' was its unvarnished truth, the truth that so many wanted to obliterate beneath either a funeral shroud or a pastel-tinted layer of red, white and blue: namely, the fact that 'memory' and opinion were divided. He was perfectly happy for the conflict of interpretations to continue, provided it was articulated in accordance with the protocols of scholarly exchange and in the spirit of a commemoration. Alongside Vovelle's even-handedness, Furet ultimately comes across as a mix of shabby publicity seeker, petulant diva and aggressive power broker (naturally he boycotted the international conference organised by Vovelle in the week running up to 14 July, having instead made representations for a 'closed colloquium bringing together a score of historians of an identical viewpoint').

But for all his determination to rise to what he construed as the occasion, Vovelle himself had to confess that his task was predicated not simply on the certifiable 'malaise of the national community over the way to deal with this major moment of our collective memory', but more drastically on the memory of the Revolution being in the public mind 'very far along the road to extinction'. It was the depressing truth that, while the chattering classes continued to chatter in their inimitably brilliant Gallic way, the nation as a whole was paying very little attention. This was probably less a reflection of the fact that the Cold War was 'over', or because the emergence of the consensual republic had extinguished political passions, and more the outcome of the long history from 1880 onwards, which, apart from times of crisis, had seen the divergence of state-sponsored commemoration and public holiday. But whatever the causes, it seemed a matter of incontestable fact that few outside the charmed circle of the metropolitan intelligentsia or the riven world of politicians jostling for position cared whether the true 'hero' of the Revolution was Mirabeau or Lafayette or Danton or Robespierre or the *sans-culottes*, whether the execution of Louis was justified regicide or brutal political murder, whether the Terror was imposed by 'circumstances' or wilfully generated by an insane political 'voluntarism', or whether the installation of 'Condorcet' in the Panthéon signified a rehabilitation of the Girondins (an appropriately diplomatic veil drawn over the fact that the Girondins had been the more bellicose members of the war party). The issues that the historians, journalists and intellectuals had variously tried to keep alive were in the wider public imagination something of a dead letter.

In another of his speeches Mitterrand claimed that to 'remember' is to 'rejuvenate' or 'renew'. The one attempt at enacting this proposition with a degree of literalness came from an unusual quarter and in an unusual form. Someone at the Hôtel de Ville had the bright idea of bringing the Revolution back to 'life' by tracing living descendants of the original protagonists and arranging a reunion. Predictably enough, it turned out to be a somewhat lowering affair, degenerating fast into sulky and ill-tempered farce. A descendant of Robespierre, a right-wing journalist, disavowed his ancestor. Louis XVI's exceptionally distant kin refused to stand alongside the alleged posterity of his executioner, Henri Sanson. A relation of Danton, discovered in Peru, declared himself to be a man of the Right, while a descendant of Charlotte Corday insisted that she had not in fact been an assassin. So much for the spirit of fraternity. But if this was to take history a little too personally, at least the persons concerned took a view. Most of France had no view at all, and for the most part in *la France profonde* the televised Goude show was greeted with a Gallic shrug. The Revolution was now more a *lieu d'oubli* than a *lieu de mémoire*.

At the time of the bicentennial *Le Nouvel Observateur* conducted a survey based on the question: 'what was the most important event of the French Revolution?' The winning answer was 14 July and the taking of the Bastille. But pressed on what actually happened on the famous day, memory tended to draw a blank. Who, today, other than in some specialist corners of the academy, remembers Humbert, Cholat, Poupart, Hulin, Elie, Maillard et al.? Who indeed has ever heard of them? Perhaps this is simply Nature's way with History; forgetting is what comes naturally to us. In the meantime, the president's 14 July garden party remains a fixture, the *tout-Paris* version of the great and the good (the cost of Chirac's last estimated at nearly half a million euros of taxpayers' money, a strange comment on what began as a dispute about representation and taxation). At first it was *le peuple*, real men on the ground, then that political abstraction, *le Peuple*; now it is (the English term is the one used) 'people' in the sense of the celebrity culture, the beautiful people, those in the news, the denizens of what is now journalistically called the *république peopulaire*.

On both left and right, earnest discourse on the republican virtue of secular 'equality' drones on, while turning a blind eye to the real challenges of 'integration' (altogether too expensive and, as some have put it, too 'divisive'). Instead, official talk of the republic one and indivisible focuses on the (non-)issue of headscarves (the bicentennial lip service to cultural 'difference' long forgotten). What, if anything, and notwithstanding the 'multicultural' panache of the bicentennial, the immigrant communities of the contemporary banlieues make of what started in the old faubourgs is not hard to guess. Even Furet's eirenic view of the post-revolutionary settlement (as the republic of the centre) was to darken, as his eye wandered over the ravaged landscapes of the banlieue, where the liberal mantra of individual 'rights' had little meaningful purchase.

One of the organisations sponsoring the idea of the bicentennial was upliftingly called Vive 89. In ironic counterpoint, the most comprehensive study we have of the issues surrounding its reality—Steven Kaplan's brilliant book—bears, for the French edition, the more forlorn title *Adieu 89*. Not, it should be noted, *Au revoir* (although its author did point out, as germane to his own intention, that in some parts of France 'adieu' can mean both 'bonjour' and 'au revoir'). Is it, then, farewell in the definitive sense *sub specie aeternitas*? Or was it Zhou Enlai who in fact got it right: it just is too early to tell? Even Quinet, who cast such a disabused gaze over the resources of memory, also wrote, in the same text: 'The dead are patient; let them wait.' In the meantime, as we also wait and in the interim ponder whether the bicentennial razzmatazz was more appropriately wrapped in Furet's shroud or draped in Goude's exotic costumery, perhaps it is best to think of it as a gigantic collage, dutifully headed by the trinity 'liberty, equality, fraternity', but captioned below in even larger type with the greeting 'Have a nice day' (the culturally dismal terminus of the spirit of the original *journée*). As a gesture to those whose taste in historical memory runs along sterner lines, there might also be a small corner in the collage reserved for Man Ray's provocative image, *Imaginary portrait of the Marquis de Sade*, which has the stormed Bastille in the background, all fire and smoke, and in the foreground a representation of the incandescent brain of the prisoner who wasn't there, the divine Marquis.

Further Reading

General

The literature of the storming of the Bastille and its more general background in the French Revolution as a whole is fittingly gigantic and irreducibly controversial. The following bibliography confines itself to what a curious reader, anxious to pursue these matters further, is likely to find most useful.

For sheer narrative flair, nothing can beat the two historiographical classics of the nineteenth century: Jules Michelet's *Histoire de la Révolution française*, Paris, 1979 (*History of the French Revolution*, translated by Charles Cocks, edited by Gordon Wright, Chicago, 1967) and Thomas Carlyle's *The French Revolution: A History*, edited by K. J. Fielding and David Sorensen, Oxford, 1989. Both accounts are written from distinctive points of view, but have in common unsurpassed storytelling verve.

Chapter One and Two

The reader should be warned that the whole question of what 'caused' the French Revolution is a historiographical and ideological minefield. The 'classic' accounts emphasise the so-called 'nobles' revolt' and the defence of traditional privileges as a causal crux, leading to the convocation of the Estates-General and everything that then followed. On the other hand, the so-called 'revisionist' account either contests or modifies this 'monolithic' view, stressing the progressive erosion of Privilege in the course of the eighteenth century, along with the influential role of many of the more 'progressive' or 'enlightened' aristocrats. One unfortunate consequence of the more extreme versions of this approach is that it renders the outbreak of the Revolution effectively unintelligible.

For an overview of the French Revolution and the antecedents of the storming of the Bastille, the following are recommended for clarity of exposition and masterful synthesis: J. M. Thompson, *The French Revolution*, Oxford, 1955; Georges Lefebvre, *La Révolution française*, Paris, 1957 (*The French Revolution*, translated by Elizabeth Moss Evans, London, 2004) and *Quatre-Vingt-Neuf*, Paris, 1939 (*The Coming of the French Revolution*, translated by R. R. Palmer, Princeton, 1989); Albert Soboul, *Précis d'histoire de la Révolution française*, Paris, 1962 (*The French Revolution, 1787–1799: From the Storming of the Bastille to Napoleon*, translated by Alan Forrest and Colin Jones, London, 1989) and *1789: l'an un de la liberté. Etude historique, textes originaux*, Paris, 1973; Claude Manceron, *Le Sang de la Bastille: du renvoi de Calonne au sursaut de Paris*, 1787/1789, Paris, 1987 (*Blood of the Bastille*, translated by Nancy Amphoux, New York, 1989); William Doyle, *Origins of the French Revolution*, Oxford, 1999, and *The French Revolution: A Very Short Introduction*, Oxford, 2001; Rurt Scurr, *Fatal Purity: Robespierre and the French Revolution*, London, 2006.

More recently, there is the magisterial study by Robert Darnton, *The Revolutionary Temper: Paris, 1748–1789*, Allen Lane, 2023.

The most detailed and substantial scholarly account of the storming of the Bastille is Jacques Godechot's *The Taking of the Bastille*. Other studies include: Guy Chaussinand-Nogaret, *La Bastille est prise: la Révolution commence*, Paris, 1988; Christopher

Hibbert, *The Days of the French Revolution*, New York, 1980; Paul Chauvet, *1789: L'insurrection parisienne et la prise de la Bastille*, Paris, 1946. Simon Schama's *Citizens: A Chronicle of the French Revolution* (London, 1989) tells the story of the storming at a cracking pace. On the history and literature of the Bastille prison, see Monique Cottret, *La Bastille à prendre: histoire et mythe de la forteresse royale*, Paris, 1986; Hans-Jurgen Lusebrink and Rolf Reinhardt, *The Bastille: A History of a Symbol of Despotism and Freedom* (translated by Norbert Schurer), Durham, NC, 1997. On the *Vainqueurs de la Bastille*, see Victor Fournel, *Les Hommes du 14 juillet: gardes françaises et Vainqueurs de la Bastille*, Paris, 1890; Joseph Durieux, *Les Vainqueurs de la Bastille*, Paris, 1911.

Chapters Three and Four

Humbert's eyewitness report is included as an appendix in Jacques Godechot, *La Prise de la Bastille, 14 juillet 1789*, Paris, 1965 (*The Taking of the Bastille, 14 July 1789*, translated by Jean Stewart, London, 1970). Humbert's text is briefly discussed in the context of a more general survey of eyewitness testimony by Jules Flammermont, *La journée du 14 juillet 1789: fragment des mémoires inédits de L.-G. Pitra, électeur de Paris en 1789*, Paris, 1892.

For those who wish to go straight to the sources, there is the admirable online service of the Gallica catalogue of the Bibliothèque Nationale. For contemporary press reports, see Jeremy D. Popkin, *Revolutionary News: The Press in France, 1789–1799*, Durham, NC, 1990.

Chapters Five, Six and Seven

On the revolutionary festivals and related ceremonies, see Mona Ozouf, *La fête révolutionnaire, 1789–1799*, Paris, 1976 (*Festivals and the French Revolution*, translated by Alan Sheridan, Cambridge,

Mass, 1991); Marie-Hélène Huet, 'Unsettled Memories: The Revolution Buries Its Dead', in Robert T. Denommé and Roland H. Simon (eds), *Unfinished Revolutions: Legacies of Upheaval in Modern French Culture*, Pennsylvania, 1998, pp. 121–37.

On Bastille Day, see Rosemonde Sanson, *Les 14 Juillet, fête et conscience nationale, 1789–1975*, Paris, 1976; Charles Rearick, *Pleasures of the Belle-Epoque: Entertainment and Festivity in Turn-of-the-Century France*, New Haven, 1985; Christian Amalvi, 'Le 14-Juillet. Du Dies irae à Jour de fête', in Pierre Nora (ed.), *Les Lieux de mémoire*, Vol. I, *La République*, Paris, 1984, pp. 421–72. On the Centennial, see Pascal Ory, 'Le centenaire de la Révolution française. La preuve par 89', ibid. pp. 523–60.

On the Bicentennial, see Steven L. Kaplan, *Adieu 89*, Paris, 1993 (*Farewell, Revolution*, Vol. I, *Disputed Legacies*, Vol. II, *The Historians' Feud*, Ithaca, 1995, 1996; Jean-Noël Jeanneney, *Paris, 2000: rapport du président de la Mission du Bicentenaire au président de la République sur les activités de cet organisme et les dimensions de la célébration*, Paris, 1990; David A. Bell, 'Liberté, Egalité, Have a Nice Day', *New Republic*, 23 January 1989.

On the general conceptual and political issues of 'interpreting' the French Revolution, see François Furet, *Penser la Révolution française*, Paris, 1978 (*Interpreting the French Revolution*, translated by Elborg Forster, Cambridge, 1981) and Eric Hobsbawm, *Echoes of the Marseillaise: Two Centuries Look Back on the French Revolution*, London, 1990. Their respective approaches are utterly different and provide the best available snapshot of just how riven the field is. For a comparative history of the two revolutions, the American and the French, see the study by Patrice Higonnet, *Sister Republics: The Origins of French and American Republicanism*, Harvard, 1988.

Printed in Great Britain
by Amazon

d0900107-d6f3-46c7-a604-7e354f9ea6eeR01